Challenges and Change in Nurse Education – a study of the implementation of Project 2000

Sandra Jowett and Irene Walton
with Sue Payne

 STANDARD

nfer

Funded by the Department of Health

Published in February 1994 by the
National Foundation for Educational Research in England and Wales
The Mere
Upton Park
Slough
Berkshire SL1 2DQ

Telephone: (0753) 574123   Fax: (0753) 691632

Registered Charity No. 313392

ISBN 0 7005 1360 4

CONTENTS

Advisory Group

Veronica Bishop	Nursing Officer, Department of Health (until March 1992)
Peggy Curtis	Nursing Officer, Department of Health (until March 1992)
Sheila Collins	Formerly Associate Lecturer, University of Surrey and DNE (Tower Hamlets)
Maureen Fraser	Formerly a member of Her Majesty's Inspectorate
John Harland	Head of Northern Office, National Foundation for Educational Research in England and Wales
Seamus Hegarty (Chair)	Deputy Director, National Foundation for Educational Research in England and Wales
Rita Le Var	Director for Educational Policy, English National Board for Nursing, Midwifery and Health Visiting
Christopher Maggs	Professor of Nursing Research, University of Wales College of Medicine (until September 1992)
Elizabeth Meerabeau	Liaison Officer (Research and Development), Department of Health
David Moore	Nursing Officer (Education), NHSME, Department of Health
Alan Myles	Vice Principal, Institute of Advanced Nursing Education, Royal College of Nursing
Robin Orton	Assistant Secretary, Department of Health (until March 1992)
Margaret Wallace	Assistant Registrar (Education) United Kingdom Central Council for Nursing, Midwifery and Health Visiting
Wendy Watson	Formerly DNE (Bristol and Weston) and retired Project Leader/ Principal of the Avon College of Nursing and Midwifery

Research Team:

Judy Bradley   Sandra Jowett   Sue Payne   Irene Walton

i

Acknowledgements

This study could not have been carried out without the active collaboration of a large number of people whom we would like to thank for their generous cooperation and support.

First and foremost we are grateful for the help of those participating in the 13 Demonstration Districts (education and service staff and students) who made us welcome on the research visits and responded patiently and openly to lengthy questioning.

Secondly, the members of the Advisory Group promptly and efficiently provided us with helpful comments on the drafts of all our reports. Their support and advice during the research are much appreciated.

Our thanks are also extended to Judy Bradley, whose warmth and encouragement sustained the research team throughout. The secretarial staff in the Professional Studies Department provided efficient and helpful support, as did members of the Foundation's library staff. Barbara Tomlins and Marion Sainsbury, NFER colleagues, made invaluable comments on the draft report that facilitated greatly the production of this final version. David Upton's editorial skills were also instrumental in this process. We are grateful to Tim Wright for his skilful layout and cover design.

The funding provided for this work by the Department of Health is gratefully acknowledged.

Abbreviations

A-LEVEL	Advanced-Level General Certificate of Education
AIDS	The Acquired Immunodeficiency Syndrome
CATS	Credit Accumulation and Transfer Scheme
CFP	Common Foundation Programme
CMHN	Community Mental Handicap Nurse
CMHT	Community Mental Handicap Team
CNAA	Council for National Academic Awards [1]
CPN	Community Psychiatric Nurse
DGM	District General Manager
DHA	District Health Authority
DN	District Nurse
DNE	Director of Nurse Education
DNS	Director of Nursing Services
DoH	Department of Health
EC	European Community
EN	Enrolled Nurse
ENB	English National Board for Nursing, Midwifery and Health Visiting
FE	Further Education
GCSE	General Certificate of Secondary Education
HA	Health Authority
HCA	Health Care Assistant
HE	Higher Education
HIV	Human Immunodeficiency Virus
HMI	Her Majesty's Inspectorate
HV	Health Visitor
ITU	Intensive Treatment Unit
MSc	Master of Science
NA	Nursing Auxiliary
NCVQ	National Council for Vocational Qualifications
NHS	National Health Service
NHSME	National Health Service Management Executive
NHSTA	National Health Service Training Authority
NVQ	National Vocational Qualification
PhD	Doctor of Philosophy
PREP	Post-registration Education and Practice Project
RGN	Registered General Nurse
RHA	Regional Health Authority
RMN	Registered Mental Nurse
RN	Registered Nurse
RNMH	Registered Nurse Mental Handicap
RSCN	Registered Sick Children's Nurse
UKCC	United Kingdom Central Council for Nursing, Midwifery and Health Visiting

[1] *This closed in 1993 as a consquence of legislation on further and higher education (G.B. STATUTES, 1992). Awards records and principal publications of the CNAA are now handled by Open University Validation Services.*

Glossary

acute services
> Predominantly hospital services concerned with the care and treatment of patients who are acutely ill.

bank staff
> nursing staff registered as available for work with nurse managers and employed as required.

Branch
> After an 18-month common foundation programme, students on Project 2000 follow one of four specialist Branch programmes (Adult or Child or Mental Health or Mental Handicap) for a further 18 months.

Care Sector Consortium
> the Body representing the health and care sector (the Lead Body) in the development of NVQs.

'carry the bleep'
> be on call, i.e. obtainable by radio pager.

City and Guilds
> The City and Guilds of London Institute is a course validating body.

clinical grading
> A system by which the content of practice-based nursing posts are assessed against defined criteria to determine which of nine pay grades should apply to the post under review.

Districts
> The 14 Regional Health Authorities in England currently contain 168 (although mergers are occurring) District Health Authorities known as Districts.

'drugs assessment'
> procedure to assess whether student nurses are competent to administer prescribed drugs.

enrolled nurses
> second level nurses, qualified to register with the UKCC following a two-year course of preparation, phased-out as part of the Project 2000 reforms.

National Vocational Qualifications
> a range of vocational qualifications accredited by the NCVQ and formulated by the different occupational sectors.

NHS Trusts
> Hospitals and other units which are run by their own Boards of Directors; are independent of District and Regional management; and have wide-ranging freedoms not available to units which remain under health authority control.

off-duties
    time when not working a shift, i.e. not on duty.

practice areas
    institutional and community settings where nurses work.

practice-based staff
    those providing nursing care in hospital and community settings.

PREP proposals
    Proposals from the UKCC for standards of post-registration education and practice: concerned primarily with professional development and post-registration qualifications.

purchaser-provider agreements
    Following the NHS reforms, DHAs became purchasers of healthcare, and Trusts and Units providers of health care. Purchasers agree or contract to purchase from providers specific services on behalf of the local population. Purchaser-provider agreements also exist between purchasers of nurse education (Trusts, Units of RHAs) and providers of education (colleges).

recess period
    non-term time.

Regions
    The 14 Regional Health Authorities in England are known as Regions.

replacement staff
    staff employed to replace the lost student contribution to service when traditional courses were replaced by Project 2000 programmes with supernumerary status for students.

rostered service
    being included in staff numbers.

skill-mix
    The relative proportions of staff within a team or unit with particular knowledge, skills or qualifications needed to deliver an agreed service.

supernumerary status
    not being included in staff numbers.

Units
    The hospital and other services of District Health Authorities are organised into management Units.

validation
    The process by which courses are assessed, by the appropriate authorities, for their academic and professional credibility, prior to being run and at regular intervals subsequently.

Chapter One
INTRODUCTION

Rationale and context for the research

The launch of Project 2000[1] in 13 Demonstration Districts in England in late 1989/early 1990 represented a substantial innovation in nurse education. Given the scope and significance of the changes, it was vital that they were documented and that the views and experiences of participants were chronicled. While there was much enthusiasm and excitement about the introduction of Project 2000, it generated a considerable amount of hard work, stress and anxiety and it is crucial that lessons for the future are identified and disseminated. The invitation to tender for Project 2000 monies stated that the first schemes were not to be pilots in the sense that their experience would be evaluated for a number of years before progress could be made elsewhere but, Demonstration Districts, 'the lessons from which could be fed to others as they came on stream' (NHS Management Board, 1988). The Department of Health's funding for the large scale study reported on here provided just that opportunity.

There was a general assumption that, as with any substantial change, Project 2000 would inevitably suffer 'teething troubles', and that optimism about a general improvement 'as the dust settles' was realistic. While there are undoubtedly issues to which this will apply, there is a need to identify aspects where there will not be this inevitable improvement, and strategies which would make positive development more likely. The purpose of this report is to provide an overview of the findings amassed during the research in such a way that they can be incorporated into future planning and development in nurse education. Here is evidence to inform the debate, gathered systematically through the initial period of change. It is anticipated that the report will be read by those with an interest in the principles and practice of nursing in the 1990s and beyond. It may also be of interest to a wider audience because the outcomes of an innovation of this scale have implications for the management of change that cross professional boundaries.

The Project 2000 reforms envisaged more than a revised course for the preparation of nurses, emerging as they did from sustained widespread debate about the future of nursing and nurse education. The basic principles for reform date back several decades e.g. Platt Report (1964), Athlone Report (1938). The Wood Report (1947), made 40 recommendations, including student grants, a CFP with later specialisation and composite training units with a principal and an education committee. Some of these have finally surfaced, with the introduction of Project 2000. Lathlean (1989) made a key distinction between Project 2000 and 'the numerous reports that have emerged over the years, many with far-reaching proposals, few [of which] appear to have had much effect on policy and action'. Project 2000 however 'has been a major exercise in policy formation and a major determinant of action which will lead to the reform of nurse education'.

The case for reform was fuelled by concerns about several issues – educational standards, service delivery, recruitment and retention of students and changes in the NHS and in the health needs of the population. The quality of previous courses for nurse preparation has been forcibly and extensively criticised, e.g. French (1989), Judge Report (1985), Dodd (1973); the reliance on unqualified student nurses to provide service has been viewed as unsatisfactory for all involved; maintaining an adequate output of qualifying nurses has been an increasing concern and the types of patient/client and the services required for them are changing, with implications for the demands made on nursing staff. The UKCC (1986) highlighted crucial deficiencies in the delivery of courses, citing 'the constant grind of up to six intakes per annum and of repeated teaching with no time for research or professional development, the frequent need to make compromises in terms of learning experiences to ensure that wards are staffed, the daily need for pairs of hands to get the work done, [which] are some of the factors which erect immense barriers to educational improvement'.

Evidence for the breadth of change Project 2000 was anticipated to set in train came from the Government's provisos to the effect that nursing must address the issues of widening access into nursing and of the role and function of the new support workers, as part of the Project 2000 package (DHSS, 1988). A succinct and informative overview of the sequence of events leading to, and the key issues to be resolved in, the implementation of Project 2000 was given in Elkan and Robinson's (1991) interim report on reform in one District. Dolan (1993) offered an account of the historical context (particularly emphasising the move from apprenticeship to studentship) and also identified a set of critical factors that highlighted the need for reform.

The significance and complexity of the investment in change were illustrated by Charlwood's (1993) belief that 'if we can provide a "higher" form of education, then we can feel confident that, even if they bring the whole edifice of nursing crashing down around us, we have given these new nurses the tools to rebuild the system we have criticised for so long'. The point already expressed about the scope of the change was made explicit in the following extract quoted at length because it encapsulates the radical nature of what was at stake as well as the impact the changes could have on the existing system.

> *The curriculum for the course supports an individual, community-based, health promotional approach to the practice of nursing, and emphasises personal/professional responsibility and accountability. It aims to produce assertive nurses, with skills in counselling and advocacy, who are able to take through to registration their expertise in all these complex areas of care and who are motivated (and capable) self-directed learners, able to develop their competence on their own initiative. All this is indeed change, and change of a very fundamental kind in that it moves the perspective of nursing, through almost one hundred and eighty degrees from a hospital-based medically modelled approach to treatment and care. Of course, not all this happened at once, but for those who trained in the 1960's and 1970's it has happened in our professional lifetime (Kershaw, 1993).*

The change process

Given the depth and scope of the proposals for Project 2000, evidence from the already extensive literature on the management of change in other fields is an appropriate starting point for setting a context for the reform under scrutiny here. This evidence is both salutary and yet, at times, encouraging. Fullan's overview of educational change (1982) made clear the challenge by stating that 'most attempts at collective change in education seem to fail and failure means frustration, wasted time, feelings of incompetence and lack of support, and disillusionment'. A constructive context of change is needed, because it is not just a case of providing opportunities for the individual to acquire the necessary skills, knowledge and attitudes needed to bring about the desired change in practice. The concern must also be with creating a climate in which the individuals learn to accept and support the proposed change as a desired and accepted way of doing things in their organisation. Kirkpatrick (1985) identified the need for managers to understand and respond to the personal as well as the institutional consequences of change, the need for effective communication and systems of feedback for staff, the need to elicit support rather than force innovation, to involve those who will be affected by the decision-making, to allow sufficient time for implementation and to develop effective strategies for planned change rather than just responding to the situation emerging.

Fullan's (1991) cautionary note about substantial change in general echoed concerns about the feasibility of change on the scale being posited for nursing. As he explained, 'unfortunately, structural changes are easier to bring about than normative ones. If we are not careful we can easily witness a series of non-events and other superficial changes that leave the core of the problem untouched.' Indeed, Fretwell (1985) identified in nursing 'an inbuilt desire for routine, order and conformity which militates against change'. She concluded that nurses have therefore become adept at producing 'a veneer of change through documentation, whilst leaving underlying practices untouched'.

Significant change is **always** demanding and many of the challenges exposed during this research are **not** Project 2000's alone but are met by all who seek to facilitate a change process. Adelman and Alexander's (1982) comment that 'the most apposite model of educational change in the 1980s should perhaps be grounded in catastrophe theory rather than evolutionary theory' could readily be applied to the circumstances in which this study was undertaken, by adding on a decade. Project 2000 has been implemented in a period of continued and massive development in the NHS, notably all the changes attendant upon the introduction of the NHS and Community Care Act (DoH, 1990), the implications of which have inevitably impinged upon the educational reforms. Indeed, Project 2000 was just one factor in the multiplicity of changes with which many of the respondents were having to wrestle. Mergers of some institutions of nurse education, which were taking place at the same time, were an added complication. The difficulty of singling out effects directly attributable to Project 2000 implementation and the danger of effects being wrongly attributed were ever present in the study.

That the reforms have been implemented at all in such turbulent circumstances is in itself no mean achievement. Given the political context in which they were introduced, those involved could justifiably speculate on the 'compromises to be achieved between political expediency, social conscience and professional interests' (James and Jones, 1992). The data that follow will reflect both the achievements and difficulties of the early stages of implementation. Undoubtedly there is much to be said on the former, but the purpose of this report is not only to acknowledge this but also to identify where there was discord and to find ways of progressing.

The Diploma course

Project 2000 is a major innovation in the preparation of students for registration as nurses. It introduces a Common Foundation Programme with specialisation after 18 months into one of four Branches for a further 18 months (Adult Nursing, Mental Health Nursing, Mental Handicap Nursing[2] and Children's Nursing), increased links with higher education, supernumerary status (for most of the course) and bursaries for students, and a diploma-level qualification. In all but one of the 13 colleges of nursing referred to in this report, students enter the courses already assigned to one of the Branches. The entry requirements for nurse education (and the principle of a wide entry gate), did not change when Project 2000 was introduced (further developments are reported on pp.49-51). Some details of the structure and content of the course are presented in Appendix 1, and a comparison with traditional nurse education is given in Table 2 (page 10). Here some of the aims and underlying principles are outlined, drawn from statements in the course submission documents and subsequent course booklets. While these principles and aims have been interpreted differently in practice on each of the sites[3], there is substantial common ground.

There is a cluster of recurring words and phrases in the relevant documents including 'holistic care', 'client as the person at the centre of the caring process', 'student-centred', 'communication', 'research-based practice', and 'accountability'. The phrase 'knowledgeable doer' was widely used to describe what Project 2000 was trying to achieve. A typical summary of the desired outcomes for practice, self-development and management (highlighting the breadth of the courses beyond the pursuit of nursing competence) from one course handbook is provided below. The diplomate should be able to:-

● critically analyse and synthesise material and engage in cogent argument;

- understand the research process and be critical of research methodology and findings that may be applied in practice;

- explain and justify practice that is based on a thorough theoretical grounding and the application of research, to their peers and a multi disciplinary team;

- practise autonomously;

- demonstrate professional accountability and commitment to continuing professional education and development;

- give safe, compassionate, competent nursing care which acknowledges the individuality, stage of development and rights of the adult and is based on a model of nursing;

- demonstrate confidence and competence in communication and teaching of adults, families and colleagues;

- assign appropriate work to helpers and provide supervision and monitoring of assigned work.

In terms of the educational philosophy underpinning Project 2000, the emphases in the relevant documentation are consistently on student-centredness (mirrored in the holistic approach to patient care) and on integrating a range of subjects into a nursing-focused course. On the first point, a typical statement in course documentation is 'the educational philosophy is based on humanistic and holistic principles with the student as the central focus. The process of learning is facilitated by the recognition of each student's individual potential and worth. Upon these principles a foundation is laid for a life-time of professional development.' On the latter it was explained that 'the curriculum is nursing-led but is underpinned by a knowledge base derived from the biological and behavioural sciences and an appreciation of the research process'.

As the course documentation outlines, all the sites have students rostered in the Branch programmes for 20 per cent of their time and all offer a very mixed placement programme in terms of location, length of stay and client group. The general direction is of experience with increasingly unwell clients as the course progresses, although there is variation in how this is put into practice. On one site students have very little contact with hospitals during their CFP, on others there are short placements there in the first term. The duration of community nursing placements also varies, from four to ten weeks, with differing levels of supervision and responsibility. The breadth of community experience, in the wider sense, is similarly varied, with different emphases on access to shops, workplaces and other everyday situations.

The guiding principles on each site, identified in the documentation, are of an overall focus on health rather than illness (certainly during the CFP), of the inherent dignity and value of the individual (be they student or client) and of service being an integrated whole, whether provided in a hospital or community setting. On the last point, the courses are commonly organised so that 'a significant feature of the practice component of the total course is the provision of non-institutional and community experience such that the registered practitioner is capable of competent practice both within and outside the care institution'.

The course on each site comprises different combinations of the physical and social sciences interwoven with practice placements. While the CFP typically contains a widely interpreted range of community (and some hospital) placements, the emphasis in the Branch is commonly on institutional placements and relevant academic work. The split is half and half between academic work and practice for the courses overall. The breakdown itemised in one Adult Branch Handbook (of a standard 2,300 hours programme), to illustrate further, is of 950 hours on the Art and Science of Nursing (largely placements and time for reflection); 500 hours on the Development and Function of the Individual (including microbiology and pharmacology); 500 hours on the Individual and Society (including psychology in nursing) and 350 hours on

4

ethics and politics in relation to nursing (including nursing management).

Data collection and analysis

The research was undertaken in six of the 13 first round Demonstration sites in England – those that started the Diploma course in late 1989/early 1990. These six were selected from the 13 on the basis of their location, size, and type of HE link.. Contact was maintained with the other seven colleges of nursing through interviews with principals and course leaders at three points in the study to collect information that could be compared and contrasted with that from the main study sites. The main data collection was by interviews with college of nursing staff, senior nurse managers, senior service managers, practice-based nurses, staff in HE and students. This was a longitudinal study in which interviews with the same key personnel took place at different points in time (although there was obviously some substitution in that individuals, or indeed posts, were not static). The variation in the number of interviewees in different rounds for some groups is because the most senior personnel were seen only in the first round (if there were two) or in the first and third (if there were three). In addition, the variation in the number of nurse educators reflected changes in areas of responsibility within the colleges' structure.

The research took place over a period of four and a half years in total, although the bulk of the funding covered the period between September 1989 and August 1992 when three full-time researchers were in post. To provide up-to-date material on implementation prior to this report, a series of interim papers and an interim report were produced. (Further details are provided in Appendix 2.) Table 1 (page 9) conveys the scale of the study. The students were interviewed four times (including once after the course) and the education-based staff three times (during the passage of the first intake). Some characteristics of the student sample, and details of the sampling are given in Appendix 3. Managers and practice-based staff were seen twice (once in the early stages of the study and once in the third year of the course). Details of the complexities of sampling for the practice-based staff are given in Appendix 4. A questionnaire was sent to all students in the six sites in the early stages of the course (Jowett *et al*, 1992a) and data on those leaving the course were collected and are presented in Appendix 5. All this information was supplemented by attendance at relevant meetings, and by the collection and analysis of documentation pertaining to the courses.

Some of the fundamental principles underpinning the research approach are presented below as an introduction to the type of data that follows. The focus of the study was on the process of implementation over time and it is argued here that a largely qualitative approach was the best way of highlighting and reflecting upon the complex issues thrown up by an innovation of the scale and dynamism of Project 2000. 'Qualitative methods' is an umbrella term encompassing a range of interpretative techniques designed to discover, describe, decode, translate, and otherwise get to grips with the meaning, not the frequency, of features of the social world. (Quantitative methods include randomised experiments, quasi-experiments, paper and pencil 'objective' tests, multivariate statistical analyses, sample surveys, etc.)

An experimental mode of inquiry with control groups would be inappropriate given the diversity of subjects under scrutiny and the need to study the **context** of change rather than just isolated variables. To base the study on questionnaire surveys would produce relatively superficial data, of limited value in terms of explaining the process being studied. As Yin (1984) suggested, detailed case study work seeks to 'explain the causal links in real life interventions that are far too complex for the survey or experimental evaluations' and may be used to 'explore those situations in which the intervention being evaluated has no clear, single set of outcomes' – statements that exemplify the methodological challenges of studying the implementation of Project 2000.

The research literature identifies a 'growing awareness that the traditional (or 'scientific') paradigm characteristic of research in the physical sciences is inappropriate when dealing with the complexities of individuals relating to each other and functioning within their social or educational settings' (Hamilton, 1977). Parlett (1972) light-heartedly described this approach as 'A paradigm for plants not people'. Finch's (1986) exposition of the strengths of the qualitative approach demonstrates its relevance to the questions being addressed in the NFER study. She identified:

> *Concern for process as well as outcome, capacity to study process over time, including the policy-making process itself, the capacity to provide descriptive detail which makes situations 'comprehensible', the study of social processes in their natural contexts; a capacity to reflect the subjective reality of people being studied, including most importantly those who are the target groups for social policy action.*

The nursing research perspective

The study of nursing and nurses has contributed to the emergent awareness of different modes of investigation. A proliferation of publications (e.g. Cahoon, 1987; Polit and Hungler, 1987; and Field and Morse, 1985) offer sound advice on the feasibility and applicability of a vast range of approaches. The aspiring (or indeed experienced) researcher in the nursing world has a wealth of material to draw from, in a climate of growth and enthusiasm. Research is accorded a high status and in the current phase of development nursing is explicitly expressing its allegiance to it.

Twelve years ago Melia (1982) challenged her colleagues to explore some hitherto unfamiliar territory. She expressed concern that nursing research tended to adopt a quantitative approach which carried a danger of missing a wealth of rich data; data which allow interpretative understanding of the phenomenon under study. Prior to that she concluded a section on research approaches in her thesis (1981) with the reminder that in the social sciences there is 'nothing particularly new about the adoption of a qualitative method'. Leininger (1987) found it '... most encouraging to see nurses become interested in ethno-methods and to envision its great potential to the discovery of many elusive aspects of nursing. It is also a timely method to use as nursing moves closer to knowing human beings in personalised, direct and intimate caring ways'. Such commentators have promoted a lively and fruitful discourse within the field of nursing research where methodological issues are high on the agenda.

The nature of evidence

The NFER evaluation of the implementation of Project 2000 consists of gathering and presenting information that is deemed useful for making decisions and judgements about the way forward, set against the stated aims and objectives of Project 2000. Only by asking interviewees to reflect on their own experiences and views in a loosely structured way that allows them to set the priorities can an understanding of the process begin to emerge. The resounding messages come through - the difficulties encountered when such a dramatic change in course delivery is established, the demands that such multi-faceted courses make on staff and students - but so too do the more subtle, sometimes unexpected, aspects of implementation. To attempt to quantify the students' reflections on their practice placements or the views of nurse teachers on the pressures of the early stages of implementation, for example, would obscure the main messages of these data. The focus is on depth, not breadth and statistical inferences.

By collecting only the limited data that are easily measurable in quantitative terms, the study would miss the opportunity to reveal and understand the complexities of implementation. Finch (1986) criticised the positivistic, 'fact'-finding approach to explaining social life on the grounds that it assumes an unproblematic conception of 'facts' and an impartiality in their collection that is unrealistic. She pointed out that precise divisions of information into categories can leave the key questions unanswered. Finch used the example of the Crowther Report (1959) on the education of young people to illustrate the limitations of a quantified approach when tackling certain types of issues. She explained that their survey data on school leaving identified

6

who leaves school at the minimum age, but the quantitative analysis of data on **why** people leave produced 'reasons' that 'beg far more questions than they answer', because in general, 'data of this kind cannot give a sense of how decisions are arrived at (or indeed whether the concept of 'decision' is even appropriate) because the individual is necessarily decontextualised, and social action divided into discrete items of behaviour (in this case 'reasons')'.

In a similar vein, Brion (1989) explored 'an unskilled assumption' ... that quantitative data are somehow 'better' and explained that 'this is not necessarily so. For example a postal questionnaire survey of local employers may yield less valid and reliable data about training needs than some carefully selected case studies and in-depth interviews.' Cicourel (1964) explained that 'standardised questions with fixed choice answers provide a solution to the problem of meaning by simply avoiding it'.

As stated, there is some confusion about the nature of 'facts' and what is 'objective' or 'subjective'. Providing respondents with a set of pre-determined categories from which to select an answer does not make their response 'objective' - it merely limits the scope of their answer to fit the researcher's schema. It may be neat, it may produce cut and dried 'answers', but it would be inappropriate for an accurate study of social processes. The degree to which the data collected 'fit' the questions asked influences the choice of mode of analysis. When students were asked for their experience of the personal tutor system, for example, it was relatively straightforward to process their responses in terms of varying degrees of support achieved. However, to do so for responses to the mentoring question would have produced misleading results. A neat breakdown along the same lines as outlined above would miss the crucial point, which was that mentoring was not particularly significant for students. The richness of these data suggested that it was the placement ethos that mattered, not whether there was a consistent mentor *in situ*. The real message was that they did not aspire to this long-term engagement. To have manipulated their answers into a numeric framework, or to have limited their opportunity to make this point, would have been to impose the researcher's meaning on to the data and would have missed the point that students may have different criteria on which to judge the value of their placements.

Parlett and Hamilton (1972) explained that a 'powerful check on the study's validity' is 'does it present "recognisable reality" to those who read it?' During the production of this final report, a draft version was sent to all 13 sites involved and the responses of senior staff suggested that Schatzman and Strauss' (1973) 'post-verification' validation was achieved. These academics posed the question: 'do the participants in the documented enterprise regard the study as accurately depicting the world they know?' One response to the draft report, from one of the sites was that 'although the report evoked for me some painful memories, it also reminded me of the excitement and challenge of four years ago. I was gratified to find that the report raises some key issues, which from my own experience, I felt were important to emphasise. I do feel the strength of the report lies in the fact that it has addressed these issues in a very detailed way'. Another respondent's view was that the report was 'well presented, comprehensive and will certainly highlight areas which must be addressed by the Department of Health, the ENB and Institutions'. A third felt that the report 'makes very interesting reading as I believe it very accurately reflects the issues and associated problems surrounding the implementation of this major innovation in nurse education'.

This study was concerned with the processes, perceptions and contingencies that culminated in particular outcomes for those engaged in the reforms. The data presented here do not permit comprehensive causal explanations of outcomes, nor statistically significant correlations between features and outcomes. The goal was to document and interpret as fully as possible the totality of participants' experience, in context. Such an approach acknowledges and tackles the complexities encountered and studies them realistically and it is hoped that the present study will make a useful contribution to the emergent understanding of what Project 2000 represents in practice. Adelman and Alexander (1982) explained that evaluation is not only inherently problematic but also necessarily so because 'if it is bland or non-controversial, if it produces scarcely a ripple in an institution's consciousness, then arguably it is not worth undertaking'. Evaluation only begins to justify the time and resources invested in it 'if it questions, or provides the basis for questioning, existing practices and orthodoxies, if it provides for a consideration of alternative analyses and solutions to the problems of teaching and learning'.

The interview questions used were designed to elicit both specific answers as well as unexpected issues. The data collected were organised into subject areas, following the pattern of topics covered in the interviews. By a relatively simple editing process the responses were organised under gross headings such as 'placement experiences', 'perspectives on higher education', etc. Having attained this structure, the analysis continued with the quest for themes or recurring regularities. Common trends and the variations between them were identified. Polit and Hungler (1987) outlined the need to 'attend not only to what themes arise but also to how they were patterned. Does the theme apply only to certain subgroups?... in certain contexts? At certain time periods? What are the conditions that precede the observed phenomenon, and what are the apparent consequences of it? In other words, the qualitative analyst must be sensitive to **relationships** within the data.'

The aim of the analysis was to portray the characteristic forms the data took and any significant exceptions with a view to describing and analysing the process of change. The challenge was to maximise the 'real-life' insights and subleties, whilst imposing a structure (sometimes a 'count') when that is judged to be the most effective way of determining the relationships between variables. For widely discussed points the analysis consisted of coding such references and counting their frequency – the latter to ensure that an accurate picture of their recurrence was drawn. An example would be the widespread reports of an initial lack of clarity about the purpose and proposed outcome of placement experiences in the CFP. It was not that all respondents used this exact phrase when reflecting on their encounters, rather that it was a feature that ran through most of their accounts. Having concluded that this lack of clarity could be described as widespread, the task was to look for counter-arguments and complexities and incorporate them into the writing of this report.

Qualitative analyses usually contain quantitative statements in some form. They may be less explicit than in quantitative material but there are generally frequency statements about the incidence of general categories. For much qualitative data the count is used to facilitate accuracy, rather than as a form of presentation. In many instances it is unnecessary to distinguish between percentage numbers, only to know that the percentage is high or low. However, not only widely held views have validity and sometimes a point can be illustrated by the particular perspective of one person. The text is illustrated largely with quotations that typified responses and where such individually held insights or reflections are included, they are identified as such.

Studying Project 2000

In view of the need to learn from the endeavours of those engaged in the early stages of Project 2000's development, a series of related studies have been established to monitor specific features of the change. Given the widespread interest there is in the progress of Project 2000, the major projects funded to date are listed below.

Staff in colleges of nursing are the focus for the Liverpool University team's study of *The Evolving Role of the Nurse Teacher in the Light of Educational Reforms* (Luker *et al.*, 1993). Staff in the practice settings are given equal prominence in the King's College, London and University of Manchester team's investigation of *A Detailed Study of the Relationships between Teaching, Support, Supervision and Role Modelling in Clinical Areas, Within the Context of Project 2000 Courses* (White *et al.*, 1993). Both studies are funded by the ENB. Similar developments in Wales are the subject of the DoH-funded project (on behalf of the Welsh Office Nursing Division) being undertaken by a Cardiff-based team *The Practitioner Teacher: a Study in the Introduction of Project 2000 in Wales* (Davies *et al.*, 1992). The experience of one institution is documented and analysed in Robinson's (1991) study based in the Suffolk and Great Yarmouth College of Nursing and Midwifery (in partnership with the Suffolk College) and another individual scheme is the subject of the study at Nottingham University by Elkan and colleagues (1991, 1992). One part of the courses (the CFP) has been comprehensively studied in the University of Belfast's NINB-funded work (O'Neill *et al.*, 1993). The National Audit Office's (1992) report on the planning and the workforce implications of Project 2000 highlighted issues needing to be tackled to facilitate an efficient transition from previous systems.

The research reported here is the most comprehensive in coverage but further studies are still needed. It should be remembered that this research was concerned with the process of implementation rather than its outcomes. To investigate the impact of the Project 2000 reforms, a longer-term study of the career paths of those successfully completing the course would be required. Even a relatively lengthy evaluation, such as the one described here, necessarily involves using short-term criteria with limited timescales, and caution must be exercised in judging outcomes.

Table 1: Number of interviews conducted				
	1st round	2nd round[2]	3rd round	4th round
Managers[1]	50	32	—	—
HE staff	31	18	25	—
Nurse educators[3]	108	79	82	—
Practice-based staff	90	92	—	—
Students	77	71	68	68[4]

1 Chief nursing officers/advisers, district general managers, directors of nursing services, district personnel managers, etc.

2 Where there were only two rounds, this meant one in the early stages and one in the third year of the courses.

3 Includes principals and course leaders in nurse education in the 13 Demonstration Districts.

4 Thirteen of these were telephone interviews.

This report draws together the views of different groups of those involved in the implementation of Project 2000. Some of the chapters focus on the data from particular groups, and others deal with broad areas of change. Where appropriate, the views of different groups on particular topics are drawn together. Chapter 2 contains data from senior staff highlighting the breadth of the changes and the wider context within which the details of implementation must be set. It seeks to set the scene for the findings that follow. Chapter 3 outlines the organisational outcomes of the liaison between nurse education and HE, and the consequences for staff and students of such arrangements. Details of the curriculum and the ways in which it may be developed and enhanced are the subject of Chapter 4, and the particular circumstances and views of nurse teachers form Chapter 5. Having dealt with several strands of the courses delivered in institutions of education, Chapter 6 details the situation in the key area of practice placements, identifying well-regarded features and areas for development. The students' views appear throughout the text, as appropriate, but Chapter 7 presents their perspectives on what it was like being on the courses and their expectations and experience of work as a qualified nurse. A summary of the main points is provided at the end of Chapters 2 to 7. Chapters 3 to 7, those with detailed data from the research, end with discussions drawing out the key points. Chapter 8 draws together broad-based comments and overviews on the changes and Chapter 9 seeks to identify the main issues for consideration and action.

TABLE 2: A comparison of project 2000 with traditional nurse education		
	Project 2000	**Traditional nurse education**
Specialisation	All undertake common foundation programme for 18 months and then either Adult Nursing, Mental Health Nursing, Mental Handicap Nursing or Children's Nursing for a further 18 months	All embark upon specialist three-year course
Name of qualification	Registered Nurse (RN) with (Adult) or (Mental Health) or (Mental Handicap) or (Child)	Registered General Nurse (RGN) or Registered Mental Nurse (RMN) or Registered Nurse Mental Handicap (RNMH) or Registered Sick Children's Nurse (RSCN)
Status on course	Student nurse with bursary Supernumerary status on placements for all but 20 per cent of the time.	Employee in NHS A member of the workforce (apart from some specialist areas)
Contact with HE	All colleges of nursing have links of some kind with an institution of HE, at a minimum to achieve academic validation	None formalised
Level of qualification	Eligibility to register with the UKCC as a nurse and a Diploma in Higher Education (equivalent under the CNAA CATS scheme to 240 points at level II)	Eligibility to register with the UKCC as a nurse
Philosophy and approach (simplified)	An emphasis on health, and holistic care – to be delivered in both institutional and community settings	An emphasis on ill-health, focused mainly on institutional settings

[1]   *A major reform in nurse preparation, details of which are given on pp. 3-5 and in Table 2 (p.10)*
[2]   *This phrase is used here to refer to the Branch, but elsewhere the now recognised term Learning Disability will be used.*
[3]   *The course providers (the colleges of nursing, the HE link and the practice-based staff) pertaining to one college of nursing.*

Chapter Two
IMPLEMENTING PROJECT 2000: THE CONTEXT FOR CHANGE

Introduction

Funding of £114 million has recently been announced to support Project 2000 in 1993/94. This will enable all remaining schemes to start, subject to successful professional and academic validation, by April 1994. Implementation of Project 2000 in England will thus have been completed in only five years compared with a possible period of as much as ten years originally assumed. All of the 13 Demonstration sites have now seen their first students qualify as HE diplomates, but they have entered a world very different from that in which the Project 2000 initiative was first conceived and launched. As well as the changes within the NHS already referred to, nursing's move to forge links with HE has taken place when that world too has been undergoing major changes in structure and funding.

This chapter draws on senior education and service managers' accounts of, and reflections on, the process of implementing Project 2000 in this rapidly changing context. (Data from principals and course leaders across all 13 sites are included.) It begins by reporting managers' experiences of the initial planning and implementation process that was involved in becoming a Demonstration District and goes on to consider issues which, for them, have been of major importance over the course of the ensuing years.

Becoming a Demonstration District

Submitting the bids

In October 1988 the Department of Health asked RHAs to identify sites to participate in Project 2000 from Autumn 1989. Plans were to be submitted accordingly by 31 January 1989 (NHS Management Board, 1988). All 14 RHAs submitted schemes and approval was given in April 1989 for 13 'Demonstration sites' from 11 RHAs. Although the aim was for all schemes to start in Autumn 1989, only seven in fact took their first students then. The other six schemes were delayed until early 1990. The timescale to deliver submissions was tight, demanding considerable effort and commitment – and no little personal sacrifice - on the part of those involved. Those approved as Demonstration sites were single District or amalgamated colleges able to meet ENB requirements relating to size of learner establishment (minimum 300) and number of Branch programmes offered (at least two, normally three) (ENB, 1988). They were also perceived to be colleges with a reputation for innovation which were already some way 'down the road' towards Project 2000 in terms of curriculum development.

Managers reported that, although in nearly all cases the initial impetus for Districts' bids to become Demonstration sites came from education, service management commitment and involvement were crucial. An initiative of the magnitude of Project 2000, with its far-reaching service implications, had to be seen to be a partnership between education and service and to enjoy the backing of the whole HA. Chief nursing officers/chief nurse advisers in post in five of the six Districts in the study at the time were seen as having a vital role in 'selling' Project 2000 to general managers and HA members. District level personnel directors, finance officers and accountants (whose functions were subsequently devolved to Units) were also involved to an unusual degree in the preparation of Project 2000 submissions. In two sites in the study, DGMs chaired District-level education/service steering/implementation groups up to the point of acceptance of their bids for demonstration status. In another case-study site the District personnel officer did so and, indeed, continued to chair such a group two years after implementation, albeit in the new capacity of Unit human resources director.

As in all major innovations, the role of key individuals with the vision and drive to foresee the need for change and for early movement in that direction, was clearly an important factor. Despite the tight timescale, most Districts concerned saw advantages in becoming a Demonstration site in order to be 'in the driving seat instead of being driven'; to raise their college's profile and prestige and hence recruitment potential; and to acquire central monies available at the time with greater certainty and, perhaps, in greater amounts than might be the case in the future.

There was awareness too, however, that those following would have the benefits of the Demonstration Districts' efforts and experience upon which to draw in order to avoid at least some of the pitfalls along the way. Above all, they would have **more time** to prepare and phase in the plethora of changes Project 2000 entailed. The high profile and expectations placed upon the Demonstration Districts were a source of added pressure as well as heightened prestige.

The Districts bidding to be Demonstration sites were expected to lead the way, but managers spoke of having been leading 'in the dark', with only a glimmering of guidance, if any, in the early stages. This was particularly the case in the vast uncharted territory (perceived by some as a 'minefield') of replacement for the student service contribution. All 13 Districts were required to make cuts, often substantial, in their original bids. Reservations about the assumptions on which replacement was based were widespread.

Guidelines and formulae, made available subsequently by the DoH Implementation Group, drew upon the efforts and experience of the Demonstration Districts. For the latter there were so many unknowns and uncertainties when drawing up and costing their bids, assumptions had to be made on a whole range of factors, not just replacement levels. Even the requirement that the new courses should be at Diploma in Higher Education level (that is 240 level II Credit Accumulation and Transfer points), was not clarified in some instances until the day of validation. Levels of student bursaries were not known until June 1989 (DoH, 1989a) and dependency additions not until October 1989 (DoH, 1989b) after some Project 2000 students had already started their courses.

Curriculum planning and validation

In terms of curriculum development, Project 2000 was not a complete or a radical change, for the Demonstration sites and colleges were able to build on previous curricula for parts of their CFP. Nevertheless, the timescale for curriculum planning, as for submission preparation, was tight. After the announcement of the 13 Demonstration Districts in April 1989, conjoint validation meetings scheduled for July 1989 (for an Autumn 1989 start) left colleges only a matter of weeks to finalise curriculum documents. Staff had to work at a tremendous pace and the image of 'laying the lines while the train is coming' captured a widespread feeling. It was inevitable that corners were cut – internal validation processes bypassed in places, for example – and that a good deal of detailed planning, as well as correcting omissions and ironing out inconsistencies, had to be done subsequently as the courses went along.

In some colleges curriculum planning, intended to be corporate, eventually relied almost exclusively upon the work of particular individuals; with problematic repercussions for coordination of subject planning and teaching. Joint planning was even more difficult, with little opportunity for input from HE staff – and little chance for staff from the 'two cultures' to work through differences in perceptions and priorities. In this, as in other respects, however, colleges were coming into Project 2000 from different starting points. In one scheme in the study, where pre-existing relations between the college and the HE institution were strong, an HE staff member was seconded part-time to assist the college with curriculum planning. In other sites links were more tenuous and HE posts, part- or fully funded from Project 2000 money in order to permit greater HE input to course planning and teaching, had not yet been filled.

As a condition of validation, most schemes were required to refine and standardise their academic assessment procedures. Another common requirement was to firm up the links between colleges of nursing and HE institutions. With the planning emphasis having inevitably been on the CFP, Branch programmes had also frequently to be clarified and refined.

Management of change

Managers expressed the view that, given the rushed planning and implementation, it was inevitable that the reality of introducing Project 2000 in the first round Districts fell short of the ideals set out for the management of change. With a change of the magnitude of Project 2000, the aims of effective communication and the involvement and preparation of all groups affected were difficult to achieve. In the early stages of planning and implementation many nurse teachers themselves felt in need of more preparation. The multiple and potentially conflicting pressures placed on them – not least the heightened academic and clinical credibility demanded of them – by Project 2000 were acknowledged from the start. Moreover, the task of informing and preparing practice staff throughout the nursing service was a Herculean one. Despite enormous efforts on the part of education and service managers, confusion and misunderstanding continued to abound as the students progressed through their courses. Nevertheless, by the end of the first CFPs, principals and course leaders saw the support shown by service staff – and the development and commitment of teaching staff – as particularly satisfying aspects of implementation (Jowett *et al.*, 1992b).

The changing context

For senior education and service managers interviewed in 1992, the pace and magnitude of change in both nurse education and service had been such that in the Demonstration Districts the now established Project 2000 was largely overshadowed by other developments. Service managers from the outset had seen Project 2000 as just one factor in a multiplicity of changes with which they were having to grapple simultaneously – with massive programmes of rationalisation and restructuring of services, skill - mix reviews and the continually reverberating clinical grading exercise. Particularly for general managers, who had sometimes been heavily involved at the strategic planning stage, the increasing pressures of implementing the health service reforms from April 1992 (especially in the three case-study Districts which had units in the first wave of independent trusts) meant that Project 2000 became very much a side issue.

For education managers too, Project 2000 had been largely overshadowed by developments in continuing education, particularly the ENB Framework and Higher Award (ENB, 1993a). In 1992, curriculum planners in the first-wave institutions were putting great efforts into developing a panoply of CATS courses and modules offering qualified nurses (including Project 2000 diplomates) a variety of 'links and ladders' by which to pursue their academic and professional development. The wider HE scene was also continuing to change, with polytechnics attaining university status and rapidly expanding student numbers.

Probably the most crucial aspects of the changing context of Project 2000 implementation, however, were problems of recruitment and retention in nursing proving strong grounds at the time for acceptance of the case for change advanced with Project 2000. Six years later the situation looked completely different. The effects of the demographic time-bomb which it was predicted would hit nursing in the early 1990s when the pool of 18-year-olds – the profession's traditional source of recruiting – would be at its lowest, had yet to be felt in most areas.

Recruitment and retention of qualified nurses had also greatly improved, attributable in the main to the combined effects of clinical grading and the deepening economic recession. Lack of staff movement, restructuring of services and skill-mix changes had led to a situation where nurses qualifying from both traditional and new Project 2000 courses already faced less favourable job prospects and future intake numbers were being reduced to achieve a better match between training places and the demand for registered nurses. Debate continued about the role and significance in the future workforce of trained support staff, the very group of staff which enabled the nursing profession to achieve long sought supernumerary status for its students, but now widely seen as threatening to dilute that profession.

Education/service liaison

With the establishment of a market economy in the NHS and implementation of Working Paper 10 (NHS Management Executive, 1989), relations between nurse education and service changed. They had come closer in the sense that student numbers were now more directly tied to service needs (although a shift of emphasis from long-term to short-term needs was also frequently noted). But they had also become more distant, with colleges of nursing having left the ambit of weakened DHAs and moved ever closer towards mainstream HE. At the same time – and in places cutting across the latter move – the drive to amalgamate colleges into ever wider regional groupings continued apace, so that some institutions fortunate enough to have been able to stand alone (in terms of student numbers and Branches they could offer) at the time of the original Project 2000 submissions now found themselves caught up in the difficult and complex process of mergers.

As noted earlier, evidence of service commitment to Project 2000 schemes was seen as one of the predisposing factors in Districts' selection as Demonstration sites – and an essential prerequisite for successful implementation. Five of the six case-study schemes had District level steering groups with strong service management representation to try to ensure service implications were fully addressed and resources directed accordingly. These groups provided a valuable vehicle for joint implementation efforts and for airing and resolving disagreements. Moreover, having had to work together on Project 2000 submissions – at the pace and pressure forced by the Project timetable – was said to have generated considerable goodwill and team spirit among staff involved. As anticipated, however, the NHS changes disrupted established communication channels.

The NHS reforms entailing the growth of DHAs' 'purchaser' remit and the devolution of District level functions (particularly personnel and finance) to units also necessitated changes in the formal structures for education/service liaison – about Project 2000 and nurse education generally. As colleges' relations with DHAs became more distant, new structures had to be established for communication with individual trusts or directly managed units.

Four of the six case-study schemes retained 'umbrella' groups for college managers and senior service representatives from all units in participating Districts. The head of nursing in one first wave independent trust spoke of the value of remaining part of such a group which allowed issues arising from the changed role of the college as an education provider to be addressed on a District-wide basis. In another District a specific Project 2000 working/steering group had been retained because according to its chair, 'You do still find that you need that interface between education and service on Project 2000 because there are continuing issues to be addressed'. At curriculum planning/monitoring level, links were universally well established with service representation reported on all relevant groups. On the whole, senior service managers expressed themselves generally happy with the level of contact they enjoyed with education over the continued implementation of Project 2000 and nurse education matters at all levels.

The divorce of colleges of nurse education from DHAs was not without costs for senior education managers. The college had 'lost a lot by way of support', one case-study principal felt, even though, with the purchaser-provider split, it no longer fitted comfortably into the HA and HE was now seen as its 'final home'. For the present it meant there was, in effect, 'an HE college sitting on hospital sites'. When the merger under way with a neighbouring college was completed, there would be 15 different teaching sites belonging to 11 Units or Trusts. Moreover, negotiations of legal leases required in the case of the new Trusts involved 'a lot of time and hassle quite out of proportion with its importance'. Another principal, in the site where a move into HE was imminent, spoke of staff feeling 'bereaved' even though it was acknowledged that the NHS was in any case changing. Going into HE was now seen as 'more stable than staying in the changed NHS'.

Project 2000 funding: costs and assumptions

It was not part of this study to look at the actual funding of Project 2000 in any detail (unlike the National Audit Office (1992) investigation which had a specific remit to do so), but the research did aim to highlight funding issues. When interviewed in 1991, principals identified the main areas of Project 2000 implementation which had proved more costly than foreseen in their original submissions, as travel, libraries and HE links (Jowett *et al.*, 1992b). In 1992 the situation had not changed. Travel and travel costs continued to present major problems, particularly in rural areas.

Library provision (computer and support facilities as well as books) also remained high on the list of locally identified needs and some schemes had managed to get a certain amount of extra funding for this purpose. Ironically in the case-study site where the college was about to move – organisationally – into HE as part of an amalgamated nurse education Unit, the switch of HE link meant that students (hitherto HE-based for the CFP) would no longer have access to an HE library. Some extra money which had become available had accordingly been used to build up library resources at the (Trust) hospital site, which would become the main base for the CFP, for students and staff, with effect from September 1992.

The cost of HE links had been cited in several of the Demonstration Districts as higher than foreseen in original submissions and several principals commented on what was perceived as the continuing inadequacy of funding in this area. In the scheme where the link was described as 'highly subsidised' by the DHA the principal felt that original assumptions about HE costs had been 'very unrealistic'. The principal in another case-study site was concerned that the costs of the link would rise considerably in the future because there had been incorrect funding in the first place and because the HE institution saw the present (three-year) facilities agreement as under-funded. HE costs for students from the other college of nursing entering the link arrangements upon amalgamation with the demonstration site had been set higher accordingly.

Another area identified as still needing additional funding was staff development – for both service and education staff. Even where some pump-priming monies had been allocated to that – or some of the extra central monies – it was seen as an area requiring 'enormous investment' and there was concern about how the necessary funding could be found to meet the on going need.

Over all 13 schemes, only one reported not having received any of the additional funding allocated in September 1991 because as a Demonstration site it had already had more than other areas. (This was £5 million allocated to Regions which were then responsible for determining allocations to Project 2000 schemes to help meet the effects of inflation, bursary increases and other locally identified needs such as library additions (NHS Management Executive, 1991a).) Another had 'not seen much of it' for the same reason. Most of the extra monies had gone on bursary increases and libraries, mainly for computerisation of facilities and staff support. There were also references to the additional funding put into libraries by the ENB. In three Districts the extra central funding had also gone into staff development – both for nurse teachers and practice staff. In one District some of the money had been used to meet the extra costs of NHS employees undertaking Project 2000 courses on their existing salaries, since the decision in June 1991 (NHS Management Executive, 1991b) that NHS staff wishing to enter Project 2000 courses should be seconded by their existing employer. In another the principal mentioned using some of the extra money to meet dependency allowance payments since the actual percentage of mature students had been well in excess of the estimated percentage originally funded.

Replacement and rostered service funding

The introduction of supernumerary status across the board for students was probably the most radical aspect of the Project 2000 changes. Indeed the original Project 2000 proposals (UKCC, 1986) were seen as calling for 'nothing less than a revolution' in the usage of the workforce in the NHS. It was subsequently conceded that the students would give 20 per cent rostered service over the three-years, concentrated in the final year. But the principle of supernumeracy remained crucial, and provision for replacement of the other 80 per cent of the former student service contribution – the numbers and type of replacement staff – was a key aspect of Districts' Project 2000 submissions and costings.

For the majority of service managers interviewed in all six case-study Districts in 1990, all the issues surrounding replacement of the student labour force on the wards – staffing levels, costs, skill-mix, support staff training and roles – were the main area of concern. Two years on – in the third year of implementation – this was still the case, with the students' period of rostered service causing particular problems in places, as predicted. (What was clearly perceived as less of an issue two years on was the impact of the new programme on staff morale. Staff attitudes generally were seen as much more positive, and greater acceptance of the new-style students – and placements – was widely reported.) For some principals too, it was a major issue. What was striking about the 1992 interviews with both senior managers and principals on this point, however, was the difference of views expressed in different Demonstration Districts.

Although all schemes had received funds for staff replacement, Units within Districts had varied in how they had used them –some employing full-time or part-time established staff, some taking on temporary bank or agency staff either on a regular basis or when needed. While replacement provision was made originally within 'a costing parameter' of certain percentages of staff on certain grades, it was always open to Districts to vary replacement grades and skill-mix within that parameter. The fact that with restructuring, individual Units and individual areas within them had become responsible for deciding how replacement monies allocated to them were spent, had greatly facilitated that kind of flexibility.

Reservations about the levels of replacement and/or skill-mix initially approved for funding were expressed in every scheme, particularly by managers in acute services, and especially where a level of less than the maximum 60 per cent RGN service contribution allowed had been agreed. Calculations had been based on a number of assumptions, two of which related to notions of efficiency:

(i)   that replacement staff who would be permanent would be more efficient than students constantly rotating though clinical placements – hence the deduction of the contentious 'efficiency factor'; and

(ii)   that the 20 per cent service contribution of the new Project 2000 students would be less efficient than that of their predecessors and would thus need to be reduced by a similar factor (Project 2000 Implementation Group, 1989).

The first point was being challenged, although no one, it seemed, wished to question the latter assumption (although there also appeared to be little awareness of a compensatory allowance having been made in the replacement calculations). Although the amount of rostered service contributed by the students at the time of the last round of interviews was still very limited, managers frequently emphasised that Project 2000 third-years could not be relied upon to the same extent as the previous students and needed more supervision.

16

Managers in a number of areas reported that the situation had begun to stabilise as wards got their full replacement quotas, more qualified staff were appointed, new support staff gained skills and recruitment of bank or agency staff diminished. However, fears voiced by those interviewed in 1990 that application of an 'efficiency factor' from year one of Project 2000 replacement would cause problems in the transition phase, when the primary need on the wards would be for 'hands', had, it seemed, to a large extent been borne out. The same applied to the concerns about replacement staff having to be withdrawn from some areas in the students' third year when they gave all their rostered service.

The most complex and confusing aspect of Project 2000 funding in the third year of implementation concerned the students' rostered service contribution – how that was being dealt with in terms of replacement and how it was being accounted for under Working Paper 10 (NHS Management Executive, 1989) and the new purchaser/provider arrangements. The position was understood to be that bursary monies in respect of the Project 2000 students' service-giving was being top-sliced by Regions and paid to Units where the students were placed. It was then for those Units to pay colleges of nursing for the student service they were actually getting. Particular problems were arising where service Units found themselves in the position of having to repay money or relinquish some of their replacement staff appointed in phases over the preceding two years. As some managers had predicted in 1990, this was especially difficult in the case of critical care areas.

It was not just institutional areas which were affected. One scheme reported having to reduce the students' community placements because practice staff had been taken out of community teams when students were allocated so that there were not the necessary staff available for supervision. Other areas, residential facilities in hospital grounds and outpatients, for example, had to be redesignated as 'community' accordingly. Because students had always been supernumerary in the community, most Districts had not had any 'replacement' or extra staff allocated. Exceptionally, one District had negotiated some extra funding for support staff to relieve district nurses of some case-load duties.

In most Districts, however, this was not seen as a pressing problem at the time, although, in one, there was some suspicion the finance department would require withdrawal of replacement staff the following year. In another District, there were grave doubts how the original intention to reduce replacement could be adhered to if wards were not to become unsafe, because of the unforeseen degree of supervision the first group of rostered students needed. According to one manager (who had already overspent the budget to ensure safe staffing levels in areas like operating theatres which had not had any replacement funding), they really needed to take another hard look at this issue and to find the money to retain the replacement staff throughout the rostered service period, if necessary. In two other schemes, however, there was evidently no question of replacement staff or monies being withdrawn.

Discontinuity in the students' allocations to some areas, so that there were long periods when they did not have any students giving service, was the other aspect giving cause for concern for acute service managers in two case-study schemes in particular. Wards, they reported, were having to use bank/agency staff to fill the gaps and to keep posts free in order to do so. The students 'come like buses', one manager said; there could be 16 learners coming into Accident and Emergency for four weeks and then nobody for four months'. In the other District it was not just the gaps in the students' service-giving which were causing problems, but for one head of nursing there was also 'a complete mismatch' between the allocations and levels of patient activity. The 11 weeks over the year when they did not have students giving service in the unit fell at times when patient activity was highest, yet the time when 75 per cent of students were rostered for service was peak holiday time for doctors and nurse mentors – and consequently low patient activity.

Again, however, there were marked differences between Districts in this respect. In some other Districts, delay in getting approval to start Project 2000 might have created a gap in the projected supply of students to the wards. But allocations had evidently been arranged so that

there **was** a continuous flow of rostered students into service areas, once that stage was reached. In one District where the students were about to commence rostered service, a change in original plans – and provision – for them to spend ten weeks in the community rather than all 30 weeks in the Acute Unit was posing the head of nursing the problem of finding staff to replace the Project 2000 students for those weeks, exacerbated by the difficulty now in shifting money from Unit to Unit.

Although some colleges had tried hard to ensure a continuous flow of rostered students to service areas, an 'education-led' programme by its very nature made this difficult to achieve. Education managers appreciated that the reduction from three to two (larger) intakes per year in some schemes would exacerbate the 'flow' problem from the service perspective, and the contradiction inherent in having a rostered component in an education-led course was frequently pointed out. There was also appreciation of, if not always sympathy with, the arduous task service managers had in monitoring the student service-giving for which they were paying: 'The service managers have all got so much headache trying to sort out what's owed to them... some... want every drop of blood back in terms of their 20 per cent service contribution. This creates problems for delivery of the course.'

The whole picture as regards the funding and provision of staff replacement for student service-giving had, it seems, become blurred by the NHS changes. Personnel involved in the original negotiations had frequently moved on. The difficulties of monitoring expenditure of replacement monies – and the risk of their diversion for other purposes – were obviously heightened in such a fluid situation. Efficiency savings, frequently imposed on Units in setting their budgets, posed one such threat. One Acute Unit manager reported 'ring fencing' the Project 2000 monies in 1992/3 to prevent their use to offset such savings. Another Unit head of nursing elsewhere who, with the devolution of budgets had retained responsibility for monitoring the overall Unit establishment, had been able to ensure replacement monies were excluded when efficiency savings were being made because an efficiency factor had already been deducted. She fully endorsed the recommendation that a single manager should have the responsibility of coordinating Project 2000 implementation in a hospital and overseeing the working out of its staffing implications on the wards (Audit Commission, 1991).

In some of the Demonstration Districts, extensive activity and skill-mix analysis, looking at what nurses did and what they should be doing, had been under way for some time before Project 2000. Elsewhere, it seems, it was only in the course of attempts to calculate, or recalculate, bids for replacement staff to carry out the work previously undertaken by student nurses that the issue started to be addressed in earnest. It was clear from the 1990 interviews that the amount of 'non-nursing' tasks repeatedly shown by such analysis to be performed by qualified nurses – and the extent of dependence upon student labour – were a real cause for concern among general and nursing managers alike.

The sheer number of students requiring supervision and assessment in hospitals and the community continued to cause senior managers concern, and there were references in all six Districts to the pressures this placed on staff and on services. Although traditional course placements were coming to an end, there were now students on various stages of the new Branch programmes as well as the CFP, conversion students of various kinds, and support staff trainees. A Mental Health Unit manager described having 'to draw the line' when small community teams found themselves 'completely overloaded with students' at certain times of the year – a situation which had 'stretched the corporate responsibility for education considerably' –but at the end of the day they had responsibilities to their clients too. In Mental Health and Learning Disability and increasingly in Community Nursing generally, it was still emphasised that the demand for student placements had to be balanced with clients' rights to privacy. In response to the situation there were frequent reports of agreements being negotiated or already concluded with colleges of nursing about the maximum number of learners particular areas could accommodate at any one time.

Support staff training and roles

The whole question of support staff training and roles, like the replacement issue with which it is closely related, has from the outset been one of the most complex aspects of Project 2000 implementation. When interviewed in 1990, senior managers in the case-study Demonstration Districts felt particularly strongly about the timing of the introduction and training of the new HCAs.

At the root of the problem, from the managers' perspective, was the fact that Project 2000 monies were available for new support staff to replace the student service contribution, but there was no financial provision for training and assimilating into the new structure the mass of existing nursing assistants. National guidelines stated that, in the absence of new grades, HCA jobs were to be graded in accordance with existing definitions for Scales A and B, but that the usual principle should apply that 'the receipt of training or the acquisition of a qualification does not of itself provide justification for a higher grading' (NHS Management Executive, 1990). With the clinical grading, however, there was the expectation that enhanced competences and roles should carry enhanced grades. Where the money would come from was not known, especially where there was a very large – over 1,000 strong – nursing assistant workforce. The decision announced in the Autumn of 1990 to leave the questions of HCA pay and grading for local determination did not completely resolve the situation.

In 1992, three years into Project 2000 implementation and with the phasing out of the previous students virtually complete, major issues had still to be resolved, particularly regarding a pay and career structure for support staff and definition of their roles. Providing a training system was optional and was only just beginning in places. Slow progress nationally on competence development and validation (including validation at NVQ Level 3 and recognition of that as an entry to professional nurse education, not announced until November 1992) had, it seems, continued to hamper local movement on these issues. In some Units, nursing auxiliaries were said to be reluctant to undertake HCA training until the potentially more advantageous 'integrated' NVQ proposals awaited from the Care Sector Consortium became available.

Because nationally agreed standards of competence for NVQs were still not available when the Demonstration Districts embarked upon support staff training, managers in 1990 had frequently voiced fears that much of the effort and resources Districts had put into developing their own competence training might subsequently prove to have been wasted. In 1992, some duplication of training effort was, in fact, reported, where bodies like City and Guilds (with which colleges and other agencies were now registered to provide such training) required further/different competences. But on the whole, it seemed, this had not proved as great a problem as feared.

By 1992, the title 'health care assistant' was used much less widely, with Districts reverting to 'support workers' or 'health care support workers' or still using 'nursing assistants', and keeping the HCA title for new jobs where roles and pay were locally determined. The problem exercising managers in 1990 – of how to find the money for existing staff acquiring higher competence levels to be given higher grades – had so far been averted by making distinctions of this kind. Existing staff were being offered NVQ training and registration – usually just to Levels 1 and 2, and in some places Level 3, although national validation was still not available at that level at the time. There was also, it seems, across the Districts a general feeling that some sort of career structure had to be developed to give support staff the incentive to train. Slow progress in assimilating existing staff into the national competence framework in some Districts was attributed to lack of movement on this front.

Student numbers

In 1992, recruitment to Adult and Child Branches remained healthy across the Demonstration sites. Child Branch programmes in particular were usually over-subscribed and size or frequency of intakes had increased in places accordingly. Recruitment to Mental Health and Learning Disability Branches was still slower in most schemes, but the picture was variable. One of the case-study schemes, where since 1991 a Branch programme in Learning Disabilities leads to both Diploma in Nursing and Diploma in Social Work qualifications, had not experienced any problems with recruitment. Expectations voiced by college of nursing principals in 1991 that, with implementation of Working Paper 10 (NHS Management Executive, 1989), numbers of students contracted by RHAs would fall, had been widely realised. With the exception of the Child Branch where shortages of RSCN nurses had dictated increases, regional contracts based on annual demand forecasting by individual Units had meant reductions in student numbers across the Demonstration sites. Thus the colleges were said to be getting more – and better qualified – applicants, a situation which respondents attributed in the main to the recession, but also to the higher academic status of the new courses. But at the same time the 'dramatic' decreases in staff turnover (which education managers, like their service colleagues, saw as a consequence of the recession and clinical grading, accompanied by skill-mix changes), meant a perceived need for far fewer registered nurses. Future intake numbers were being reduced (usually in the region of 10-20 per cent for the Adult Branch) to better match training places with the demand for qualified nurses.

Several senior service managers commented upon the greatly heightened unpredictability of the job market since the health service reforms. The whole situation had 'become more unstable as purchasers made their presence felt', according to one head of nursing. All Units in that District were said to have expansion plans but 'it would depend on the money coming from the purchasers'. There was more volatility as well as more versatility with the new contract arrangements, and in these circumstances some managers expressed themselves very sceptical about the soundness of workforce predictions.

Some college principals interviewed in 1992 also expressed reservations about the annual demand forecasts made by Trusts and directly managed Units on which regional needs were based. Such forecasting was still 'an imprecise science' in one principal's words. Elsewhere concern was expressed about the short-term nature of projections made by non-nurse general managers who failed to realise the implications of dropping intakes.

Job prospects for Project 2000 diplomates

When senior service and education managers were interviewed in 1992, job prospects for the first Project 2000 students to qualify were uncertain. However, there were some Units – in three case-study Districts – where service managers envisaged being able to place the Project 2000 qualifiers without too much difficulty, and most Units were determined to make every effort to place the first Project 2000 nurses. In one of the case-study schemes, the principal predicted (in May 1992) that the employment situation should not be too bad, because the main 'host' hospital was then short-staffed. It was also reported, with great satisfaction, in that scheme that eight of the first group had been (informally) offered grade 'D' jobs in the community. In another District, it was thought that the Adult Branch students should manage to find jobs, but that in Mental Health and Learning Disabilities it was really going to be 'a struggle'. In a part of the region where large institutions for both client groups were scheduled for closure, there were already said to be real problems with re-deployment of existing staff.

The once widespread practice of offering new qualifiers short-term contracts had virtually ceased, and formerly centralised interviewing systems in particular Districts or particular units had given way to what one course leader termed a 'free-for-all' situation whereby students had to just look out for – and apply for – any jobs available on individual wards. Respondents in some schemes envisaged the Project 2000 students, by virtue of their broader-based education as well as the job situation, looking further afield for their first jobs, to other sectors (private, voluntary and social services), as well as to other parts of the country and abroad. One principal saw colleges of nursing having to take the universities' approach in future and say to students: 'Come and do the course, and then you'll have to go and find your own job.'

For students who would succeed in finding employment in their locality one Demonstration District already offered a system of one year contracts which included two six-month placements with supervision and study days. This system (which the principal had observed in Australia on a study visit) was said to have been very well received by all concerned. 'Preceptorship' schemes to provide support (UKCC, 1993) were also envisaged or even in place occasionally elsewhere. But at the time of the last interviews with principals and course leaders, rumours that Project 2000 qualifiers would be offered grade 'C' jobs were also causing consternation in some Districts, although in the case-study sites at least, these subsequently proved to be unfounded. One course leader expressed the view that all Project 2000 students should have been given an extra six months' bursary – an 'internship' in effect – to consolidate their experience.

Summary of main points

- The timescale to deliver submissions to start Project 2000 was tight, demanding considerable effort and commitment – and no little personal sacrifice – on the part of those involved.

- Service management's commitment to, and involvement in, implementing Project 2000 was crucial.

- There were many unknowns and uncertainties for those charged with drawing up and costing their bids for Project 2000, particularly with regard to replacement staff to cover the diminished student service contribution.

- All 13 Districts were required to make cuts, often substantial, in their original bids.

- The tight timescale for curriculum planning meant that internal validation processes were sometimes bypassed and that a good deal of detailed planning and amending had to be done as the courses were running.

- The management aims of effective communication and the involvement and preparation of all groups affected were difficult to achieve.

- Project 2000 was just one factor in a multiplicity of changes with which NHS staff were having to grapple.

- The effects of the demographic time-bomb, which it was predicted would hit nursing in the early 1990s, had yet to be felt in most areas, resulting in less favourable job prospects for Project 2000 qualifiers than had been envisaged.

- The main areas of Project 2000 implementation which had proved more costly than foreseen were travel, libraries and HE links.

- Most of the £5 million given by the DoH to Project 2000 schemes, via Regions, in 1991 was spent on bursary increases and libraries, mainly for computerisation of facilities and staff support.

- The main area of concern throughout the study for service managers was the replacement of students' service contribution. Staff in the Demonstration Districts varied considerably in their views on this issue but all experienced difficulties.

- The assumption that replacement staff who would be permanent would be more efficient than students was being questioned. The assumption that the 20 per cent service contribution of Project 2000 students would be less efficient than their predecessors was being borne out in practice.

- Rostered service arrangements (introduced in the third year) were complex and confusing for managers.

- Project 2000 monies were available for new support staff to replace the student service contribution, but there was no financial provision for training and assimilating into the new structure the mass of existing nursing assistants. Major issues still had to be resolved, particularly regarding a pay and career structure for support staff and definition of their roles.

Chapter Three
NURSE EDUCATION
AND HIGHER EDUCATION –
A PARTNERSHIP FOR CHANGE

Introduction

In this chapter a chronological outline of the organisational changes made to the links between nurse education and HE during the period of the study is presented. Details of the contribution made to Project 2000 by HE are given in Appendix 1. The views of all participants – HE staff, those in nurse education (including principals and course leaders across all 13 sites) and students – are represented here which, taken together, offer a detailed picture of the process of implementing this key aspect of the new Diploma course.

The HE perspective

The HE institutions liaising with nurse education varied considerably in their expectations of their involvement in Project 2000 and in their previous relevant experience. What emerged strongly from an analysis of the process of developing the links was that there was no obvious blueprint for success and that those involved were taking on a considerable task in seeking to develop a combined strategy to provide the new Diploma course. There was clear acknowledgement by the HE staff interviewed almost three years into the course that the collaborative enterprise they were engaged in presented a **continuing** challenge both organisationally and at the level of course delivery.

Organisational structures, liaison and progress

The early stages

As is described below, the prospect of embarking on Project 2000 was viewed with a general feeling of optimism and goodwill. However, the task of actually establishing the links was reported to be extremely difficult in four of the six Districts studied. In one HE institution a senior member of staff closely involved in the liaison described it as 'a nightmare' and reported serious misunderstandings over organisational and structural relations between the two institutions involved. There was mistrust, and concern was expressed that the college of nursing was intending ultimately to 'go it alone'. In another scheme HE staff explained that relations were 'strained' because of a lack of clarity regarding roles. To bring in the new course 'overnight', when there were no prior links and not enough time, was believed by them to be 'courting disaster'.

In the two Demonstration sites where relations at the organisational level were described as having been easier, lecturers explained that previous joint enterprises had helped to smooth the path and that the proposed extended links were not seen as a threat. In one of them a group of four very senior members of staff (two from the institution of HE, one from the Health Authority and one from the College of Nursing) had collaborated for some considerable time before the introduction of the course and one of them emphasised that if they had not 'pushed' for what they were seeking and 'been of a like mind', the course would 'not have taken off'. The complex nature of the collaboration was illustrated in the other relatively smooth link at this level, where senior staff in HE reflected that the process of negotiation had, in fact, been 'too

23

nice' and that there had been 'mutual respect' without an understanding of what it was actually based on or an awareness of each other's cultures and traditions. There had not been a forum for **proper** discussion and the college had 'soft-pedalled' on the academic issues because of a desire to establish harmonious relationships – a strategy that was later regretted.

Progressing with links

The variation amongst the schemes apparent in the early stages increased over the period of the study. Within two years substantial changes has taken place or were to take place in the very near future in four of the six schemes (and were under consideration in a fifth). By this stage plans on one site to amalgamate with HE had come to fruition and what had been the colleges of nursing were now two schools in the HE faculty structure (with a newly appointed head of faculty from a nurse education background). A second scheme was developing with a view to the college of nursing becoming an Institute within the 'link' institution of HE in April 1992. At the other end of the spectrum, one link now only consisted of course validation. There was no student contact at all, although staff from the two institutions involved worked together at a number of meetings – the Academic, Examination and Course Boards, the Curriculum Development Group and the Academic Standards Committee. In the fourth scheme (where the college of nursing has purpose-built accommodation on the HE site) it had recently been announced that the existing pre-registration course and the other proposed nurse education courses were to be transferred to another institution of HE, and the original HE partner's only future obligation was to continue to validate and teach on the course for current students. Thus, links built up over the years were being severed and nurse education staff thrown back into the turmoil and uncertainty of a situation where they were having to apply for available posts in the new wider organisational structures. Amalgamation with another college of nursing in the Region was scheduled for September 1992 and it was anticipated that these merged institutions would become a department of nursing within the new HE link institution.

In the two remaining schemes less ambitious linkages were envisaged in the immediate future. In one, where the college of nursing already had formal associate status, a joint working group was looking at the possibilities for a closer form of association. Concerns were expressed by a senior member of HE staff here about the speed of proposed developments with some nurse education staff seeming to want to 'run before they can walk' in terms of courses they might offer. It was felt that sufficient staff with appropriate qualifications were needed before such moves should be contemplated. In the other, the link had been formalised with the college of nursing now having associate status. A new Memorandum of Association covering all activities between the two institutions had been signed and a Joint Planning and Consultative Committee established, which it was anticipated would encourage further growth in the longer term. A senior member of staff here said that the proposed orientation programmes in HE for nurse teachers would be a priority until a 'free-flow of interchange' was achieved between institutions. Such exchanges were said to be vital in developing academic and administrative collaboration (an administrative assistant having recently been appointed to facilitate the latter).

Where the link had progressed to incorporation into a faculty this was a reflection of the very positive projections made in the first interviews with HE staff. This link illustrated what Gibbs and Rush (1987) described as '... the forging of a partnership on both sides [which] will lessen the likelihood of the host dominating the new member'. There were many areas for development here as will be discussed below, but the basic organisational framework had coalesced as expected. The institutional gain here was, as one lecturer explained it, the sheer size of the new faculty which meant that it would be able to 'flex its muscles and have a major input into how the college develops'. In the scheme where HE staff had been constructively involved in course development from the start, they were on target for institutional mergers in April 1992.

In the 'validation only' link some of the influences contributing to this contraction were identified by HE staff as being an initial dependence on the working relationship between two key individuals and a subsequent change of personnel who brought conflicting views on the potential of the link. The early informality meant that it was difficult to recognise who was responsible for what, and HE staff (who were all experienced in nurse education) felt that 'bits and pieces' of the course were being bought from them and they could see no scope for development. Practical and financial limitations served to exacerbate the more fundamental restrictions on development – staff losses had 'hit hard', involving those most directly involved in Project 2000, and space to accommodate students was also at a premium. Regret was expressed that potential benefits for students had not been realised – when on site they had literally been using space in the HE building and had not had access to facilities or the HE 'atmosphere' in any meaningful way.

In the scheme where nurse education was being withdrawn, HE staff saw their plans for expansion curtailed by decisions made outside their sphere of control, and disappointment at wasted efforts and lost opportunities was expressed. A senior member of staff reinforced the point that they had taken the 'hard route of complete integration' with nurse students based on the HE site and he regretted that the good intentions and hard work had been in vain. A feeling of having facilitated the development of the nurse education centre (giving them a 'leg-up' to meet their new HE partner) for very little reward was expressed by these staff.

Although informal relations were good on all sites, for some staff there was unease about how to progress without more formal input. As one lecturer explained 'when things work well it is through goodwill and informal structures ...what you can do as an individual is so limited'. This unease was not expressed in the scheme where HE staff had been involved from the outset and a sense of steady progress towards a shared goal (with nurse education) permeated their comments. At worst, a lack of structure to involve HE staff resulted in them feeling 'marginalised', notably when channels of communication were inefficient. Disruption to courses of lectures by placements, multiple intakes and misunderstandings about the use made of the recess period (and the need to safeguard it) were further difficulties. It was clear, as one lecturer put it, that there were 'still two quite different outlooks and cultures' which were 'difficult to weld together'. One key figure expressed total frustration with some of the practicalities (involving both HE and nurse education colleagues) which had to be endured in a situation where there was still uncertainty about the Project 2000 input continuing.

Further developments in collaboration

Towards the end of the study, the major organisational changes in terms of links with nurse education had been consolidated and refined. One striking feature of note was that three of the link institutions were in the process of transferring from polytechnic to university status. The two colleges of HE were also in transition – with one of them becoming a faculty within an existing polytechnic (which then became a university) from September 1992, and the other attaining designation as a university in 1993.

On the site where the colleges of nursing had previously amalgamated to become two schools in the HE faculty structure, the anticipated development had continued apace. The key role played by the coordinator in HE (a member of HE staff, part of whose timetable had been allocated to the development of the scheme from the first year of the course) was applauded, although how much longer the post would be required was unclear. He explained that the 'mechanisms are now in place', emphasising in particular the value of a clear structure of line management. The need now was for nurse education colleagues to become more 'proactive' in asserting the course's place in the faculty structure and for key decisions about the location of resources and financial management to be made.

A senior member of the original HE staff in this link reflected that the amalgamation had now 'normalised' and his colleagues from the former colleges of nursing had constructively 'joined-in' the period of substantial change. Their involvement had been facilitated by the evolving status of the institution of HE – 'the river was moving anyway'. (Nurse teachers' full involvement in the HE move to modularisation had also made amalgamation timely and constructive. Similarly **all** faculties had recently appointed a Reader as part of a process of addressing the college's academic profile, so nurse education had taken this on as part of the wider programme of development in HE.)

In the scheme on target for the college of nursing to become an Institute within the link HE establishment by April 1992, the pace of change had accelerated with the latest goal described by a key senior member of staff as the movement of nurse education 'lock, stock and barrel' from September 1992, with the college principal transferring as head of school and associate dean. Two project officers had been given responsibility for facilitating this radical move (one concerned with HE and the other with the NHS side) and had played an invaluable coordinating role in dealing with the myriad personnel and budgetary decisions crucial to an efficient transition. These posts ensured that negotiations were completed with the appropriate level of thoroughness and the expense was said to be readily justified. There had been three project teams – for personnel, finance and estates – and it was said to have taken six months' steady work to negotiate and secure approval for a good transfer package. 'Ring fencing' of the NHS money was considered crucial. The development of links produced personnel and financial dilemmas (notably the retention of mental health officer status) which in the absence of any central guidance were the subject of local deliberation, and reinvention of the wheel seemed to be the order of the day.

Careful strategic planning in the scheme above also helped in promoting an environment of staff not feeling that change had been 'forced' upon them. There had to be a systematic breakdown of financial ingoings and outgoings to assess the feasibility of what was proposed (although it was emphasised by one senior member of HE staff that this was not primarily a money-making enterprise – the vast amount of time and effort could have been expended elsewhere – and that nurse education was **positively** welcomed by him and some of his colleagues). The organisational and academic sides of the courses had been split managerially, with the former head of the CFP becoming head of operational management for pre-registration education. The college had realised the importance of creating a specific post and department as the magnitude and complexity of the administration required on a course like Project 2000 had become apparent. As with the scheme outlined above, moving in as such a substantial entity meant that nurse education would play a significant part in the future of the receiving institution and would make a formidable section in its own right which would serve to 'protect' its interests.

The link that previously consisted only of course validation was now, as one newly appointed member of staff expressed it, 'starting again' and in this still fluid re-evaluation of the options contact had gone 'back to basics'. There were now different personnel in post in both institutions and there was felt to be a dual commitment to steady progress although its cautious nature was illustrated by another senior member of staff's description of 'piecemeal actions towards approximate goals'. From this institution's perspective there was much to be gained by maximising their chances of securing firm links with nurse education – each such collaboration strengthening their position in the health care education market.

In the fourth scheme (where the college of nursing had purpose-built accommodation on the HE site), the proposed amalgamation of the college of nursing with another and the incorporation into a new partner institution of HE were on target for September 1992. For HE staff in the original link there was obvious regret at losing the Diploma course and its spin-offs that 'fitted in beautifully' to other areas of their development, as one senior member of staff explained. He would, with hindsight, have been 'more proactive' in terms of establishing course teams and participating in the validation exercise and was disappointed at the numerous possibilities for staff development and research that now eluded his staff. A senior colleague commented that it was hard to lose 'a fully validated course with all the teething problems ironed out'.

In the two remaining schemes with rather less ambitious links to date steady progress had been sustained. In one where there had been formal associate status the school of nursing was now classed as an accredited institute. Possible designation as a school of the link HE institution formed the basis for a renegotiation of the optimum form collaboration should take. Here,

26

senior administrative appointments, extant since 1990 (two deans and a registrar), had taken over direct staff line management responsibilities from senior nurse education managers as the latter's departments disappeared – a move designed to bring the management structure in line with that in HE. In the other link there was still associate college status and it was unclear to what extent substantial change was seen as feasible and desirable, although a senior nurse educator now felt that links were continually improving, they did have a greater insight into each other's operations and there was less nervousness around. She was convinced now that their original model (operating as two separate institutions) did not work and the progress made in collaborative work had made her much more optimistic than she was two years ago about a workable partnership.

In both the latter schemes, as elsewhere, there was a sense that any **real** integration was impossible while the two institutions remained administratively as well as geographically separate. As one principal expressed it, relations would 'never be completely right' until they were 'under one umbrella'. There were no longer naive assumptions that integration of staff or students 'would just happen' and there was also greater insight into **why** that was so. In both colleges, however, there remained a desire to retain a degree of autonomy. One course leader's main concerns were not about a move into HE, but about the time-span and the college of nursing retaining its identity: 'It's not the fact that it's going to happen but that it will happen too quickly, just when the students and staff are beginning to feel more comfortable with the course'.

Opinion was divided on the merits or otherwise of the link HE institution having a background in nurse education. On one site it was declared that not being constrained by the vested interests of pre-existing nurse education expertise had been very beneficial in the creation of the link. In the sample sites, the two most developed links were where there was not significant nurse education experience in the HE institutions, and in the two least ambitious there were established nurse education specialist staff. However, in one of these a senior member of staff emphasised that there would be problems of ensuring quality assurance if you did not have a nursing expertise in HE and felt that this had not been thought out properly in other links he had knowledge of. Even where, as in his link, there was such expertise, responsibility from a distance for quality assurance for 900 students was far from unproblematic. This difference in perspective highlights one of the essential dilemmas of this course, namely the extent to which it is a nursing course serviced by HE specialists in other fields and strengthened by that or whether it is a Diploma in HE where nursing plays a central role.

HE links in the 'other seven' sites

Links with HE institutions had also developed, at least formally, in most of the other seven Demonstration Districts, although unlike the six main study sites there was none where the link institution had changed or where there had been full integration into HE yet. In the scheme with the closest organisational link – in the sense that the college of nursing was already established as a Division of Health Care Studies within a college of HE – it had not proved possible to get an office base for nurse teaching staff on the HE site as hoped, because of lack of space. The tutors with prime responsibility for each intake were now spending substantial periods of time there with the students in the first year and that was seen as contributing to smoother integration.

In the site where the level of HE funding had been particularly problematic and no HE input had been made to the CFP, it had taken until June 1992 for the link to get properly off the ground and a new formal memorandum of cooperation signed. The extra funding finally secured for the year 1992/93 for that purpose (on a non-recurring basis) was being put into four posts with a teaching and research component at the HE institution, plus the college's contribution to partnership funding for a paediatric post there (50 per cent HE, 25 per cent college and 25 per cent Children's Nursing Unit). In the negotiations taking place about these posts, the college was understandably concerned to ensure it got its money's worth; the previous funding of two HE posts having been withdrawn for that and other reasons. However, the future form and destination of the HE link remained undecided in that scheme pending the outcome of a poll which the principal was carrying out of staff views on the various options. As for the three schemes involving (existing) universities, links in two of them were still fairly static, although the students in one were now able to use the university library and links with the Sociology Department had increased. The links in that scheme consisted of separate contracts with individual HE departments rather than the institution as a whole and those contracts were said to be quite different – almost as if 'with different institutions'. In the case of the Sociology Department, the contract included advice and development for nurse teaching staff, and a series of seminars – once a month for six months – being put on for them by university staff for the first time that year was said to be very much appreciated.

In the second university link where there was disappointment with the pace of developments – and with what the college of nursing was getting for its funding of the link generally – this was attributed at least in part to delay in appointing a chair in nursing as proposed. Two joint appointments had not been filled either. Ironically, what was seen as a strength of the original negotiations in this scheme – the link institution's lack of a Department of Nursing or of previous experience of nurse education – was now perceived as a drawback. The result had been a link described as 'all one-sided' (although there had been an increase in the university teaching input in the bio-sciences). In the third scheme linked with a university, however, relations continued to develop well, with plans for integration in October 1994 involving the creation of a joint HA/university/institute of health sciences, which it was envisaged the university's department of nursing might join. (It was pointed out that the link there was with the university **as a whole** – not just the latter – small – department – and it was to the **education** department the college was looking for honorary contracts for its teaching staff.) All five joint appointments were filled and the holders contributing to Branch as well as CFP teaching programmes.

In the two remaining schemes, one linked with a polytechnic, the other a college of HE, colleges of nursing had continued to move closer to their link institutions in formal terms. One college would progress from associate faculty to affiliated college status with effect from 1 September 1992, retaining considerable autonomy over its own development. However, the expected ministerial guidance on the future management of colleges of nursing was awaited before deciding whether to integrate completely or continue 'to stand beside HE in a much looser arrangement'. In the other scheme, a joint working group was looking to complete integration by April 1993, with the college possibly becoming a new faculty of health in the HE institution. Basing a second joint appointment in the college of nursing had contributed to an increase in HE teaching input. The holder of the first such appointment, HE-based, had been drawn into other initiatives and had not made any input to Project 2000 teaching as hoped. In the 'other seven' sites, as in the case-study sites, what little integration of staff and students was happening in real terms was described as slow, with the pressure on HE institutions of increased numbers of their own students precluding or severely limiting the possibility of space being made available for Project 2000 students. The situation was not expected to change with formal integration as long as the nurse students and teachers remained geographically separate from their HE peers. (In the last mentioned scheme a round trip of 100 miles to the HE institution was involved for those based at one site.)

Management structures in the 'other seven'

Management structures in the 'other seven' sites were also evolving, with the trend towards separation of operational and academic course management there too. As in one case of the case-study schemes, one CFP head was about to move to an academic registrar post. The need for strong administrative leadership – with an academic perspective – had become increasingly felt as the course grew in numbers and complexity: 'The placement officers have found it extremely difficult to interpret the needs of Project 2000 students and they need contact with someone who knows the course inside out.'

In that scheme too there was also the realisation that now 'the development phase' was past, it was no longer necessary to have separate teams for the CFP and Branch which, the principal said, felt as if they had 'developed two separate courses'. Now they were to be integrated into one team for the Diploma course under a single head at associate director level. There were also to be senior lecturers with different roles from senior tutors. Instead of having two senior tutors responsible for the CFP, two for the Adult Branch and one for each of the three specialist Branches, there were to be two senior lecturers with responsibility for academic planning across the whole course (for September and April intakes, respectively). In addition to senior lecturers for each specialism there would also be a senior lecturer for institutional placement – and clinical teaching (primarily for the Adult Branch) and one for the community. These new posts were described as 'academic posts where people will be expected to know what's going on in a practice and to be well up in current research'. Across the Districts, it seemed, senior tutors' roles had been changing in different ways, in some cases assuming more specific management functions, as responsibilities for teaching particular intakes or courses were increasingly delegated to designated tutors. The trend away from senior tutors heading teams in particular specialisms towards multi-specialist-teams of tutors contributing to both CFP and Branch programmes had also continued.

As well as conforming to HE structures, changes in the skill-mix of staff at management level in colleges of nursing, including new finance, personnel and marketing officer/director appointments, were also seen as the result of the wider changes in the NHS and the colleges' new 'provider' status. Liaison and liaison structures between education and service had changed accordingly. As already noted, colleges' relations with DHAs were now more distant even where an umbrella group for education had been retained at District level. At Unit level, however, new structures were now in place and contacts were increasing with both heads of Units and directorate managers.

Benefits for HE

Most HE staff involved felt that having nurse education affiliated in some way was desirable for the future development of their institutions and they generally supported Judge's expectation (1986) that 'one day nurse education will take its proper place within the family of HE and a better family it will then be'. In one HE institution, a senior member of staff described the course as 'the biggest academic development in 20 years' and, in another institution, it was said to be a 'prize' and a potential starting point from which many other initiatives might come. Staff reflected Sheehan's (1986) finding from his survey of nurse education courses in universities, polytechnics and colleges of HE that there were expectations of and positive attitudes towards increasing involvement. Staff's commitment to the courses did not diminish over time (in spite of sometimes feeling that teaching on it was like a 'production line' where you 'took a deep breath' and carried on) and this buoyancy and optimism was sustained as the course progressed.

One lecturer, who had been consistently involved, spoke of the extensive range of new developments and challenges that he was fortunate enough to be involved in (indeed, towards the end of the three years he added the proviso that he hoped the nurse educators knew 'when to stop'). A senior member of staff closely involved throughout an extensive link spoke of the positive impact of nurse teachers' 'keenness' for education and teaching, emphasising that there was not a unified 'HE culture' and that he had more in common with incoming nurse teacher colleagues in this respect than with existing HE peers in some faculties. (He welcomed the opportunity to 'liberate them [nurse teachers] from all that drudgery' of constant intakes and limited time for reflection and study.) Another spoke of exciting course development whereby HE colleagues were now thinking how their work could fit into the health-related expansion. They were at a stage where 'additionality' (the whole being greater than the sum of the parts) was beginning to emerge from the close associations being formed across faculties. There was one site where developments in reciprocal teaching were a feature of recent times and HE staff here spoke of their 'satisfaction' in seeing this take off.

29

There was sustained evidence across sites of good, productive working relationships. One senior member of staff explained that he 'cannot praise enough' the attitudes and enthusiasm contributed by those amalgamating with his institution. He enthused about planned and proposed joint research projects and the 'refreshing' approach his nurse education colleagues brought (although he was conscious that he was dealing only with senior staff as yet and not the 'rank and file'). In a less extensive link another senior colleague commented that given the two different cultures and the unhelpful disparities in size between the two institutions, relations had 'worked admirably well'.

Staff were also positive about working with these students and it was clear that where they had risen to the challenge presented by the new courses, there were rewards to be had. As with any group, the students' response was 'mixed', but several lecturers outlined gains for their own professional development from the teaching undertaken. Staff felt that these students had distinctive characteristics as a group, notably their desire for 'relevance' in what was being taught and their strong vocationalism. As one lecturer explained, they were different because they were not, unlike undergraduates, 'intimidated by the weight of knowledge that they don't have'. There were challenges in the teaching role in that typically undergraduates 'see you as an academic' whereas the Diploma students ask you to 'make the practical links'. (This feedback from students was not universally received, with some lecturers commenting on how infrequently students approached them. Some students reported that lecturers were inaccessible and this was exacerbated by tightly scheduled lectures.)

A senior member of staff in an institution where there had been some resistance to involvement believed that despite the difficulties, working on the course was still 'intrinsically a good thing to do' and a more recently appointed colleague of hers welcomed the insight the course afforded into a different group of students with a vocational orientation. Staff in one HE institution were said to have benefited because the course had 'opened their eyes to other ways of teaching and other forms of knowledge'. Making connections with health care in the material covered was considered beneficial to one's own academic development and reading. Some nurse education colleagues were said to have expertise in 'sandwich-type' course structures and in-course evaluation that could be drawn upon.

Institutional benefits were evident from an equal opportunities perspective with the resultant influx of female staff at a senior level (which significantly altered the composition of some senior management teams) and the student body was said to be similarly revitalised by the introduction of non-traditional students in line with current trends in HE (PCFC, 1992). Rather than having to justify the presence of these students, the point was made forcibly on some sites that it was other courses with more traditional patterns of recruitment that had to explain 'why they are missing out on half the market for students'. Conversely, one lecturer with a nursing background voiced concern that the level of individual support and awareness of student progress that could have been promoted in traditional nurse education, with its small intakes, could be lost with the move into HE without concerted efforts to sustain it and that this could be a regressive move in terms of realising the potential of some groups of students.

When the nurse teachers were asked directly what they saw as the benefits for HE staff from liaison with nurse education, a range of aspects was mentioned across the six sites – applied teaching, assessment strategies, organisational skills, financial gain for institutions and teaching expertise were mentioned, with the last one being the most frequently expressed (a point not referred to by HE staff themselves). The point about teaching expertise was made strongly on four of the sites, with the most critical comments coming from situations with relatively limited contact where some of the HE input was described as 'grim' and the qualified teacher status of nurse teachers and the presumed greater expertise this afforded were contrasted with the situation in HE. On one site HE staff's openness was applauded – they were said to have '... discovered an awful lot about nursing' and to have 'taken on a lot of learning'.

The nurse teachers' perspective

There was wide variation in the extent to which those interviewed were working with colleagues in HE, which depended on the post they held and their area of curriculum responsibility. For the key players in each institution providing nurse education the link was clearly of significance in their working lives and in some cases had substantially altered it. This applied most strikingly where the college of nursing had joined a faculty structure in HE. However, even here the link had had minimal impact on some of those interviewed (and those in this sample were the nurse teachers most closely involved in Project 2000). The repercussions for staff of the 'validation only' link were negligible. Although some nurse teachers in all schemes were members of HE committees as a result of the link the overall level of contact was low.

There was said to be a gradual expansion of involvement in the more developed links. Where nurse educators had become part of a faculty, there were opportunities for grass-roots contact, notably joint staff development days and team-work to establish modular degree courses. In the scheme due to merge with HE in the coming months, whilst acknowledging that there were serious anxieties and reservations amongst some of their colleagues, the general mood was one of optimistic growth where 'the barriers have gone' and the HE contribution was now a 'very good and natural part of the course'. This emergent collaboration (and the difficulties of working across sites) was captured by the nurse teacher who explained that 'we are becoming more and more part of them. But we are always based on different sites and we do feel like a satellite out here'. A senior colleague emphasised that nurse teachers still did not feel that they can 'just walk into the (HE) staff room and make a coffee'. Collaboration was not automatically achieved. One nurse teacher with an office in an HE institution explained that 'I am based there but I hardly ever see anybody. There are no opportunities to integrate and no forum to do this. We are a pretty isolated unit here.'

Attitudes to the link

Although somewhat apprehensive about their own involvement, the nurse teachers interviewed were almost unanimously optimistic about and supportive of the link with HE. As with their colleagues in HE, the general tone was of potential benefits to be gained and of agreement with the principles underpinning the arrangements. Their positive expectations mirrored those of commentators from nurse education. Le Var (1988) expressed the view that: 'For the improvement of nurse education and patient care it is essential that we grasp the possibilities offered and establish firm partnerships between nurse education and further and higher education.' In 1988, Owen wrote of several clearly identifiable gains for nurse education that had been possible in collaboration with HE but would have been 'difficult or almost impossible to implement in a health service school of nursing alone'.

The most enthusiastic responses to the links in the present study came from nurse education staff who had been closely involved from the outset. One senior member of staff where there was integration into a faculty reported that the link was 'going very well indeed' and that 'there is a very nice feeling of being at the start when something is being built... You don't feel as though you have to fit in because you can actually influence what goes on and it is new and exciting.' There was said to be a certain 'inevitability' to the direction developments were taking. A principal spoke of the 'logical step' integration represented which her staff were meeting with 'a mixture of excitement and anxiety'. These mixed feelings were most clearly evident in the 'new start' link where potential gains from contact into HE could be glimpsed but past experience had left its mark.

Staff's responses were less enthusiastic where plans were not being put into operation so smoothly or speedily. They were aware that what had been anticipated had not materialised, although they still saw merit in the principle. The contraction of the 'validation only' link was summed up by one nurse teacher as: 'We didn't know what we should ask for and they didn't know what they should be able to give.' The least positive reflections came from the scheme set to transfer its allegiance to another HE institution. Here there was little positive comment on the link towards the end of the first three years (representing a shift of perspective from the mid-course interviews where gains were more readily identified). Undercurrents of uncertainty about the future form nurse education would take surfaced at this time, and on this site the intention was for increasing independence for nurse education (within the organisational structure of an HE institution) with less 'reliance' on HE. For the handful of staff across the schemes who expressed opposition to the link, concerns were the 'them and us' attitude said to colour HE staff's contact with nurse teachers (with the latter cast as 'poor relations' who 'have to justify their academic credibility') and the totally different philosophy perceived to underpin HE that was thought inappropriate to the development of nurse education.

Benefits for staff

When nurse teachers reflected on the experience of liaison with HE, a number of benefits for themselves were described at both a global and individual level. Senior staff were generally enthusiastic about the staff development gains and the effect on morale. One of them reported having more professionally confident teaching staff as a result of the HE work and described them as 'a completely different team' in this respect. Nurse teachers in general enjoyed the professional collaboration that had taken place and the 'new blood' and 'different ideas' that came in as a result. Some staff pointed to the benefits of 'learning the system' of organisation and procedures to facilitate the smooth development of the Diploma and other innovative courses. Even if the future was still uncertain, contact with HE had been of benefit. One nurse teacher explained that 'it's unknown territory and I've got to wait and see. But we have no need to be fearful about the move into HE. We can hold our heads up high.'

Again, the strength and scope of the link were crucial in determining the scale of benefits for staff. Those with fairly substantial contact in the more developed links were pleased with the 'academic' enhancement they saw emerging. One perspective on this was that they had the opportunity to 'realise that there is more to life than the school of nursing' and that with the continuing 'influx of new ideas' the situation 'can only get better'. On a site where steady progress was being made towards closer working together, the 'credibility' that such association would give was welcomed. The generally enthusiastic tone of the comments of staff on the site due to amalgamate with HE in September 1992, was most forcibly illustrated by the nurse teacher who said of the link: 'We wouldn't have been able to move on without it and it's healthy.' Here again the emphasis was on academic development and a move towards a 'less institutional, insular set-up'. As elsewhere, the career opportunities for nurse teachers that such developments opened up were valued (although these comments were usually tempered by concerns about conditions of service and the future role and status of nurse teachers). With widespread 'academic drift' acknowledged to be taking place, it was said to be essential for '...nurses to feel comfortable in HE'.

A senior member of staff said that colleagues did not seem to be clear about precisely what was on offer to them in HE and that she did not really know the way round this although 'some people have really "taken off" and their staff development is wonderful and all that enthusiasm is being brought back to the school and is helping it to develop'. What staff were in a position to say at this stage about the basis on which individuals had been relocated in terms of salary and conditions of service indicated that satisfactory arrangements had been or were being made. In the scheme where this was most advanced, a senior member of staff described her and her colleagues as 'having got a good deal' (there had been some difficulties pertaining to staff with Mental Health Employee status), although there was still a lot to do in terms of clarifying staff's roles and teaching commitments. She likened Project 2000 to 'a volcano erupting' where 'the lava is still coming down' and 'so many new issues keep rising'.

Problems encountered

Despite the tentative nature of many nurse teachers' contact with HE, the sense of being part of a potentially far-reaching developmental process was clear. Across the Districts, it seemed, there was still a good deal of anxiety among staff about the effects of a move into HE on their Conditions of Service, and the need for the negotiation of personnel matters to be handled with great sensitivity was underlined. The strains that this can lead to were neatly illustrated by a senior member of staff where the decision to become part of a faculty in HE had been made. Here the stability achieved was appreciated because: 'It's not courting each other any more and wondering who you are offending and it's actually a very successful marriage after a long engagement!' (Referring back to the uncertainty staff had experienced, which was still prevalent elsewhere, it was explained that staff had been asked to comment on proposed structures for amalgamation without knowing whether they themselves would be part of it.)

Some 'spin-offs' were seen as problematic. One nurse teacher spoke of the anxiety and pressure created by an expectation that all teaching staff would obtain degree status within the next few years. One principal described the very big culture and value change that nurse educators had to undergo. The value of research as part of one's work was said to be not widely acknowledged in nurse education and colleagues would need to 'tolerate diversity and realise that you progress by breadth of experience'. One senior member of staff who described her institution's move into HE as 'the best thing that could ever have happened' because of the opportunities it provided for nursing and for individual members of staff, added that 'the only thing missing is the time for staff to develop into what HE wants'.

The negative reflections that came out most strongly towards the end of the study (with the first intake near to completion) were from the more tentative arrangements where a lack of development appeared to have promoted confusion and apprehension. Where organisational structures had not developed significantly as the course progressed, staff expressed a rather jaundiced view of the current position. One nurse teacher reported 'no development, it has never really been established' and another disappointment that the proposed 'cross-fertilisation' was not happening. Meetings designed to bring staff from the two institutions together had been instituted on one site but their impact was said to be short-lived. Here the link was said by one respondent to be 'just a facade'. The jaded tone of these responses was most clearly expressed on the site where a new start was being established. Staff were rather cautious about the best way ahead although they could now identify senior staff who were making efforts to make the link work.

Practical difficulties concerning accommodation and timetabling were highlighted throughout the study – difficulties which it was felt should have been resolved much earlier still persisted. The limitations on effecting collaboration where multi-site institutions were involved were similarly emphasised throughout. In the more advanced links, there was some reference to the need to resolve pension entitlements before transfer, of the 'politics' at the senior levels that staff on the ground were uninformed about and of some 'disputes *vis-à-vis* teaching styles and the issue of cost-effectiveness'. At the nurse teacher level, staff sometimes had an incomplete understanding of what had been agreed at a more senior level, or why some practices had ceased, and this caused confusion. Where the link had become 'validation only', individuals had been told by colleagues in HE that further liaison was not possible or that rooms were no longer available to them and were uneasy about the way this had been done and unsure about what had led to it.

Changes in management structures were commented on by senior staff on two sites as having restricted their autonomy and they needed a period of readjustment because 'it now takes **so** long to get things sorted out' in the larger, more removed decision-making process they were part of. One senior member of staff in the college of nursing due to move to another institution of HE emphasised the complex nature of the arrangements, notably the 'educational pull-out' in that the course 'belongs' to two 'units'. The constructive personal relationships enjoyed by staff were of particular benefit in this time of transfer given that 'it could have been exceedingly difficult with different people'.

The student perspective

Views on the link

The students' comments on the questionnaires they completed during the early stages of their courses showed that they, too, approached the prospect of liaison between the colleges of nursing and HE with a certain amount of optimism. They saw advantages in having access to study resources and facilities, most notably the libraries, and thought that contact with HE would enrich the course, mainly by providing contact with a wider range of staff. They identified gains for nursing itself and for course content and depth of study, and they welcomed access to social resources and facilities. Early concerns raised at this stage (some of which were based on experience and some of which were speculative) were that the relevance and standard of the HE input could be unsatisfactory and that practical problems such as distances to travel and the development of efficient channels of communication between the participating institutions could inhibit successful liaison. Caution was also expressed about the extent to which meaningful integration into HE was feasible for students based on a different college site.

Following up the students' views of HE in subsequent interviews with them showed the robust nature of their early predictions, although what became clearer as the study progressed was the widely differing encounters with HE across the six sites. For students in one scheme, for example, there was very little to say other than that they now had access to a larger library, whereas for others contact with HE was a continuing part of the CFP (and sometimes beyond). When asked to comment on the advantages of the link, a widely held view (that of three-quarters of the students in the schemes with sustained contact) was that the access to specialist staff was a significant gain. This was expressed in comments such as 'The staff are not biased by their nursing experience and have a broader view and a more specialised one'.

During the CFP the consensus was still that there were gains to be had from the link. Only ten students (of the 77 interviewed) were opposed to the contact, with the rest equally divided between those who did not feel particularly strongly either way at this stage and those for whom the link was a very positive component of the course. The more substantial links were generally those with most students in the latter category. The students' concerns about some of the teaching in HE are discussed in Chapter 4 – their other reservations centred on practical arrangements, notably travelling and timetabling.

When interviewed in the CFP, about one-third of students spontaneously referred to a sense of pleasure at having access to a campus. The 'change of atmosphere' was welcomed. (One view of the potential advantages for students (Owen, 1988) referred to access to library resources and technology as well as 'real life experience with normal healthy young adults of their own age'.) It was a certain satisfaction of association that was described – most markedly by those at each end of the spectrum of previous educational experience. A graduate, for example, spoke of 'access to intellectual life and a sense of being seriously engaged in what you are studying' and a mature student with few qualifications to date said that contact with HE had had a powerful effect on her and provided a 'new lease of life'.

The students' reflections on the HE input to their course altered significantly by the time they entered the Branch programme in that contact had decreased (in five of the six sites) to such an extent that respondents spoke about the links retrospectively. In the scheme where there was the most sustained contact with staff from HE, lectures were now given in the college of nursing and most students were positive about these arrangements (with five of the 20 regretting losing their visits to the HE site). There were a few comments about lectures being at 'too high a level' but on the whole the contributions were valued. One student's comment summed up a generally held perspective: 'The content of the lectures is really worth having and I prefer them coming here.'

In another scheme students had moved from their base on an HE site to hospital bases and the convenience of these arrangements was much valued – the seemingly endless bussing between sites that the students found so tedious had ceased. At this stage of their course the students here were looking forward to their practice and did not express regret about leaving the HE site (although one of the six emphasised her appreciation of 'having got a lot out of' the HE input).

There were two schemes where the initially limited contact with HE had ceased and the students there did not see it as having influenced their course. On one of these sites students' responses were neutral – the liaison that took place between staff did not impinge on them and apart from a few comments about potential access to the library they had nothing to report (only one of them made a positive statement about liking the link being 'part of the course'). In the other link where initially limited contact had dwindled (in this case to 'validation only' with the cessation of student contact), students were more critical of the process. Rather than the non-existent link outlined above they saw their institution's efforts as having failed. They were disillusioned by the process and expressed disappointment at how little the link had provided. These were not comments on the quality of teaching they had experienced previously but on the difficulties of gaining anything over and above this specialist input – the HE site was difficult to travel to and was perceived as 'hostile'.

Where the link had initially provided a major input to the course which had subsequently ceased, students expressed mixed views on the gains – they saw the contact as a definite section of their course but, while a few regretted its demise, most were more muted in their reflections and uncertain when looking back about what had been achieved. This split seemed to have left students confused. One student offered an overview of what had taken place: 'I thought that the first year was very enjoyable and it was like a university-style education and I know that people with preconceived ideas about nursing didn't like it, but I was very happy. There is a problem because it's as though the course has created a monster. We have had this HE approach and now they suddenly want us to become nurses.' A few students here referred to library facilities (although there were difficulties with transport to use them), but the most general reflection at this stage was that links 'haven't been a big deal after the first six or eight months'.

In the final scheme, where consistent input on the major HE site during the CFP diminished during the Branch, students were, on the whole, positive about the content of what had been provided, but were still negative about travelling and timetabling arrangements. For students travelling across an authority there were considerable logistical implications and these evoked heartfelt complaints. This dissatisfaction was summed up by the student who said: 'I used to dread going to the college even though I enjoyed some of the teaching and have benefited. You don't feel like an individual there at all and it is so vast. Having all this mess-up about the rooms really reinforces this and doesn't give you much confidence in the place or in how much they really want us there.' Throughout the study, it was students from the most sustained links who reflected positively on the impact of the input from HE and the contribution made to their learning. As one of them suggested: 'I think that the gains have been so many and I did think those early links were useful and I'm very sorry to be losing that. There is a wealth of specialist knowledge there and it's as if we have been given a little bit then it's been drawn away just at the moment we would appreciate it.'

Being students

Whilst some students enjoyed the atmosphere and some of the teaching was applauded, the students did not feel part of the institution of HE. No one reported social integration with other students – the limited socialising that took place in HE institutions was either with their Project 2000 peers or, in a handful of cases, with friends who happened to be students there. This was so even when students were based on the HE campus. Indeed, where students were bussed around at set times, the actual distance between sites was irrelevant. Even a few miles were sufficient to deter participation in campus activities for students without transport.

Very little use of the HE facilities was reported in the early stages of the course – a point made even more sharply as students entered their Branch programme. There were students who did not particularly want or expect to enlarge their leisure activities in this way, but others felt frustrated by the half-way house situation the link generated. One 'positive in principle' respondent explained that '...it's a pain in a sense – the one day a week means that you don't get into the swing of it – we seem to be here, there and everywhere – don't get a chance to mix'. In one scheme where students spent a decreasing amount of time in HE during the CFP, a few students had joined up for activities that they had to abandon as their timetable had altered. This institution of HE was described as a 'big carrot' that was dangled before the students but which the constraints of time and distance kept out of reach. Such situations contributed to a sense of being 'a student in name but not reality'. As one of them put it: 'The (HE institution) doesn't apply to us.'

Very little use of student union membership had been made. As one student explained, she had joined because 'at the beginning of the course it all seemed very exciting to be going along there'. There was evidently confusion amongst the students about the position regarding renewal of membership and there were very few who stated confidently that they had completed this procedure. On one site someone from HE was said to have come to the college of nursing to facilitate students' re-registration and a few students had taken the opportunity to do so. On other sites most students had not got round to it and some were unclear about whether they had to do anything at all. As would be expected, given the minimal impact the HE culture and facilities had on students across sites at this stage of the course, formal procedures relating to them were not a priority.

It was clear as students entered the Branch programmes that it was not that there was resistance on their part to HE contact; rather it was that the structure and sequencing of their courses seemed to have marginalised what impact HE could have realistically. Even in a link where there had been very regular input on the main HE site during the CFP, students had not internalised a sense of attachment and towards the end of the courses had 'moved on'. The majority of students had used the HE library, but for many of them this meant limited contact – only a few visited the library on days that they were not on site anyway. Distance was obviously one issue here which was exacerbated by the reduction in timetabled contact with HE in the Branch programmes. In one scheme where students would have had to travel to the library themselves (because they visited HE so infrequently) only three students (from several intakes) had used the library at all. In a similar situation, students who had used a convenient HE library on occasion were dismayed to discover that it had been moved across town, which would limit their access. As one student in the link where student contact had ceased explained: 'It's a great shame but none of the students use the facilities at (HE institution). It's too far to use the library, even if there are exams coming up. Students don't feel welcome at the (HE institution) – they feel they are not seen as part of [it], but just a group of nurses who come down for lectures. It should either have been good links or they should not have bothered.'

The staff viewpoint

The benefits identified for students by staff were largely of a subtle nature, focusing on intangible HE gains such as 'confidence', 'career options', 'status' and the facility to develop as 'independent thinkers'. The use of more concrete advantages was acknowledged to be limited and student integration was agreed not to have taken place to any significant degree. In a very well developed link the situation was described as 'not a good deal for students' because they appeared to have very little contact with HE and had to deal with the confusion of multi-site inputs. There was said to be continuing conflict because students 'will **always** see the "academic" as separate from the nursing'.

Library usage was acknowledged by staff to be limited, and some respondents expressed frustration that although students **could** attend functions and use amenities they did not do so (although it was recognised that distance and packed timetables did not encourage this). On one site there was an awareness that students felt that the HE library was too far and one member of staff commented that they needed to find ways of freeing up sessions so that this 15-minute walk was feasible. Blocks of time on the HE site (rather than one day a week) had been introduced in one scheme to provide continuity for students, although it was said by one senior member of staff that the distances between sites necessitated a realistic perspective on what could be achieved.

In one scheme re-establishing links after a difficult start, students were timetabled to spend one day a week in HE, with the morning free to use the library and the afternoon to pursue any other activities they might wish. The extent to which this had made an impact on the students' experience was not yet known. The principal emphasised how difficult the distance between sites made student contact and explained that 'if you are serious about them being students there should be residential accommodation on that (HE) site'. The notion of different cultures was seen as limiting the extent to which students would be able to develop a sense of belonging on different sites. Although there was widespread acknowledgement that it was a 'good thing to get away from the hospital' and have access to another complementary setting, the limited rate of progress on the scale of benefits to date was evident.

One senior member of staff who enthused about the link in principle and its impact on staff reported that: 'Integration of students is the area we feel we've failed most on.' Here, because of switching to another HE link, the situation for incoming students will be different from that to date. Although institutional amalgamation had developed apace, the reality for students will be of no contact with the new HE sites (apart from an occasional trip estimated to involve a three-hour journey), in contrast to the situation during the course of this research where with less clearly established links **organisationally** students were based on the current HE site. The member of staff quoted above commented that because of their experience on an HE site so far he had mixed views about access to the much acclaimed HE culture and was not unduly perturbed about the imminent change. The different patterns of attendance from other HE students, the bussing to and from sites and the distance between the HE and nurse education bases were reported as problematic. In addition, some HE sites were seen as unwelcoming because of their lay-out and location. The decreasing amount of time spent on HE sites as the course progressed was also a concern.

Although HE staff did not feel that student integration was taking place to any significant degree, one senior member of staff made the point that the changing climate of HE made traditional expectations of an HE culture redundant for many groups of students anyway. Another said that whatever the current limitations the contact with HE had to be 'a great improvement on all hospital-based courses'. Addressing the students' timetable was potentially one way of influencing their time in HE, but staff were well aware of the practical barriers to making integration of the type originally hoped for, a feasible option. Practical deficiencies such as restrictions on the amount and timing of access to laboratory space had an impact on the students' experience and group transport arrangements provided an additional constraint.

Summary of main points

● Those involved in forming links between nurse education and HE were taking on a considerable challenge in seeking to develop a combined strategy to provide the new Diploma course.

● There was much enthusiasm for developing the links, although establishing them was reported to be extremely difficult in four of the six Districts studied.

● The variation amongst the schemes apparent in the early stages increased over the period of the study, with one scheme starting all over again and others amalgamating with institutions of HE.

- Although informal relations were good on all sites, for some staff there was unease about how to progress without more formal input. This unease was not expressed in the scheme where HE staff had been involved from the outset and a sense of steady progress towards a shared goal (with nurse education) permeated their comments.

- It was felt that no significant integration was possible while institutions remained administratively as well as geographically separate.

- Most HE staff felt that having nurse education affiliated in some way was desirable for the future development of their institutions. There was sustained evidence across sites of good, productive working relationships.

- Institutional benefits were evident with the resultant influx of female staff at a senior level, and the student body was said to be similarly revitalised by the introduction of non-traditional students in line with current trends in HE.

- Senior nurse education staff were generally enthusiastic about the staff development gains and the effect on morale. The strength and scope of the links were crucial in determining the scale of benefits for staff.

- The negative reflections that came out most strongly from nurse educators towards the end of the study, were from the more tentative arrangements where a lack of development appeared to have promoted confusion and apprehension. The more developed the link the more positive the responses were.

- Practical difficulties concerning accommodation and timetabling were highlighted throughout the study.

- The students approached the prospect of liaison between the colleges of nursing and HE with a certain amount of optimism. What became clearer as the study progressed was the widely differing encounters with HE across the six sites.

- By the time they entered the Branches, contact with HE had decreased (in five of the six sites) to such an extent that students spoke about the links retrospectively.

- Whilst some students enjoyed the atmosphere and some of the teaching was applauded, the students did not feel part of the institution of HE. No one reported social integration with other students. Library usage was very limited.

- Aside from the geographical constraints, the structure and sequencing of the course marginalised what impact HE could have realistically.

Discussion

It was clear that the links established between nurse education and HE had emerged with varying degrees of uncertainty, unease and caution. There had been differing degrees of clarity in perceptions of the options and potential of the links, and a range of very different arrangements appeared as a result. There were initial difficulties and continuing challenges, made harder in some situations by decisions made outside the institutions involved. There were clearly 'winners' and 'losers' at both institutional and individual levels. The speed with which the early stages had to be accomplished added yet another difficulty to an already demanding task. The existence of two distinct cultures was apparent throughout the research. There were so many unknowns and misunderstandings about both intent and potential outcomes that the undoubted achievements and progress made on each site should be applauded.

The thread of optimism and keenness that ran through the interviews with all groups of respondents and was sustained over time is a tribute to the level of commitment that exists to promote the optimum way forward for nurse education. It would be misleading to see the exposition of difficulties and continuing dilemmas presented here as a rebuttal of the principles underlying what is being sought. The early predictions of substantial change were largely being operationalised on target and in situations where there had initially been a tentative welcome to liaison with HE, there was now steady change in the same direction. Some staff had seen anticipated developments come to fruition with a corresponding degree of satisfaction and although there had been **significant** set-backs on two sites, new arrangements had been set in motion. What this process illustrated was not the inadvisability of liaison with HE but rather the complexities of formulating such a radically new course in the variety of situations where sophisticated systems of checks and balances are required if staff are to keep afloat in the ever-changing seas of NHS reforms and HE realignments. It was felt by some HE staff that their nurse education colleagues had not always realised the scale of the change and the amount of re-adjustment liaison with HE would necessitate.

The most established schemes now saw the Diploma almost as a springboard from which a multitude of other initiatives had come and from which a dramatic revision of the part to be played by nurse education in the institution had emerged. The Diploma had been instrumental in providing course development experience from which other initiatives had flourished. As one senior member of staff in a well established scheme with amalgamation imminent expressed it: 'If Project 2000 had not worked so well there would not have been the motivation for this big move.'

It is easy with hindsight to scrutinise the best guesses senior HE staff made in terms of deciding when, how and with what degree of commitment they should seek nurse education's promise. For some, an initially strong and sustained pursuit had borne prized fruit. For others, an explicit approach (materially in terms of accommodation if not initially in terms of the curriculum) ultimately had produced little. The link has ceased because of a management decision taken at Regional level, on the grounds of cost efficiency. Caution, even when set in the context of enthusiastic optimism, emerged as a justifiable strategy. Committing large amounts of time and other resources to this enterprise was a shot in the dark based on varyingly accurate predictions of the ultimate outcome. When should an institution of HE, for example, commit themselves to upgrading or expanding their laboratory space (an obvious key capital expense) for Diploma in Nursing students – a commitment that would need to be based on an assumption of long-term collaboration?

There had undoubtedly been gains for nurse education staff that reinforced their initial levels of optimism, although the pattern of these gains was still patchy. Arrangements were in hand to extend collaboration amongst grass-roots staff in the most developed links. The opportunities available for staff development and academic enhancement were widely espoused and examples of personal and institutional gains were regularly quoted. There was considerable excitement and enthusiasm for advantages still to come. For HE staff there had been rewards to be gained from some of the teaching and the embryonic research and development work with colleagues from nurse education was warmly welcomed. Their future role in relation to nurse education was perceived quite differently amongst, and sometimes within, different institutions and the options are discussed in Chapter 4. There were clearly staff development issues in relation to course delivery that were being addressed.

The situation was less clear-cut for students in that, although the input was widely appreciated by them, there was a feeling of distance – both geographical and psychological. They did **not**, as Reinkemeyer (1966) found in her study of undergraduate nurses, feel 'attracted by the academic atmosphere and repelled by the traditional hospital training programme'. It would be difficult to provide a convincing counter-argument at this stage of development to any student who asked 'Why don't the lecturers from HE just drive over and give us the lectures in the college of nursing?' While there is obviously great potential for growth, as the enthusiastic comments of some students testified, sustained effort will be required to achieve it. In the least substantial links, contact with HE was very much regarded as an early phase of the course. The disillusionment and disappointment expressed by some students because the link had not realised its potential emerged as the Branch programmes took off. There was still a belief by staff that HE was a good idea for the students but a reappraisal of what the links **could** realistically mean for them was taking place. Interestingly, there was an indication that greater institutional linkages (involving amalgamations across bigger distances) could mean **less** access to HE for students in practice and various strategies for enhancing what **was** possible were under discussion.

The links needed to be set in the context of changes in HE where demographic, economic and philosophical factors were combining to produce a rather different perspective on the student population and provision for them. While not wishing to exaggerate the extent to which this changed perspective has been assimilated by HE, it is the case that access for a more diverse group of students is an issue receiving serious consideration. Encouraging young people with non-traditional qualifications and older people who may lack formal qualifications at all to enter HE is now a legitimate goal for many institutions.

At a time of widespread educational institutional amalgamation, these early experiences suggest that providing the widely proclaimed advantages of HE culture will require more than good intentions and some lectures on HE sites. The most positive reflections came from the more substantial link schemes, which sound an optimistic note for future development. However, without an early incorporation of HE facilities into their schedule, it is unlikely that students will benefit from this aspect of provision. Physical distance is an issue that will not be surmounted when the HE link is a peripheral activity.

At this stage of development it was clear that the varying speed of development of links with HE on the six sites had resulted in a widening of the gap between the types of link established. At one extreme, organisational structures were set and work was now continuing on effecting the day-to-day collaborative working arrangements required. In other instances, structures for change were still under negotiation. Although there was still a good deal of optimism surrounding both the principles and practice of collaboration, it was in these less developed situations that staff expressed a somewhat disillusioned perspective. There was a sense of possibilities in the air, but uncertainty and unease about potential benefits were evident over the period of research.

Chapter Four
CURRICULUM ISSUES

Introduction

Having already considered some of the issues surrounding the implementation of Project 2000, this chapter focuses on the resultant courses in some detail starting with the way in which they were planned and developed. Pervasive concerns about integration and content are highlighted, as are issues about course delivery and assessment. The views and experiences of teaching staff and students are presented alongside each other in an attempt to offer an overview of these multi-faceted courses in this most crucial phase of their introduction. The role of HE staff to date and the options for their further collaboration are explored. The enormity of the task of developing the Diploma course is evident from the data presented here and the need for further clarification and consolidation must be seen in the context of the already considerable achievements of those working on it.

Course planning and development

The issue to emerge most strongly in the early interviews with staff providing the courses was the speed at which the development work had had to be done. One head of department in HE praised the nurse teachers for the amount of work they had put into establishing the courses because 'they really did work long hours for very few rewards as well as keeping up existing courses'. This interviewee nevertheless held the view that as an exercise in collaboration and course development it was 'an example of how not to go about it'.

Because of the time constraints imposed by the system of funding and validation, joint course planning between nurse education and HE had not been easily achieved and was only accomplished to any significant degree in two of the six Districts studied. (In one of these it took place after a re-submission of the course for validation was requested.) Early collaboration has now been officially recognised as of merit in that 'the involvement of a CNAA approved higher education establishment is seen as very important in achieving and maintaining a Dip HE standard. Higher education staff should be involved with curriculum development from an early stage' (CNAA/ENB, 1992).

Although there was some consultation in the early planning stages with service staff, curriculum planning was largely an 'in-house' affair. The work had been undertaken by a 'lot of different little working parties doing different things'. There were echoing references to 'working in the dark', which produced discontinuities across subjects, and from the CFP to the Branches. In addition, a small number of teachers referred to a failure to 'spread the word' to others in nurse education because of an element of territoriality which had grown up with the development of the courses.

There was a sense of having to adapt or circumvent established practices in HE because of the tight timescale. One senior member of staff spoke of making the best of a bad situation, having to meet a deadline for the commencement of courses that limited what could be achieved. He said that the nurse teachers were understandably unfamiliar with the CNAA procedures and there had had to be a great deal of pragmatism and 'papering over the cracks'. He would have preferred a delay of a year to go through the usual procedures, but this had not been possible given the nurse educators' desire to become a Demonstration District. Concessions had been made in order to be ready for the 1989 start. A colleague of his explained that there would normally have been a two-year lead-in and staff would have been working on a **joint** submission, the management issues would have been sorted out and there would have been team commitment to the course. He was then in the difficult position of having to establish that team commitment, months after the start of the course.

One senior member of HE staff contrasted the current fluidity of the course with what he perceived as the much more robust status of the newly validated midwifery course which had gone through an extended period of collaborative planning. Whilst applauding the current phase of staff development he saw his nurse education colleagues engaged in, he explained that it should have been instigated earlier because it was needed to write the curriculum. On one site, a key member of staff expressed his frustration at the slow pace of curriculum development where there appeared to be acknowledgement of the need for critical reflection and yet no dynamic mechanism for effecting it.

In one Demonstration District where staff from the two institutions had collaborated in the planning, there was, for those members of staff most actively involved, a sense of partnership evolving. A planning group containing a broad cross-section of staff from the two institutions had been established some considerable time before Project 2000 had been funded and there had been joint working groups to develop the curriculum as the course began to take shape. One lecturer explained how he had met with nurse teacher colleagues over a period of about 12 months, with more frequent sessions as the start of the course approached, and he described this work as truly interactive and constructive. In this scheme a member of staff had been seconded from the institution of HE to the college of nursing for approximately two-and-a-half days a week for about four months of the course planning stage. It was agreed by all those involved that this arrangement (which had been financed by the nurse education centre) had been well worth it. The lecturer had played a key role in developing the course, contributing his considerable experience in HE to what the nurse educators were producing. He described this process as moving the different parts of the curriculum through from the ideas stage to, for example, 'the 30-hour course that is taught on Wednesday', always with a view to the CNAA house-style with which he was very familiar.

Concerns identified in the first round of interviews about a lack of involvement in CFP planning emerged again in relation to Branch planning and, taking a wider perspective, to course management. As the courses progressed, it was apparent that HE staff were uneasy about their 'servicing' role which, to varying degrees, they felt had emerged, particularly when they had formal responsibility for parts of the courses. In general, they expressed a desire to enhance the course academically within a quality assurance framework. One lecturer described this as: 'We see ourselves as flying the flag for CNAA and HE standards. We have the integrity of the subject to defend.' Concerns about limited developmental input into the Branch, coupled with the fact that there was very little teaching by HE staff in the Branch, raised people's concerns about this 'safeguarding' role. As one lecturer explained, it was impossible to monitor students' progression through the courses, when the major commitment from HE was in the CFP. The four days he had with each intake during their Branch were 'absolutely pointless' because there was 'nothing to build on or link with'.

There was an unwelcome feeling of being a figure-head, and lecturers commonly expressed a desire for more input than just sessional teaching and 'decorating the submissions'. This concern about limited collaboration was heightened by having originally become involved in the courses 'so late in the day' that the 'curriculum still bore all the imperfections consequent upon that'. The one scheme where staff did not express concerns about the appropriateness of their contribution was where they had played a significant role in the early course development and were automatically involved in Branch development. Plans here centred on matters of course improvement and development rather than on their role. Senior staff on two HE sites expressed very strong reservations about the course structure that their nurse education colleagues espoused. In one case there was also said to be 'slippage' towards a curriculum model that had been challenged previously by HE staff as an inappropriate approach for identifying progressive levels of achievement through the courses.

Course integration

There was some concern expressed by staff in HE about the Diploma courses being 'overloaded', resulting in 'great problems in making the different units coherent'. Without an extension of team teaching it was difficult for staff to see their contributions as part of a whole, and it was consistently said across HE sites that these were rather confused courses with loose ends. One lecturer had originally tried to make connections for the students to aid coherence but had found it frustrating taking on this extra task simply to provide students with the odd sentence linking elements. A lecturer on another site bemoaned the difficulty in achieving coherence given that revision is '**still** done unit by unit, rather than the whole course'. The need for coherence was identified in guidelines (CNAA/ENB, 1992) which stated that 'it is important that a course is designed and presented as a totality and not as discrete theoretical and practical elements. There must be a clear demonstration of interaction between the elements, including the assessment strategy, to achieve coherence throughout the whole programme.'

Curriculum planning groups for discrete parts of the CFP rapidly diverged to concentrate on particular course subjects, and thereafter tended to work in isolation. Although curricular issues were discussed across the different units or parts of the CFP, many nurse teachers acknowledged subsequently that there was not enough consultation between subject groups. This resulted in common themes between courses not being linked, and some teachers detected a certain disjointedness and incidences of duplication – these problems were reflected later in curriculum planning for the Branch programmes. One nurse teacher described the different course subjects as being 'separate boxes with overlap', rather than a truly integrated course structure.

When the students were asked to reflect back on the areas covered in the courses, it was clear from their responses that they would have liked them to have shown more cohesion and unity. Areas of study did not always seem to be presented in any logical sequence and were sometimes difficult to relate to without sufficient background and context. Some parts of the courses would have been appreciated at earlier stages and others had been only partially understood if taught during the early stages before the relevant (or sufficient) practical experience had been undertaken. As one student explained: 'When I first did philosophy at the beginning of the course it took such a long time to sink in. You couldn't get your head round it. But at least now on the wards you can think things through, and begin to see things as they really are.' Working through the 'basics' again towards the end of the courses (feeding and visits to residential homes) was seen by students as symptomatic of poor organisation.

Students reported difficulty in absorbing the breadth of information generated by the range of subjects – a quarter described themselves as 'overwhelmed'. With only a limited awareness of the philosophy and pedagogical rationale underpinning their courses, students found it difficult to visualise the whole. There was also disjointedness as in 'I have a sense of it being all over the place and don't feel that we are looking at a set of subjects related to nursing. It is a very difficult course to absorb as a whole.'

This sense of alienation from what was presented to them was clear in the comment that 'we would do something in life sciences that wasn't linked in any way to the implications for nursing and you could do fluid balance as an area without relating it to the loss of fluid in the body and what you need to know about it and what you need to tell patients so you couldn't connect different parts of the course'. Another explained that 'when we did the biochemistry it just didn't seem to make any sense and it would have been much better to have it now, near the pharmacology'. The pressures inherent in courses of this nature that seek to cover such a range of subject areas for a vocationally focused group are clear when the criticism made in the previous comment is set beside the charge from another student that the courses offer only 'a very superficial look at complex issues'.

The students were asked for their views on the relationship between 'theory' and practice that they identified on the courses and nearly half of them felt that a mismatch did exist. When asked to elaborate on what forms this gap took, students identified several different dimensions. A major concern was the sometimes unsatisfactory sequencing of the academic input and the practical placements. As one student expressed it: 'Yes, we get the practice far earlier than the theory and that happened right through...they left it all to the ward to teach us and that is not right and we should have got what we need in school and then had an opportunity to go out and practice.' Following through this sequencing, students reported being taught aspects of practice towards the end of the courses that they had been undertaking on their placements for some time, with nurse teachers seeming unaware of this and assuming otherwise in their teaching. The converse, of having an input in the college of nursing without any opportunity to put it into practice or to do so only at a much later date, was equally frustrating.

While this concern about sequencing was the main thrust of their reflections on the lack of integration on the courses, other aspects of the gap mentioned were a 'pure' academic input that was not directly related to nursing and a contradiction between 'good' practice as identified by staff in the college of nursing and practice in the placement areas. The first point was explored in the comment that 'at the [HE institution] you would do the blood system and drugs but you were not taught how this applies to drug therapy and what the nursing implications are and how it affected what you did with people and what you advised them. If you were lucky you would pick up this information by chance on the wards but certainly you were never taught it.'

The following quotation illustrated both the second point about contradicting practice and the absorption of one of the learning objectives of Project 2000. The student explained that:

> *I can see that it's very difficult for the tutors to tell us to contradict the ward. We might know that you should keep a thermometer in for six minutes to take a temperature accurately and yet know that everywhere we go it's only kept in for three minutes, but it's very hard for tutors to actually tell us that the wards are doing bad practice because we would get disillusioned. What the course does is arm us with research so that we are not in a position of saying you don't do it like that because we have been taught differently, but you don't do it like that because the research says otherwise. We've been taught to back up what we say and that's the best way to broach this gap between how things should be done and how they are actually put into practice out there.*

The students who felt that there was not a mismatch between 'theory' and practice focused in the main on practice in the placement areas matching to a satisfactory degree what they had been taught. One typical comment was: 'No, what we do is backed-up by what we see on a ward.' This different perspective obviously depended on individual student responses as well as on the variety of practices they would have been exposed to on the many placements on offer – no one site differed significantly in the proportion of students who felt that the gap existed.

Course structure and content

Discussion of the courses with those involved yielded a considerable amount of concern about what the basic underpinnings should be. To illustrate the diverse views held, one senior member of HE staff from a nurse education background felt that 'letting all these subjects in shows a lack of confidence in Project 2000' and that the course should be blocked into nursing units with other subjects feeding in. Conversely, a senior member of HE staff on another site explained how a course committee 'dominated' by nursing interests stymied course development and resulted in disproportionate significance being attached to students' comments when they mirrored nurse teachers' (as he saw it, restrictive) emphasis on relevance and subject integration.

Some nurse teachers expressed reservations concerning the curriculum as it stood. A senior member of staff commented that 'everything must relate to nursing, and if it doesn't we've got to think very carefully why we are including it'. Elsewhere, a member of staff had misgivings about the status of health education in the courses. Because it was an integrated topic, there was an assumption that it was being covered in the different subject areas when this was not necessarily the case. Teachers in community studies in two separate schemes felt that there was not enough rigour in this aspect of the courses. Another teacher commented that subjects were not always coordinated properly so as to allow progression throughout the courses.

While a handful of students had changed their Branch, it was not the case that students approached the CFP with an open mind about how they should specialise. (Across all 13 sites, only one did not allocate students to Branch groups for the CFP.) When students were asked about the organisation of the courses into two parts – an 18- month CFP and an 18-month Branch – two major themes emerged. One was the widely held perception that this was in practice an **Adult** (rather than **common**) foundation course – a view expressed by students across the specialities. The other main point was that the common part should be reduced in length – to a generally agreed 12 months. As one student expressed it: 'It would be all right if it was a genuinely **common** foundation but you are in your Branch from day one and so the CFP just means that you lump us all together and doesn't mean that it's truly common with a view to you deciding what you want to do at a later date.'

There were comments from the teachers in Mental Health and Learning Disability specialisms to the effect that the CFP did not present a true picture of commonality of the different disciplines. Teaching was said to be preoccupied with the health issues of adult nursing and students were not getting a complete range of placement experiences. One member of staff worried about the implications of this situation in terms of the motivation of students in the Mental Health and Learning Disability specialties, to which it was already hard to recruit.

Given this, 18 months seemed very drawn out for those in the numerically smaller specialties who were keen to develop those areas of interest that had drawn them to a particular Branch. Adult Branch students were aware of this and also, of more direct relevance to them, of an emphasis on 'wellness' in the CFP that seemed disproportionately lengthy. There were several references to repetition and a sense of time-filling which was particularly frustrating when students looked at the course as a whole and identified periods when a heavy work commitment was required. What the students suggested was not a reformulation of the CFP principles but a restructuring that made the best use of what was a relatively short period within which to qualify. As one student suggested, the CFP was 'good in principle, but it needs to be shorter and consolidated. Its good to have all the Branches together to get an idea of the whole but you do need clearer objectives.'

An in-depth reflection in the third year on the outcomes of the CFP from a Mental Health Branch student sounded an optimistic note for the achievement of some of the goals of Project 2000. She was aware of the considerable gains she herself had made on the course and proposed that:

> *The CFP seems to be very dim and distant now but an awful lot of what we did then we won't use although of course it may have helped to shape our attitudes. I really enjoyed the sociology and psychology and that's very relevant and I think that this will be more significant for the general nurses in that I think they are so different from the traditionally trained ones without realising it and I think that the work in the CFP will have been absorbed by them whether they know it or not and they will have gained a great deal.*

The students' answers to questioning about the material covered in the courses focused on relevance and accessibility. Whilst there were comments about the high-quality teaching and personal qualities of some members of staff, the strongest comments centred on relevance – students in the main were uneasy where this was not apparent and more receptive when it was. An important criterion for judging what was provided (across subject areas) was: 'What has it got to do with actual nursing?' The desire for more anatomy and physiology teaching expressed by several students was consistent with this. At its worst, this urge for relevance alienated students and weakened their commitment to the courses. As one student explained 'Unit One was very slow and it was horrendous to be in school so much. That is when people started to talk about leaving and we didn't really seem to be doing anything. It is part of the course to be got out of the way.'

There were carefully considered comments from a few students to the effect that the courses had 'swung too far' in terms of content. As one of them explained: 'They [nurse teachers] refuse to hold on to what might be good features of the old course. It's as if everything has to be new and different.' There was certainly a belief from some students, across sites, that insufficient attention had been given to physiology and practical skills. New areas such as communication and quality assurance issues seemed to be correspondingly over done.

This unease about course content was strikingly illustrated by the student who recounted: 'The other day a new group [of Project 2000 students] was in town doing their "observing and perceiving" and there was us in the gym exercising for "health and fitness". There were 140 Project 2000 students in that day and not **one** student was learning a **thing** about nursing.' In a similar vein, in the United States context, Davis (1975) explained that 'when during these first few months students are occasionally taught a "doing" kind of technique or procedure, a flurry of class enthusiasm ensues'.

Movement into the Branch programmes represented a significant turning point in how the course was seen. Students across sites reported a sense of relief and of settling into what they perceived as more relevant material. This response was illustrated by the comment that 'I do have a sense of knowing what I'm here for as we take on more relevant work'. A few students reflected from this position of optimism that they could see the CFP in a more constructive light now and could see their earlier work as part of a whole. As one of these students explained: 'The CFP is much clearer now and I can see how it fits in and can refer back.' Conversely, a few made negative expressions about the CFP and were pleased to have 'got through it at last'.

Starting the Branch programmes provided the opportunity for students to reflect more generally on course content – this phase took on the nature of a watershed and although only a few students drew out these points, they make a useful contribution to an understanding of how courses might develop. Contradictions were identified in the philosophical underpinnings of the courses. Students spent their time learning about health and the 'normal' and yet some of the placements (even early ones in some cases) were with people who were ill or 'abnormal'. The placements exposed them to ill-health and yet they knew nothing about disease and were supposed to be focusing exclusively on 'wellness'. The difficulties this created for students were summed up in the comment that: 'If you spend three weeks on a "disease" ward you have to get **yourself** genned up because nothing is taught about disease on the course.' The shift of emphasis in the Branches fitted into their need to have a frame of reference they could relate to for the course content. As one student expressed it: 'It is better on the Branch because we are being taught about illness. Take the heart, for example – they talk about normal, illness, pathology and patient care. We needed this kind of linkage from the beginning.'

There was concern in HE (and pockets of such in nurse education) that the curriculum was so broad as to be essentially only taking a superficial look at a wide variety of subjects. The most confusion for staff centred on the life sciences input where a re-evaluation of the level and breadth of what was on offer was a feature of several sites. There was concern that the original input had been over-ambitious and on two sites the summative assessment had been moved to later parts of the courses to allow students more time to absorb what was widely acknowledged to be a potentially very demanding part of the courses that had not been appropriately 'pitched'. The options and possibility of 'back-up' sessions (before and during the courses) and distance

46

learning materials had not been fully explored on any of the sites, although there had been some moves in that direction in places.

Students expressed disappointment when they had been unable to comprehend or assimilate what was on offer. The clearest example of this was some of the life sciences work – the area that received the most critical comment from students, with widespread concern (from two-thirds of the students) being expressed in the two schemes where the life sciences formed a regular part of the HE input. Students expressed strong reservations about what they had been able to learn and were demoralised and confused. 'Remedial' life science sessions had caused confusion – students were unclear whether you only had to go if you had a 'problem' and it all seemed 'random and people don't know what they are for'. In these two sites it was only those with a science background who were coping – one such student's overview captured generally held views about the science teaching saying, that it:

> ... stands out as something that needs a lot more work doing on it. It was **very poor** and taught at far too high a level. I have O-level chemistry and yet was totally baffled. At least I understood what a molecule was which was not so for most of the group. People were asking me why the lecturer was putting K for potassium when it starts with a P. The whole thing really needs re-thinking. It is a very useful subject but not the way that it was taught here.

Teaching and learning

The students' comments on the teaching methods used on their courses at both institutions were remarkably consistent across all six schemes (although, of course, for some students there was very little HE input to consider). Students saw the institutions of HE and the colleges of nursing as **very** different in terms of ethos and teaching style. Obviously, there was variation that reflected the skill and experience of individual members of staff, but students identified the key characteristics of the two institutions and were vocal about the impact on their learning. Lecturers were seen as subject specialists – who had studied and worked in a particular field for some time. Such staff were described as 'professional', and were said to 'inspire confidence' because of their obvious depth of knowledge.

Whilst this expertise was valued it could also serve as a disadvantage – the students were adamant that they would not (with a few notable exceptions) approach a lecturer to seek clarification nor would they ask questions during sessions. The time was organised so that lecturers 'stood up, lectured, left' and such inaccessibility created anxiety. One student summed up a general concern about this 'cut and dried' approach by explaining that 'it is as though they have been asked to give us a lecture and they are simply going to come and do it', (an approach she contrasted with that of the college of nursing where 'we are **their** students and they want us to do well'). There was, however, a general sense of some of the college of nursing teaching being so informal that it left students frustrated and feeling they were time-wasting – particularly when a spiral curriculum was experienced as repetition rather than a progressive programme of study. There were several references to the difficulties of 'adjusting from the cosy school of nursing to the HE – it's a case of adjusting your thinking'.

When asked to comment on course delivery, the main points to emerge were concerns about group work in the colleges of nursing (discussions in small groups with a major contribution from students, and a feedback session), and self-directed study. A widespread sense of unease about what was achieved and a feeling of saturation were consistently expressed for the group work in each of the six schemes. The arrangements were said to be 'laid-back – they don't give you enough idea of what is expected or aims and objectives'. Drawing on the students' knowledge and experience was said to have been taken too far, with uneasiness which arose from 'not knowing the validity of what the other students have presented, never mind the depth'. A feeling of addressing issues from **every** angle and 'spending a whole day doing something that could be done in an hour' led to a good deal of negative comment on group work. It was said that 'tutors are almost frightened to let us go and give us spare time'. Students saw such analysis as a useful teaching strategy but felt that it was used for subjects that would lend themselves to more straightforward presentation and that there was simply too much of it – students' lighthearted comments about 'groaning when we see yet another flip-chart' illustrated this last point neatly.

As the course progressed there was reorganisation within intakes for teaching purposes and a few students commented that they were now in a smaller, potentially more productive group, but the overwhelming message across sites was of dissatisfaction with this method of delivery. Only a few students were positive about group discussions, citing them as confidence-building exercises. There were accusations of repetition and of low-key sessions that seemed to achieve little. In one scheme all but one of the nine students were vociferous in their complaints about plenary sessions. They claimed that such sessions had continued despite repeated requests from students about their limited value – a situation that had generated considerable frustration for those interviewed. To illustrate the need for balance, it is instructive to note that in one scheme (where students were less vociferous in their complaints) the point was made that sufficient time needed to be left after group work for feedback because otherwise you could be left 'feeling up in the air'.

The students emphasised the need for mixed approaches to teaching and the need to refine current practice. There were a few comments about the need for lectures to be sharply focused and lively (so that students don't get 'bogged down by information being fired at you'). Groups needed to be well organised so that staff 'don't just let people ramble'. The following quotation emphasises, again, the ubiquitous frustration, this time explained in terms of a perceived educational philosophy.

> *They don't like to see us sitting behind desks and yet we get very fed-up having nothing to lean on and we are actually happy behind our desks. They get really neurotic if we are not all sitting in groups interacting in the way that they would like. What we actually want is a good mix of styles where you do group work where it's appropriate and sit behind a desk and make notes when it's actually a straightforward lecture to convey facts.*

Many teachers commented on the lack of classroom accommodation, which ruled out preferred teaching methods and led to a preponderance of over-large groups. These conditions were felt to obstruct group participation, demotivating staff and students, and to pose difficulties for teachers attempting to monitor the students' grasp of a subject. Students acknowledged the demanding task their teachers faced in administering such complex courses – several of them expressed concern about the size of intakes and the longer term problems as numbers build up. The non-availability of rooms of an appropriate size was a continuing difficulty. There was some concern about the situation (already 'a nightmare' in some schemes) worsening once colleges of nursing were up to their full capacity of Project 2000 intakes. One scheme was expecting to expand into extra accommodation at one of its sites, and another District was searching for new purpose-built premises.

Staff in HE were unsure about the overall expectations of the courses in terms of workload and the extent to which students had time for study, although there was a widely held impression that they had highly structured days. An increasing number of nurse teachers commented that the timetable was too packed with classroom teaching and that there was not enough personal study time to encourage an adult learning model of education. There was uncertainty amongst the students about what their responsibilities for learning were. Some topics had been dealt with briefly and they were unclear about what they should do to pursue them further, or if indeed they should at all. This unease about self-directed work was compounded where students had been told that complex issues or areas of study with which they had been presented were not 'necessary'. One student explained that she was left with a 'feeling that I don't know what I actually **do** need to know'.

The concept of personal study had been absorbed and operationalised to widely differing degrees by individual students – a few openly acknowledged taking it as 'free time' and others struggled to achieve what seemed to them to be about right – very few were complacent about this feature of their course. Students complained about a lack of structure for what they were 'supposed' to do, which resulted in one student's comment about 'constant concern about the number of books to read.' Such study was the focus for much angst – students were guilty about not doing 'enough'. They criticised themselves for a 'lack of discipline'. Gaps between teaching sessions were seen as symptomatic of poor organisation and were not, on the whole, used for private study. Students complained of not being given notice of free periods in advance with the result that they did not have work with them and 'had to go to the coffee lounge'.

This was an area where there was a need for clarification. In one scheme, subject teaching had been rearranged into blocks which had given continuity and there were now set days for private study. This latter development would have been commended by students in another scheme, more than half of whom expressed concern about the 'wasted' study time on their course. They would have appreciated the more compact framework outlined above. Overall, one - third of the students spontaneously referred to the need for study time to be planned and used constructively – students needed to know when it was and what they should be doing with it. This anxiety about not doing enough was most marked on one site where most of the students reported some degree of aimlessness. There was a sharp contrast with another site where students reported a sense of purposefulness from the clear structure of set work (with some reporting this as reaching counter-productive levels). Students here focused on the need to pace their work steadily and plan ahead, and some argued forcibly for study time in order to do justice to the set work. One posited the view that 'I think that at the school they feel that they **must** fill up the time and they are so reluctant to let us work on our own'.

One sub-group which emerged at the mid-point of the course was that of mature entrants (across three sites) who had made a major commitment to achieving on the course, which was reflected in high grades, and who felt under tremendous pressure to keep attaining this standard. These were the respondents who spoke of 'panic' and 'terrible pressure' and who were anxious (despite assurances from tutors in some cases) about any drop in the standard achieved. The other instances of negative comments related to the erratic spacing of assignments (most markedly in one site).

Entry requirements

The increase in more highly qualified applicants and the decrease in student places were combining – in a pincer-like movement – to squeeze and threaten the wider entry gate which was always seen as an integral part of Project 2000. The limited development of part-time Project 2000 courses reported elsewhere (Bond, 1992) was another manifestation of this. The course leader in one case-study scheme confirmed – with regret – this trend with respect to the part-time option her college offered: numbers were expected to reduce with effect from October 1992 and this 'slightly more expensive' option to cease altogether in the future. Yet there was still said to be considerable demand from women with dependent children whom the course had been put on to attract when recruitment was seen as a problem.

Across the Demonstration sites principals and course leaders reported that they were reviewing or proposing to review their entry requirements. They were able to be more selective and were seeking to ensure that students whom they accepted would be able to cope with the academic course work, by, for example, suggesting that applicants do prior 'access' courses or provide other evidence of higher level study. The level of students' scientific knowledge and understanding continued to be one of the main areas of concern. One college had developed its own distance learning package in the sciences which students were recommended to buy and work through before commencing the course if they had not studied them previously. In that college, and elsewhere, students were also being offered 'remedial' work in the sciences early in the courses. In one scheme this took the form of a basic science course in the first term which someone experienced in teaching science at that level in FE had been specifically contracted to do.

Conditions were being attached to GCSE entry in places (concerning subjects and/or number of attempts) and use of the 'DC 'test was very much more restricted. In the first year of Project 2000 implementation, only one of the six case-study colleges, for example, did not accept the test as an entry qualification. In 1992 one of the other five colleges had effectively stopped using it (offering it only to candidates over 45 years old) and another confined its use to applicants with three GCSE passes. In one case, work was already underway to develop a level 3 NVQ entry route, although official confirmation of the acceptability of such a route (announced in November 1992) was still awaited at that time.

Respondents revealed some uncertainty and ambivalence about continued use of the DC test and the wide entry gate generally. The strong motivation of many mature students entering by that method was widely acknowledged, as was their subsequent level of achievement. Typical comments from course leaders were that 'there are a lot people on the course now who never previously demonstrated any academic ability, but who are bright, motivated and do very well. The profession can't do without these sorts of people' and 'a lot of the mature students with families find the academic work hard, but we've been pleasantly surprised how they stick in with the right support.'

Attrition

Concerns about the number of students not completing their course of preparation have been widely expressed. The UKCC (1986) stated that training wastage on RGN courses was about 15 per cent, with a further six per cent not taking up nursing posts in the NHS (three per cent passing but not registering with the UKCC and three per cent not finding NHS employment.) One of the proposed benefits of the introduction of Project 2000 was said to be a potential reduction in wastage (UKCC, 1987). In fact, 22 per cent of Project 2000 students in the first intakes in this study did not successfully complete the course they started. The variation across sites was from 13 per cent non-completion to 39 per cent, with no particular pattern detectable (see Appendix 5). (A pro-forma was sent to students who left the courses, asking why they had left, and their responses are included in Appendix 5.) For the second intake the figure for the number of students who did not successfully complete the course they started was reduced to 14 per cent. The ENB's figures for discontinuations from courses (ENB, 1992/ 93) show little difference between Project 2000 and traditional courses. The comparable figures for HE institutions involved in the delivery of Project 2000 ranged from 12 to 18 per cent. These figures may be compared with those for students studying for first degrees in polytechnics and universities where the drop-out rate for 1989/90 was 16 per cent and for 1990/91, 15 per cent (DFE and OFSTED, 1993).

Attempts to unravel the complexities of why people leave courses have been made for some considerable time. Macguire (1969) reviewed over sixty research reports on attrition among student and pupil nurses, concluding that 'the presenting problems seem much the same in the 1960's as they seemed in the 1940's and attempts to deal with the presenting problems have met with singular lack of success'. Following an analysis of stress, and coping strategies in student nurses, West and Rushton (1986) suggested reasons for withdrawal from courses concluding that 'many young people with initiative and enterprise find the rule-bound and restrictive ethos of nursing incompatible with their personalities' They added that their research was conducted in 'two of the more enlightened schools of nursing in the country where efforts were being made to prepare learners optimally for nursing. Even here we found that learners receive too little feedback on their performance and are often placed in situations for which they are not yet adequately trained'. In the same vein, Lindop (1989) called for 'fundamental change' in practice-based staff in that 'it would seem that a more caring and positive approach to them (students) is required, along with a realistic appraisal of just how stressful their clinical experience can be'.

In this study, concern was expressed about the a tendency to 'over-assess' students in the early intakes. In one scheme, where wastage was said to be running at about 14 per cent overall – and to cover a large number of exam failures – the students affected were described as 'victims' of the college's early 'inappropriate' assessment system. Another course leader concerned about the exam failure (particularly the biological science exam early in the course) spoke of 'losing good nurses for the wrong reasons'. The case of a student with a degree in social science who failed the biological science exam twice and had to leave was cited as an example. In another scheme, where wastage averaging around 11 per cent over the first three intakes was reported (with failure to achieve at the end of the CFP a major contributory factor),unseen examinations in the sciences at the end of the CFP were to be substituted by prepared pieces of work for the next intake.

Assessment

Reservations about the assessment strategies used were voiced by HE staff throughout the study and this was one area where a considerable overhaul was widely anticipated. There was variation in policy regarding the number of attempts allowed at each assessment. According to one college's regulations, students were allowed two attempts at an exam and then a third attempt as an external candidate. A few students were said to have returned to the course after succeeding at that third attempt. Elsewhere, two failed attempts meant discontinuation, although exceptionally a third attempt was allowed on appeal. There was widespread disquiet that the course was over-assessed, and some unease about marks being subsumed in a way that gave a misleading view of students' level of attainment and made it impossible to work on any areas of weakness they exhibited – a limitation exacerbated by the infrequent sessions lecturers had with students. One senior member of HE staff commented that not enough attention was paid to the all-round performance of students when borderline results were discussed. Combining subject areas for assessment was disapproved of by several lecturers, with one expressing the view that the early integration of subjects was 'over-ambitious and totally unrealistic'. This lecturer was surprised that differences between HE and colleges of nursing in assessment methods had persisted 'given that HE was meant to be the model'.

Although a number of nurse teachers expressed satisfaction with the overall academic assessment strategy as it stood, the majority of them identified areas for improvement. Some felt there to be too much pressure on the students, and were aware that some students were overwhelmed with the amount and depth of study required of them. One nurse teacher remarked: 'The fun of nursing just isn't there – nor the luxury of being in college.' Another described the assessment system not as continuous, but rather as a series of hurdles which occurred quickly in succession during the courses, with little respite. Staff from four of the colleges of nursing said that they regarded summative assessments as inappropriate for the early part of the courses, and wanted formative work to take precedence during the first year. Other criticisms concerned timing and sequencing of particular assessments, not enough weight being attributed to individual performance in groups and seminars, and lack of examination information for students.

There was some confusion amongst the students about the academic level of the courses. Some parts of the courses were more difficult than others, but most students were reasonably comfortable with what they perceived would be required of them. Where students were anxious about the level of work, this was either because they had returned to study after a break or because they had not settled into a routine of study so that 'there is constantly work on your mind and a feeling of a great deal to do'. Students on one site had been surprised towards the end of the CFP to learn that they had not reached Diploma level yet – a statement which was said to have raised anxiety levels and weakened morale. The extremes that anxiety can reach were articulated by the student who, although doing particularly well on the assessed work, explained:

> *I don't really know what the standard is, and this is something I am extremely worried about. I ask and they tell me that I am already working at that standard and I shouldn't worry. I've had more anxiety about this than anything else. I have asked for essays to do myself so that I can have an idea of what I should be covering and so that I can get feedback on what I am doing. Nobody actually seems to know what a Diploma is. They tell me I am worrying because I am a mature student but that just doesn't help. I am told that a Diploma means a different way of thinking and that I can do it, but I still feel very anxious.*

The level had been a surprise for some of those coming on to the courses with above- average qualifications. One such student had thought it would be a 'real doddle' and had found this not to be the case. Conversely, a graduate had found it frustrating to work below her capacity. An interesting insight into vocational expectations was provided by another of the graduates. She expressed surprise that, although the entrance qualification was five GCSEs, students were expected to do essays with references – something she had only had to do for her dissertation at university. She had anticipated that this course would be a 'half-way house' academically. She was not as motivated to write essays as she had been as an under graduate and had 'got a bit sick of it'.

In the main, nurse teachers felt confident that the teaching and assessment on the course was at Diploma level. Where there were initial concerns over academic level, issues had been clarified through work with HE staff and external examiners. However, some of them had misgivings about this issue. They were aware that academic standards differed across subject areas on the course. Others confessed to being unsure of what Diploma level actually meant – nurse teachers with personal experience of HE were included in this group – in the absence of guidelines or comparable examples. Two members of teaching staff attributed this latter concern to a lack of confidence on the part of nurse teachers themselves. A small number of staff were openly critical of the level of academic work.

A number of nurse teachers were plainly enthusiastic about the high quality of academic work being produced by students, and there were commendations of the development of critical analysis. However, others voiced fears that some of their students were not coping well with the academic demands of a Diploma course, and were 'just hanging on by their finger nails'. One respondent commented: '... some students **will never cope**. We've got to be honest with ourselves as teachers and ask: - where are we taking this person to?' Nurse teachers in three of the schemes were concerned about HMI or external examiners' criticisms of the standard of students' academic work.

Most districts had existing or planned degree course options which would be available for the Project 2000 qualifiers to 'top up' their Diploma courses. However, the question of how any full-time options would be financed was still far from clear in places. Only two colleges had a definite number of funded degree course places on offer for which students from the first intakes had been selected. They moved on to the one-year full-time courses, with specialist options, on completion of their Diploma courses in October 1992.

The role of HE

Given the varying degrees of involvement of HE staff in planning and providing the Diploma courses and the turbulent times being experienced in both sectors, the part HE staff would play in further work was seen as of central importance. Staff in HE were, on the whole, of the opinion that they and their colleagues had a crucial role to play in the Diploma courses because of their depth of involvement in subject areas. (The notion that an interest in and some limited

52

study of a subject area qualified nurse education colleagues to teach it was a particular source of unease.) On the site where liaison was being tentatively re-established, a senior member of HE staff envisaged a potentially innovative future strategy where there could be 'a lot of the basic theory done by HE' – emphasising the subject specialist, discipline-based approach. With the appropriate approach, he anticipated no difficulties in the life sciences elements (his academic background), and explained that the goal was not 'academic brilliance but good workers in health'. This can be contrasted with the view of a senior manager on the HE site which had withdrawn from much of the life sciences work in the CFP (there was never any in the Branches) who commented that bio-chemistry had become so low level that it was unsatisfactorily 'bitty' and unrewarding to teach. In this course the life sciences elements had been radically reviewed (removing immunology and biochemistry and instituting a basic science course) and it was said that nurse tutors were eminently suited to providing this contribution.

The changes proposed by nurse educators in the extent of HE input on some sites were facilitated by the increasing number of nurse teachers achieving graduate status and by them 'finding the confidence to teach most of the curriculum themselves anyway'. A senior nurse teacher felt that, following transfer into HE, it would be invidious to have HE staff making too much of a contribution to the course and 'embarrassing' to have course managers in the future coming from outside the nurse education department. He anticipated that the course would be 'completely self-contained within four or five years' because 'it really isn't viable to move into HE if you've got to look outside for contributions'. Guidelines developed for the courses propose that serious consideration be given to their subject bases as 'students need to gain some understanding of contributory disciplines such as psychology or physiology, their systematic approach to knowledge, and the gathering and analysis of data, so that students begin to acquire the skills of problem solving within these disciplines and develop these skills in the field of nursing' (CNAA/ENB, 1992).

Summary of main points

- The issue to emerge most strongly in the early interviews with staff providing the courses was the speed at which the development work had had to be done.

- Joint course planning between nurse education and HE had not been easily achieved and was only accomplished to any significant degree in two of the six Districts studied.

- There was a sense of having to adapt or circumvent established practices in HE because of the tight timescale.

- The arrangement whereby a member of staff had been seconded from the institution of HE to the college of nursing for approximately two-and-a-half days a week for about four months of the course planning stage was agreed by all involved to have been well worthwhile. The lecturer had played a key role in developing the course, contributing his considerable experience in HE to what the nurse educators were producing.

- HE staff expressed a desire for more input than just sessional teaching and the one scheme where they did not express concerns about the appropriateness of their contribution was where they had played a significant role in early course development and were automatically involved in the Branches.

- It was difficult for HE staff to see their contributions as part of a whole and it was consistently said that these were rather confused courses with loose ends.

- The students felt that areas of study did not always seem to be presented in any logical sequence and were sometimes difficult to relate to without sufficient background and context.

- There was a considerable amount of concern from staff involved about what the basic framework of the courses should be.

- Many students felt that it was an **Adult** (rather than **common**) foundation course and that the CFP should be reduced in length to 12 months.

- The students' concerns about the course content focused on the need for relevance and accessibility. Starting the Branches was a significant turning point as students across sites reported a sense of relief and of settling into what they perceived as more relevant material.

- Students saw the institutions of HE and the colleges of nursing as <u>very</u> different in terms of ethos and teaching style.

- Students expressed consistently concerns about group work in the colleges of nursing, and self-directed study.

- At this early stage, the introduction of Project 2000 has not had the hoped for impact on the number of students leaving their course before completion, although the decrease in the figures from the first to the second intake is encouraging.

- Staff in nurse education were reviewing their entry requirements for the Diploma courses.

- Reservations about the assessment strategies used were voiced by HE staff throughout the study and this was one area where a considerable overhaul was widely anticipated.

- Given the varying degrees of involvement of HE staff in planning and providing the Diploma courses and the turbulent times being experienced in both sectors, the part HE staff would play in further work was seen as of central importance.

Discussion

Despite the fact that staff in the colleges of nursing had been progressing towards a course that bore some of the key features of Project 2000, it was undoubtedly the case that there was a counter-productive rush in development and planning that staffs' best efforts could not overcome. The inevitable 'in-house' model that emerged limited the extent to which colleagues' expertise and experience could be utilised, which had unsatisfactory and long-term effects on the course. The evidence presented here made clear the need for a systematic review of both the breadth of content currently covered and of ways in which more sharply focused parts could be integrated into the whole. The merits of coherence and of logical underpinnings were clear from all sides. Identifying the fundamental structures to be built-on and the rationale for including materials on the courses and for assessing them would serve to remedy some of the concerns expressed here. The unease was epitomised by suggestions for reformulating the split into foundation and speciality – an issue that may be addressed to good effect.

Clearly, from the variety of comments on the Project 2000 curriculum, there remain some profound educational questions which nursing still has to resolve. Some of the uncertainty in course development arose from the assumptions of staff involved about nursing expertise and how it is learned, and the problems of translating the 'knowledgeable doer' and the reflective practitioner' into actual learning experiences. With nursing-related subjects jostling to occupy more space within the curriculum, how far should pure 'nursing' subjects give way? How can the competing goals of breadth and depth of the course be fulfilled given a restricted timescale? And how is the alleged bias of the CFP toward adult nursing to be addressed? Furthermore, if the Branch programmes are so well received and are in reality a return to the structure and ethos of previous courses as has been suggested, then to what degree can nurse education be said to have embraced the changes implicit in Project 2000? There is a need for the CFP to be presented with clarity as a preliminary part of the whole – a multidimensional communication exercise is called for. Another consideration raised was that of the need to consider students' preparation for placements in the CFP within a framework that emphasises wellness and health. The students' confidence in now feeling 'better prepared' as a result of input in the Branches brings into sharp relief the need for clarity about the purpose of learning experiences.

Concerns expressed by HE staff in the early stages about their place in the overall scheme grew as time passed. There was change afoot on all sites, which raised differing degrees of uncertainty *vis-à-vis* their future contributions to the course. Is it the case that, once in HE, nurse education will no longer 'require' contributions from what would now be regarded as subject specialists in HE? Is the goal a jointly run course or a 'buying-in' of what is required from HE? Have the links served a transitional purpose in the sense of acclimatising nurse educators to HE to such an extent that they are now indistinguishably part of it? How are the fundamental differences still evident as the first intake came to the end of the course to be resolved – differences including assessment, course structure and subject integration? Is there still a place for a significant subject specialist input in terms of staff with qualifications in and significant experience of teaching particular areas? The strident defence of teaching **qualifications** (identified in the chapter focusing on links between HE and nurse education) by some nurse teachers as guaranteeing a certain level of expertise contrasts on some occasions with a seeming disregard for subject qualifications as a prerequisite for playing a major role in subject delivery.

It was clear that many students were unprepared for or unaware of what was expected of them. Many had suggestions about how the structure could be improved which offer guidelines for future practice. The central message was to work towards a balanced approach that capitalised on the undoubted strengths of both HE and the colleges of nursing. This 'healthy balance' of teaching approaches raised issues about how best to meet students' learning needs. The 'impersonal' HE and the 'approachable' college of nursing were consistently described and there were obvious implications for student learning – neither side had got it right in terms of pace of work, level of direction about further study and pitching the level of work realistically. Sessions on study skills had been provided, but the key messages had often not been communicated or absorbed – discussing these approaches very early on in the course may have meant that students were unable to assimilate them and, of course, some issues only emerged as the students progressed.

The students had suggestions to make about restructuring the courses both in terms of the form the **common** foundation should take and the optimum way of sequencing and coordinating material. All groups of interviewees highlighted the need for continuing developmental work to identify what the chief priorities for course content were and to ensure that channels for effective communication and collaboration were established. The ubiquitous gap between theory and practice seemed to revolve around sequencing and could be tackled via better channels of communication. The students' workload and the academic expectations placed on them were sometimes poorly thought through and an analysis of these would need to be incorporated into any system of review and development.

In some colleges the assessment system was seen as a priority area to address and revise when Project 2000 courses were due for resubmission. In other colleges, it seemed, a considerable amount of revision and development of assessment strategies had already taken place as the courses evolved. A reduction in the number of summative assessments was the main measure planned or effected. There was a desire to move to a system where there was greater profiling of students' overall performance and/or where students could accrue results rather than face a succession of assessment hurdles, each of which had to be surmounted in order to continue the course. This, it was felt, would help to relieve the academic stress on the students – and the counter-productive period of pre-assessment anxiety when they were unable to attend to other learning. Such moves would also relieve pressure on teaching staff for whom the workload involved in marking and moderating summative assessments was described by one course leader as a 'nightmare'.

Students' experience of the workload and the opportunities for private study varied across sites, although there was widespread concern about the spacing of projects and assignments which seemed to result in an uneven pace of work, sometimes reaching both extremes. The overall picture, not withstanding this unproductive spacing, was of some sites where students felt decidedly under-extended and others where stress levels had reached counter-productive levels (certainly towards the end of the course) as students struggled to complete set work to an appropriate standard. What emerged very clearly was that students were not on the whole satisfied with the balance between **set** work and independent study and there was much angst and uncertainty. Where there was a great deal of time for independent study, it was common for students to experience that lack of direction as demotivating and demoralising. There were reports of having 'switched off' or 'become lazy' and also evidence of lost opportunities to engage students in sustained academic work and capitalise on their desire to learn.

There is, most strikingly, a need to re-evaluate the use of group work (and plenary sessions). The students' comments show the mismatch in expectation between the recipients and the providers. At worst, the former experienced group work as being taught by other students in a non-progressive and potentially anxiety-provoking way – a far cry from what the latter may have been intending from a philosophical stance (Rogers, 1983).

The students' emphasis on accessibility drew attention to the difficulty of delivering the course to such a varied intake, in terms of previous experience and academic background. If this course is to educate rather than train, then this is obviously an issue for sustained consideration. If the goal is to realise individual potential, then there is a clear need for structures to facilitate this. Some examples are clarification of and time for private study, sufficient constructive, personal tuition, 'remedial' sessions, and 'streamed' lectures/seminars. If nurse education concentrates on entry qualifications, rather than on the process and potential of the course for change, it may lose valuable recruits and may also miss the opportunity to reduce attrition rates that Project 2000 was thought to offer.

---

[1]   *A verbal reasoning and mathematics test, developed by Denis Child, used in the selection of entrants without the standard entry qualifications of five GCSEs (or their equivalent), to nursing courses.*

Chapter Five
NURSE TEACHERS
AND PROJECT 2000

Introduction

The nurse teachers interviewed in this study provided insights into the process of implementing Project 2000 and into the changes under way in their role and function, and the data collected from them are presented here. Their experiences highlighted (sometimes dramatically) the consequences of innovation introduced to a tight deadline and the individual adaptations required of the key players. The process that the nurse teachers are working through is discussed below and some aspects of their role that need clarification are explored. The debates about their work in the placement areas and their responsibilities *vis-à-vis* students illustrated key factors that need to be addressed as nurse education identifies more precisely its new practices and approach.

The pace and extent of change

Nurse teachers from all Districts commented on the rushed planning and implementation of Project 2000. The pace was described as 'ridiculous'. Most nurse teachers were still responsible for running and teaching other pre- and post-registration courses and found themselves overburdened with work once curriculum planning started in earnest. The excessive demands made upon teachers' time and the resultant frustration for students were summarised succinctly by the student who explained that 'they [the traditional students] see all the resources and time going to Project 2000 and they have been forgotten. And Project 2000 students feel that all the resources and time are going to Project 2000 and **they've** been forgotten too!' Nurse teachers habitually worked late evenings and weekends, and did not take annual leave entitlements. One of them remarked that it had been 'crisis management on a daily basis'. Similar reactions had been evident from nurse teachers previously involved in setting up courses in the six ENB Pilot Schemes (Leonard and Jowett, 1990).

The continuous pressure of imminent deadlines for implementation left nurse teachers in the Demonstration Districts feeling stressed and 'frayed at the edges'. Several commented that the sick rate among staff members had risen as a direct result. Although many staff enjoyed this challenge, some admitted that pressure of time had been such that they had been unable to make 'a proper job' of curriculum planning and found that there was no time for creative thinking or reflection. A number of teachers in the two Districts which had their starting dates deferred to January 1990, said they 'heaved a sigh of relief' at the prospect of some breathing space. Moreover, the knock-on effect of the rush meant that the course structure and teaching were still being planned well into the CFP. An experienced member of staff interviewed in the second term of the courses still felt somewhat at sea: 'My chin is just lapping against the waterline'. In the third year, as the time of re-submission for further validation approached, it was hoped that there would now be a more considered approach. One teacher expressed a desire to 'get it all clear now' so that it was not 'a series of incremental changes' but was 'starting from the beginning and putting time into the whole and producing something new'.

The consequences of such a short planning timescale manifested themselves in a variety of problems in staffing. In some cases teachers felt that the choice of staff to be involved in

Project 2000 curriculum planning had been arbitrary, with people falling into roles by default. A children's nursing tutor in one college of nursing discovered that the whole children's section of the CFP had been planned without her involvement. There were cases of nurse teachers who suddenly found themselves having to teach on courses to which they had given no contribution at the planning stage; conversely there were teachers who had worked on curriculum planning for their subjects and were then excluded from teaching them. In both cases this led to frustrations for the staff involved. A nurse teacher regretted that there had been no feedback on her curriculum work which had subsequently been omitted from her new course, saying that she would have preferred to learn from her mistakes rather than have someone else simply rewrite her contribution. A senior nurse educator admitted that these problems of under-utilisation of staff were regrettable, but had been inevitable in the circumstances. Shortage of time meant that planning work had to be completed in the quickest and most expedient manner and this meant that full and detailed consultation with all staff was impossible.

In the third year of the courses nurse teachers were still aware of the demands of course development when there were regular new intakes of students. One of them described the process as 'doing up the motorway when the traffic is running on it' and another explained that 'we have done as well as we can, but it's very difficult to get job satisfaction. Every time that you feel you have got on top of it, you get another group in'. The earlier expressions of less than satisfactory practices because of the rush were reinforced by a concern expressed by several teachers that while 'inevitably there are some problems that you can only smooth out as you run through the course... some of them were a product of the speed of implementation'.

As the courses progressed, some staff mentioned an increase in certain areas of their workload such as administration, personal tuition, preparation for teaching, planning, consolidation and reflection, which were not allowed for in the timetable and meant that more work had to be taken home. Teachers were reluctant to complain about this in case they were seen as unable to carry out their responsibilities competently – 'there are real fears about the capacity to cope'. The difficulties some staff faced were illustrated by the nurse teacher who, even in the third year of the course, found on her return from a period of study leave that: 'Largely I fumbled through by myself. But things had not been addressed which I found out by chance. For example, when I took over this group, no one's work had been presented to the Board of Examiners because no one here realised that we had got to do it. We are completely forgotten down here [a reference to a multi-site operation]'. Again, in the third year, sustaining the course was said by one nurse teacher to mean that 'everyone is so stressed that the environment of this college of nursing has made people become highly critical of each other's work'.

A respondent in one scheme regretted that the opportunity for teaching staff to take time out for team-building and sharing, which had existed in the early course planning and implementation phase, had not been available subsequently as work pressure mounted. It was considered vital for staff to have a vehicle for sharing their stress and anxieties. Some members of staff pointed out that time which could theoretically be spent in professional development disappeared in practice as more pressing work commitments spilled over.

Preparation for Project 2000

Preparation of the nurse education staff for the changes of Project 2000 progressed on both a formal and an informal basis. In some Districts, teaching staff had regular updates from principals on Project 2000 information as it emerged from the statutory bodies. But in the early stages of planning, nurse educators in all Districts by and large felt unprepared for Project 2000 and unsure of their roles within it. As more information became available, colleges of nursing were able to run induction seminars or study days for their staff.

However, there was a general feeling among nurse teachers that they would have welcomed more in the way of formal preparation. The Project 2000 sessions were few and far between, and one staff member commented that they were too superficial to be helpful, giving little insight into what was required of a Diploma course. Another nurse teacher felt that teaching staff understood the concepts of Project 2000, but were given no idea of the practicalities involved in the changes. Elsewhere it was remarked that 'teaching staff were informed when they should be educated', and that teachers had little or no prior knowledge or information concerning organisations such as CNAA, NHSTA and NCVQ.

Course management

In some Districts the previous pyramid of management in the colleges of nursing was reorganised to give a 'flatter' management structure in preparation for the changes. Such a move had also been mooted in the six ENB Pilot Schemes (Leonard and Jowett, 1990), as a way of developing 'job enrichment' by changing the traditional hierarchical organisation (a strategy outlined in relation to nurse education by Murnaghan and Murnaghan, 1990). There were two schemes where the management structures had been modified to fit in with those of the HE partners and one where a newly established college of health studies was due for a structural reorganisation following yet another merger. In a fourth, amalgamation with another college will necessitate further internal reorganisation with its attendant uncertainties and confusion for staff. Even in the third year of the research a senior member of staff described this as 'a time of great instability'. As such amalgamations continued, so too did uncertainty among staff about their roles, and where – **or if** – they fitted in with the wider structures.

There were times when the additional organisational structures set up in colleges of nursing for Project 2000 planning and organisation actually hindered the process. One tutor had to report to three different people, and did not know to whom to relate on certain issues, which in itself wasted time. Also, there were occasions when aspects of implementation could not proceed because the appropriate senior person was not available to give the go-ahead. One senior member of staff lamented the hierarchical and distant structure put in place for amalgamation with HE. Instead of a structure where four senior tutors essentially ran the course and 'made decisions', there was now a course management team ratified by a committee structure that seemed 'wishy- washy' and obstructive.

The experiences to date illustrated what an unwieldy course the Diploma was and how difficult it was to facilitate. In a situation where there were different 'lead posts' for the CFP and the Branches, it was felt that without an overall perspective, different managers were 'reinventing the wheel' and competing against each other so that it became 'an awful situation, there is no sustaining of expertise'. Conversely, on another site where there was still overall responsibility allocated by cohorts it was suggested that one person should do all the planning for the CFP and another for the Branches, in anticipation that 'they would flow nicely'.

A number of individuals from three of the schemes were unhappy with the ways in which they and their colleagues had been treated by managers. These teachers referred to pressure from senior staff who did not fully appreciate the difficulties which those involved in the day-to-day running of the courses faced. As one of them commented: 'We are under pressure from management all the time, and some people are beginning to crack under the weight of work'.

Some individuals were seriously disadvantaged by the new structures that had emerged. One teacher who described herself as a 'prime mover' in curriculum development was concerned that the new arrangements were fragmentary in that there were not clear responsibilities for an overview of the course and that staff at her level would no longer be involved in development work. There were frustrations because of the lack of coordination in that some staff were now 'going over ground' which she had covered three years ago. Such exclusion of staff has previously been cited as a serious hazard of educational change (White and Coburn, 1977).

Other staff felt that their contribution to Project 2000 had gone unrecognised, and that their experience and expertise were disregarded at times. By the third year, one member of staff reported that some of her colleagues 'look ill' because of the demands made upon them. She felt that staff had 'given our pound of flesh to Project 2000' and was dismayed to hear that there was a 'glowing' section on her part of the course in a recent report on the college that had not been made available to her and that this praise had not filtered through to the relevant colleagues.

The experience of change

There was substantial, although by no means universal, feeling among nurse teachers in the early stages of the courses that change was being imposed upon them. They frequently felt left out in the cold, and that they were not being listened to by their senior colleagues. It is important to note here that the nurse teachers interviewed were by definition the very staff who were most involved in the changes. One of them described the staff in her college of nursing as 'very upset and negative' about Project 2000 as a result of the way the changes were announced. She did not attribute the negative feelings among staff to Project 2000 itself, but argued instead that it was 'the whole climate of change that is disturbing them'.

There were layers of change that had important repercussions for some individuals. In the third year of the course one senior member of staff reported that research links with HE were proposed (with all the attendant implications for staff), whereas in reality many nurse teachers were still working for first degrees (which had to be achieved by 1995). One site had extended the teaching day from eight am to eight pm and after an imminent merger staff would be spread over 15 sites – practical developments with significant outcomes for teaching staff's working arrangements. In the scheme where amalgamation into HE was most advanced, a new pressure of involvement in other HE courses was emerging which, as one nurse teacher expressed it, meant that 'you are having to learn a whole new ball-game'.

In the third year, one nurse teacher reported that although her post had not changed as such, 'the whole nature of my work has developed'. The extent to which some individuals' posts **had** changed was illustrated by the senior tutor whose role now was to play a major part in the development of an administrative section that was 'almost a registry'. (This section was being established almost three years into the course because the process of implementation had highlighted the scale of administration involved in a course of this size and scope.) Elsewhere, a nurse teacher's view in the third year of the course was that: 'The organisation and planning are mammoth tasks and you have to plan **well** ahead so that you get a system that will flow. If only they had everything on computer the whole thing would be bearable.' By this stage a senior member of staff explained that 'the climate (of working practice) is quite different' and that she had recently arranged for a notice-board to be fitted to display colleagues' publications, which 'would not have been appropriate a couple of years ago', but was now because the college was a 'dramatically different institution'.

Communication

Although senior managers in the colleges of nursing were on the whole confident that information was cascaded down to all levels, this did not always appear to be the case in the early stages of implementation. For example, one nurse teacher found that information on Project 2000 placement areas and objectives was not available and, therefore, related lectures could not be coordinated with placements. Other teachers complained that they had not been made aware of curriculum work in other sections of the CFP, and that details were not forthcoming. One nurse teacher said that in their college of nursing there was an 'attitude that "this is my information", and therefore people [could not] draw on the experience of the first cohort as there [was] no information or opportunity for exchange of ideas'.

One teacher said that there was the rhetoric of democratic participation from senior staff, but that basically the management's line was simply to tell staff what they were to do. There was mere lip-service paid in the beginning to internal discussions concerning Project 2000 and, from then on, 'the wheels are in motion and staff just have to keep in step with the pace'. One example of this occurred in another District where nurse teachers were asked by education managers during a team-building session how they thought their college of nursing should be reorganised. The teachers discovered later that this had already been decided and cleared at Region. A teacher in a District elsewhere said that the poor, one-way channels of communication were the most disappointing aspect of his work. There was communication from above, but no vehicle for communicating upwards.

In some colleges of nursing, a 'them and us' situation seemed to develop initially between the first Project 2000 planning team and other tutoring staff. Similar feelings of anger and hostility among excluded nurse education staff were revealed in a previous study of curriculum change (White and Coburn, 1977). In the present study there was some feeling among the initial Project 2000 group in one scheme that subsequent planning teams appeared to be 'going their own way' and 'reinventing the wheel'. In another District, a teacher also noted a certain amount of resentment from other nurse teachers toward the people involved in Project 2000 work. But as time progressed, teaching staff reported that there was more communication both on informal and formal levels. For example, in one scheme study days were arranged for all staff in which Project 2000 teachers shared information and experience. In another, there was a procedure for seconding staff to the original teaching teams from those teams to be delivering the course to later cohorts.

Work in the placement areas

Nurse teachers in management posts were not usually substantially involved in work in the placement areas, and communication with their counterparts in service management was frequently the extent of their liaison with practice-based staff. However, their 'junior' colleagues in some of the schemes were expected to spend as much as 20 per cent of their time in given areas of practical responsibility, although only a minority were able to achieve this. Across all Districts it was felt that the level of contact possible in the allotted time, given present tutor: student ratios and all the other demands on tutors' time, was insufficient to attain any real clinical credibility or even, in places, to provide the support needed by students and staff. Many nurse teachers were aware that they could not spend as much time in practice areas as they should – half-a-day per week or every few weeks being the norm. Nurse teachers maintained a precarious balancing act, trying to juggle the various demands on their time. It was a continuing source of regret and frustration to many that they had to spread themselves so thinly. One teacher remarked that 'a clinical responsibility looks nice on paper, but doesn't work in practice' and another who would 'hate to lose the skills' illustrated the dilemma staff faced, stating that 'it's just a matter of having the confidence to say that those times (to spend in placement areas) were committed'. A small number of teachers admitted that ward liaison was 'just a flying visit' to see if there were any problems.

The majority of respondents saw their role in areas of practice as involving liaison and teaching work with both students and practice-based staff. A smaller number of nurse teachers made visits to practice areas principally in order to see students, while others regarded this work as being largely to provide support and advice to practice-based staff. Work with students on placements included introducing them to practice areas, giving small group or individual tutorials, guiding students in their written work, discussing their learning objectives and experiences, and organising visits to other relevant areas for observation. The role, *vis-à-vis* practice-based staff, involved giving updates on changes in education, advising and assisting staff in their own academic work, clarifying students' learning objectives and assessment documentation, and advising on professional development. Many respondents were involved in the educational audit of practice areas, as well as student evaluation of placements. Three respondents were additionally involved in conducting updates for practitioners on Project 2000 or preparation of supervisors.

The overriding impression from the students' responses to a question about contact with staff from the colleges of nursing while on placements was of brief sessions – a chance to 'chat' and make contact. The visits were not critical in determining how students rated their placement experiences (only one student made the point that college staff were more 'up-to-date' and could enhance learning), and only a handful of students had actually worked **with** a member of the teaching staff on their placements. What **was** valued was the support and explicit commitment to their progress that teaching staff could show – particularly when placements were problematic, because teachers could assist in clarifying (and potentially becoming involved in) difficult situations. It was this 'understanding' that was sought. As one student explained, '...my tutor did make sure that I had the opportunity away from staff to say anything that I needed to say. I appreciated that because unless you have this one to one contact you just can't express anything that's troubling you about the placement...'

One student's comment summed up the general mood of her colleagues and raised a reservation that may explain why more routine contact (rather than crisis management) was not widely sought. She said: 'I do think as long as your assessor is good you are probably all right without contact with the school but where there are problems you really wish you had someone. You do feel under the microscope when someone from the school comes and it makes you very nervous so they do need to handle you very tactfully.' Towards the end of the course, students expressed a desire for a more structured programme of visits and although direct supervision was not wanted (indeed many would have regarded it as 'insulting'), the 'safety net' role was widely appreciated. The potential of a more rigorous system was summed up by one student:

> *There's not much point in them [nurse teachers] coming and asking how you are but I think there might be a place for them coming if it was planned and purposeful. We did have someone [a teacher] come to a ward where there were a lot of heart operations and we were expecting something from them on that and we actually got a session on Parkinson's disease, so it seemed to be purely random and I'd like it to be better planned.*

A crucial distinction should be drawn between liaison work in the practice areas and practice credibility, gained as a result of sustained practical experience. These two concepts were sometimes blurred in discussion, which tended to obscure the extent to which the latter was attainable. Nurse teachers were divided on the issue of what their role should be, and this applied across all the case-study sites. Illustrating one approach, a nurse teacher boldly asserted that she was 'not a clinician now but an educationalist' and that credibility could not be attained without sustained, regular work in the practice areas. Being 'de-skilled' was inevitable but she was able to bring 'critical analytical thinking to the situation' because she was 'distanced from it'. The decision **not** to have a practical role was 'a choice made some time ago' when she moved into education. The alternative perspective was illustrated by the teacher who felt that nurse teachers 'first and foremost are nurses'. A senior member of staff saw it as 'vital' that credibility was sustained, arguing that teachers '**must** maintain a hands-on commitment and must get out on to the wards to do this'.

While the majority of teachers wanted contact with the practice areas, an increasing proportion of them were sceptical about the relevance and feasibility of a practical aspect to their sphere of work. As one of them expressed it: 'The very thought is mind-blowing.' As the study progressed, rather more of them had no expectation of a 'hands-on' role, since they did not see this as a prerequisite for nurse teaching, and in some cases (particularly in the areas of Community, Mental Handicap and Mental Health Nursing) as neither practicable nor appropriate to patients' needs. They felt they could add little to practical teaching, which was said to be best accomplished by expert practice-based staff.

A number of individuals, across schemes, felt that joint appointments would be the most effective way for nurse educators to do justice to the educational and practical spheres of teaching experience. One anticipated a system with a small core of educationalists and a large number of lecture-practitioners because 'you need to be aware of what is happening to the knowledge that they are giving the students, otherwise the theory will be sterile'. Others were uneasy about joint posts, having witnessed the conflicts arising from colleagues in this situation being 'pulled in different directions' by the full-time expectations of both the educational and service aspects, with no clearly defined areas of accountability or responsibility. The RCN's (1993) discussion document is of particular relevance here as it presents a 'radical scenario' of nurse teachers as regularly, (perhaps on a two - year cycle, a three - or five - year cycle) switching between teaching and specialist nursing practice, or the management of nursing services, or research related to any of these'. Such teachers would have 'academic and clinical credibility' and would be, 'first and foremost' practitioners, accustomed to 'flexi-careers'.

In one scheme, a system of 'sabbaticals' had been introduced, whereby teaching staff on a rolling programme could spend one month practising in their own area of specialty. Two respondents who had recently finished such placements spoke positively of the experience. It had been 'like a breath of fresh air', according to one. They also valued the closer relationship with practice-based colleagues which this spell had facilitated. In another District, staff were expected to spend two weeks per year working in their allocated 'link' area. These and other options for contact with the placement areas were under discussion on all sites and the key points were encapsulated in one nurse teacher's reflection that 'we need to decide a role. In one day a week you can't keep up credibility and all you can do is **basic** skills. What do you **add**? Tutors **like** to be there and we need to decide whether this is the best use of their time and who gains what.'

The personal tutor role

The role of the personal tutor was described as facilitative, providing both academic and personal support. Academic support consisted of advising on draft assignments, directing students' reading, and some 'remedial' teaching. A gradual trend towards the use of specialised subject tutors rather than personal tutors was evident here. Many staff emphasised the personal support they provided, although some were reluctant to engage in counselling, and staff in one scheme which had previously benefited from three counsellors were concerned to find that this resource was reduced in the third year of the course. In one District, the emphasis of personal tuition was consistently on the support of students in their practice placements. Teaching staff would endeavour to spend some time with each student in practice allocations to give personal and tutorial support, and also to ensure that the student had been allocated a mentor, that learning objectives for practice had been identified, and that assessment procedures were being properly carried out. Learning contracts were used to varying degrees in all of the Districts, and a number of teaching staff commented on their usefulness in relation to students whose academic achievement was causing concern (which suggests that their role was corrective rather than to facilitate individualised learning. The phrase 'learning contract' was used in situations where students were simply given a list of objectives to be achieved within a given period).

The allocation of personal students to nurse teachers varied considerably across and within the schemes. Senior members of staff tended not to be involved in this work, although a small number of them had elected to play a role here. It was common to find that nurse teachers had between 6 and 10 or 16 to 20 students, at one time (although two individuals had 28 and 48, students respectively) and that the increase in numbers any one tutor had put increasing pressure on them as the course progressed. Frequency of contact with personal students varied depending on teacher time, the students' academic and personal needs' the extent to which students chose to use the system' and the individual students' stage in the course.

The majority of staff saw their students on a regular basis, occasionally in groups, the frequency ranging from weekly to six-weekly depending on the individual tutor and the needs of students.

A number of others kept 'an open door policy', students approaching their tutor as and when they needed. A small number of respondents reported difficulties in arranging tutor-student contact, either because students were situated on different sites, or because timetables were too packed to allow for this work. A minority of staff visited their personal students in placement areas, and one respondent mentioned taking an active part in the assessment of students' practice.

Staff in three Districts reported a gradual bureaucratisation of the personal tutor system, and some teachers in these sites felt that this was creating a personal tutor role with more emphasis on surveillance than support. Personal tutors were required to monitor students' sickness and absence records, their academic and practice assessment achievements, and sometimes keep careful documentation of their contact with students as well as of the learning contracts. Over half the nurse teachers in one of these sites were aware of a contradiction in their role as personal tutors – staff were required to monitor academic progress but were not involved in marking their own students' written work. On another site it was said that there was a dilemma 'with tutors thinking they can accomplish counselling within the role when they also have a disciplinary function'.

A small number of respondents expressed uncertainties over the exact requirements of the personal tutor role, and these were frequently individuals who were uneasy about the changes in the organisation of teaching, curriculum and management of students which the introduction of Project 2000 had necessitated, and the way in which the role of the personal tutor had adapted to these changes. Factors such as 'loss of control over the curriculum' and the 'profound distancing from the students' were being experienced. These had occurred as a result of large student intakes, specialisation of teaching, and students being dispersed over different college sites. As a result it was difficult to build up relationships with 'people you don't teach or only [teach] in large groups'. One teacher lamented that, having lost direct influence over the curriculum now, she could no longer 'modify it to individual needs' and had now 'lost common ground with the students'.

The students were consistently generally positive about the personal tutor system. There were a few instances reported of very regular contact (sometimes weekly); students did not expect this frequency – although assignments often stimulated more frequent meetings. The attitude expressed by many was summed up in: 'The support is there but you have got to go and ask for it.' Students in one scheme were particularly positive about the system of tutorial support (only two of them did not describe regular productive contact) and here staff had arranged frequent sessions with personal tutors (for individuals and groups) at the start of the course, which appeared to have established the principle of support – something that was still open to individual interpretation in the other five schemes.

While it was common for students to value the sense of 'support being there', opinion varied on how frequent contact should be. At best the system drew such comments as: 'I would have left the course without him. He has given me confidence and helped me through very stressful times.' Reservations about the support focused on gaps in some tutors' knowledge about some course requirements; difficulties in contacting staff and the poor quality of the interpersonal relationship formed. Students were aware of pressures on staff time and were reluctant to approach them without a pressing need. Students were similarly aware of contradictions in the relationship. As one of them reflected: 'It is hard to develop rapport when you know they are assessing you.'

By the third year, what emerged was that while the students may have expressed overall satisfaction with the arrangements, the academic liaison was not as established as could have been expected on such a course. The tone of much of the comment about personal tutors was 'low key', and students had limited expectations of what that role should provide for them. The position was explained by one student who, although fairly positive about the personal tutor she had, commented that: 'I just like to get on and do things on my own. She is always there if I want her, but she's got a lot of students and she wouldn't actively encourage you to go and see her. I don't know how it would have been if I was the sort of person who required more academic support.' While there was generally an expectation that support would be made available when and if required, it was a sustained academic relationship that was conspicuously absent from these students' reflections.

Staff development

With very few exceptions, nurse teachers found that their workplaces were encouraging environments for staff development. Opportunities to attend short courses and study days were available and in two colleges of nursing each staff member was routinely allocated time intended for professional development and personal study. (There were indications of an extension of these working arrangements, as for instance where closer liaison with HE would mean staff working to only 33 weeks of student contact.) The majority of nurse teachers in all the schemes found the Individual Performance Review a helpful tool with which to measure their own professional development. One interviewee's comment on the implementation of Project 2000 that 'certainly teachers have grown in the process and they are now more able and flexible. They have all grown and gained all sorts of skills' reflected a widespread acknowledgement of some of the advantages of introducing such a course. An individual reflection in the third year was: 'I have come on a ton personally. Because we have been working at a higher level. It's an entirely different way of teaching... but it's been a very exciting period for me personally'; and a more generalised comment about the link with HE was that 'it has done our self-esteem no harm at all. It has shown us that we are better teachers than we ever thought we were.'

It was apparent that graduate status had become increasingly important in nurse education over recent years, and the rush to study for degrees had gathered momentum. Over a quarter of the nurse teachers at the start of the course had a first and/or higher degree, and more than a third of teachers were in the process of studying for first or higher degrees, with several more hoping to enrol in the near future. In instances where funding and study leave for courses were slow in becoming available, individual staff members took the initiative themselves. Clearly there was considerable pressure on nurse teachers to achieve graduate status, frequently with a view to obtaining higher degrees. The pressure came not only from current thinking within colleges of nursing but also from outside in the climate of professionalising nursing. One nurse teacher remarked: 'The teachers aren't here teaching - they're all out at college just to get more standing in the eyes of the poly!'[1] There was some feeling among the remaining nurse teachers that too many people were attending courses at once, which left more work for others and slowed things down at a time when the pace of developments was rapid.

Many nurse teachers saw their future roles developing in specialist fields, moving away from the traditional 'generic' working practices in nurse education. Such a move reflected not only the broadening pre-registration curriculum, but also a feeling that nurse education should emulate HE in this respect. A small number of nurse teachers who had recently joined colleges of nursing found that teaching teams in some subject areas already had full contingents, and that their own choice of subject specialities was restricted. Other nurse teachers feared that specialisation outside the theory and practice of nursing would result in their loss of identity as nurses, and these teachers would rather have 'kept their hand in' across all areas. One nurse teacher argued that the move towards specialisation contradicted the holistic philosophy of Project 2000, which would suggest multi-disciplinary teaching, and that it was 'madness' for teachers to teach just one discipline within it. There were mixed feelings on the whole issue, people being glad on the one hand not to have spread themselves so thinly and superficially over a broad curriculum; but on the other hand there was concern for professional development in a climate of change where career progression was uncertain.

Summary of main points

- Although many nurse teachers enjoyed the challenge of implementation, some admitted that the pressure of time had been such that they had been unable to make 'a proper job' of curriculum planning and found that there was no time for creative thinking or reflection.

- The knock-on effect of the rush meant that the course structure and teaching were still being planned well into the CFP.

- In the early stages of planning, nurse educators in all Districts by and large felt unprepared for Project 2000 and unsure of their roles within in.

- There was substantial, although by no means universal, feeling among nurse teachers in the early stages of the courses that change was being imposed upon them.

- In some colleges of nursing, a 'them and us' situation seemed to develop initially between the first Project 2000 planning team and other tutoring staff.

- Nurse teachers were divided on the issue of what their role in the practice areas should be. While the majority of teachers wanted contact with the practice areas, an increasing proportion of them were sceptical about the relevance and feasibility of a practical aspect to their sphere of work. The RCN's (1993) proposals are of particular relevance here.

- Across all Districts it was felt that the level of contact possible in the allotted time was insufficient to obtain any real clinical credibility or even, in places, to provide the support needed by students and staff.

- The role of the personal tutor varied and there were differing conceptions of what it should entail.

- Despite the many demands on their time, most nurse teachers found that their workplaces were encouraging environments for staff development.

Discussion

Nurse teachers were genuinely divided and ambivalent over what their role should be in relation to monitoring student attendance, personal tuition and a practice-based role. Staff were perplexed when expectations of them appeared contradictory. There was a realisation that these issues were being hotly debated in the corridors of colleges of nursing and in the wider nursing world, but also a sense that discussions had reached an impasse and needed clarification.

On the whole, respondents across the Demonstration sites still saw the personal tutor system as a valued part of the course for both staff and students. But it seemed that the difficulties attending it had increased commensurate with the increase in student numbers and their dispersal between sites in ever-widening college units. The need for realism as regards the support personal tutors could offer their students, which was pointed out by some respondents in the second year of the course, had been reinforced more widely as the demands of successive intakes built up across the Districts. Individual staff were expecting (to varying degrees), to provide students with broad-ranging academic support, while the trend towards specialism was resulting in the contracting and deepening of staff's areas of expertise. They were also experiencing conflicts over their jurisdiction, in terms of academic and personal support and with respect to discipline. It seems that teachers were employing the frame of reference of personal tuition relative to previous courses, and that a role for the personal tutor in Project 2000 has to be more clearly defined.

A number of nurse teachers from across the sample were dissatisfied with the rationalisation of the organisation of teaching which had been stimulated by Project 2000. With previous courses, the nurse teacher controlled the curriculum for an entire intake, set the timetable, did most of the teaching, and could modify their teaching to students' individual needs. Now teaching staff seemed to have 'lost 'ownership' of the course and as a result they felt distanced from the curriculum as a whole, and from their personal students.

The practice-based responsibilities of nurse teachers are presently under discussion across sites, and staff are aware of the need to collate information about the current situation and to establish new guidelines for practice. Teaching staff were by and large unable to meet the required levels of liaison with practice, and for many 'hands-on' clinical credibility was not a realistic goal, which produced feelings of frustration and guilt for some. The general view was that such credibility could only be achieved in any meaningful way if other arrangements pertained – clinical sabbaticals for teaching staff, teacher-practitioner posts, or other joint appointments. A reduction in the teacher – student ratio in institutions of nurse education would not necessarily alleviate nurse teachers' difficulties in fulfilling these expectations. The pressure to extend academic knowledge and expertise is likely to take precedence in teachers' prioritisation of the different aspects of their work.

This was a period of considerable challenge for nurse teachers in the Demonstration Districts. Not only were teachers still coming to terms with the changes in their role, but also pressure was being encountered from other sources: the threat of amalgamations and changes in management and organisation; and the new conflicts around the role of the nurse teacher which educational change had wrought. Indeed, in commenting upon the several different facets of their role, there is a danger of building a composite model of the ideal teacher that would be impossible for anyone to attain. Many respondents in the present research bemoaned the fact that there was so much change to contend with – change which followed so swiftly on the heels of previous change that there was 'no time for the dust to settle'.

Nurse teachers were increasingly finding themselves in the unenviable position of being pulled in opposite directions. On the one hand, teaching staff knew they must join the race for academic credibility in specialist disciplines or be left behind; on the other, there was the pressure to extend their practical expertise. In a climate of change, uncertainty and competition, some nurse teachers felt that they had to develop in both areas rather than polarise towards their particular area of interest.

¹ Refers to a former polytechnic

Chapter Six
PROJECT 2000 IN PRACTICE

Introduction

It is in nursing practice where the seeds of Project 2000 will bear fruit. This chapter records the first students' passage through their practice experiences, from the perspectives of service staff and the students themselves. The views of other groups of respondents on the students' placements (senior service and education managers and teaching staff), necessarily based to a large extent on feedback from students and colleagues, are recorded elsewhere and/or are drawn upon in the concluding discussion. Practice-based staff were interviewed on two occasions – in 1991 and 1992; the students were asked about their placements in each year of their course. The '1991' perceptions of staff directly involved in supervising and assessing the first Project 2000 students in their early practice placements have already been described in detail (Jowett et al., 1992b), as have the views of managers at senior nurse level and of the students themselves. The perceptions of staff and students in 1992 – the students' final year (and the last year of the main research study) – are presented here in particular detail.

The practice-based staff perspective

The first round interviews

From the 1991 survey of practice staff opinion, a fairly positive picture of the students' early placements emerged across the six Districts. All the publicity surrounding the introduction of Project 2000 and all the rumours which continued to abound until the first placements got underway, inevitably fuelled the anxieties of both students and staff. When the first students appeared in the practice areas, many of the fears on both sides proved to be unfounded. For the most part, the students did not just want to stand and observe (as their 'supernumerary status' had been widely misinterpreted to mean) and did not project themselves as the intellectual 'super nurses' rumour had conjured up. Clearly, it had taken time for staff to adjust to the new students' different level of understanding and experience, different needs and different status – particularly the greater degree of autonomy that that status gave them. But as they were getting used to having the CFP students, and as expectations of the placements were becoming clearer, most respondents were feeling happier.

One of the main problems identified by hospital-based staff was the brevity of the CFP placements – both overall and in terms of hours/days worked during the allocation – usually two or three days a week at most. One-day placements – already abandoned in one scheme – were the extreme example. The short time the students were in their placement areas was seen as unsatisfactory from everybody's point of view – students, staff and patient/clients. The uncertainty staff had felt about what was expected of these early placements was another of the difficulties most frequently referred to. Misconceptions about 'supernumerary status', and confusion about what the students could or could not do, had been major contributory factors.

The problems surrounding student supervision were also highlighted by all groups: the large numbers of students; the difficulties of finding enough supervisors and arranging for student and supervisor shifts to coincide if students were working different hours and not working weekends; and the heightened demands, in terms of time and responsibility of teaching and supervising students with not even basic practical nursing skills or experience – or a basic understanding of how a ward worked.

Community personnel shared hospital staff's concerns about the sheer numbers of Project 2000 and (in the community even more than hospital areas) other students/trainees requiring supervision. (Over two-thirds of those interviewed mentioned this as a particular problem.) The very real danger of overload for all community nurses was particularly acute for very small CPN/CMHN teams. The inappropriateness of a succession of different students accompanying community nurses on home visits (another common concern) was also stressed, in particular in those specialisms. They also spoke of the extra time and effort needed to teach students lacking basic practical skills and experience of hospital work and equipment. With the first allocations in particular, there had also been problems of students failing to keep appointments, or turning up late or unexpectedly (mentioned by about a third of interviewees), and of a lack of communication/coordination generally.

The nature and extent of community staff involvement in supervising and assessing the students on their early placements differed in the six schemes, as did the timing, duration and organisation of those placements as a whole. By the time of the 1991 interviews, only students in three schemes had done what might be termed 'traditional' community placements, i.e. allocations of a week or a few days organised and supervised by particular district nurses or health visitors. In two of the other schemes, the community nurses' role was more that of facilitation, with students loosely attached to particular health centres in order to get an overview of services offered and gather information for neighbourhood studies/community profiles.

In the sixth scheme, the students were allocated to particular community nursing teams, initially just for one day, returning to the same team and patch for a week on each of their successive practices. Allocations to CPN and CMHN services in that scheme followed the same pattern. Elsewhere, 'community' experience in those specialisms for CFP students took various forms, with periods ranging from one to six days spent with CPNs or CMHNs in some of the schemes offering relevant Branch programmes. In other schemes the scarce resource of CPNs/CMHNs had to be reserved for Branch students.

The second round interviews

CFP allocations – hospital areas

Asked, in 1992, about the CFP placements, respondents almost universally reported continued improvement as staff had become accustomed to the new students and had a clearer understanding of what was expected of their allocations and assessments. The overall tone was increasingly positive. Clarification of the meaning of the students' 'supernumerary status' had greatly assisted this process, for instance knowing that the students could be involved in the practical work of the ward, under supervision. A common qualification, however, was that this was still dependent upon the individual student's confidence, ability and motivation/interest.

But reservations about the CFP allocations were still widespread. Approximately half those interviewed in hospital areas still referred to problematic aspects – again, mainly the brevity/ fragmentation of the placements, the number of students, and the amount of supervision and teaching expected of staff. The information provided by colleges about students coming on placement – the amount of detail and notice given – was also the subject of some criticism.

Respondents acknowledged that some changes for the better had already been made to the structure of CFP placements. Nevertheless the time students spent on the wards, both in terms of the overall duration of placements and the hours worked per week – two to three days at the most – was still considered to be too short for students, staff and clients/patients. The lack of continuity was seen as affecting the students' ability to build up their skills and confidence and their rapport with staff and patients. This applied especially in areas with fairly rapid patient turnover. As the sister in a five-day general surgery ward commented: 'It destroys the students' confidence because they are coming to a fresh situation every week.'

Respondents in Mental Health and Learning Disability areas tended to have particular reservations about the short placements, not only because of the time necessary to build up relationships with clients and the disruptive effect on their lives of a steady stream of students, but also the time needed to overcome the initial fears and prejudices which some students showed, especially if they came without any particular interest in the client group and/or not prepared for the kind of conditions/problems they could encounter. There were particular concerns that students were not getting a realistic view of these specialisms in their short 'taster' placements: 'They don't grasp some of the concepts – they find it strange. We are not going to change their minds (about psychiatric nursing) in eight days.'

The number of students on placement at a time was mentioned in the second round interviews as a problem by some respondents across the six schemes. The CFP students still needed a lot of teaching and supervision, it was frequently stressed, especially in the early stages and, in the words of a respondent on a busy surgical ward, it could be 'very draining'. Numbers had peaked in places in late 1991 when overlap with students on previous courses (RGN, RSCN, etc.) had resulted in instances of as many as 16 students at a time (on a medical ward, where according to the sister, they had outnumbered the staff for a period!). Again, such overloading could present particular problems for patients in areas like acute psychiatric admission wards. Having at times had five staff and five students on duty with 15 residents in the fairly small and domestic-like in-patient areas of one such unit had definitely been a case of 'over-kill' – of clients being 'over-therapied'.

Several respondents confessed to finding it difficult and confusing having the Project 2000 students coming on allocation at different stages, working different hours and having different study days. The paucity of the information provided by colleges prior to the placements – sometimes just a list of students' names and year, not specifying whether they were CFP or Branch students (or, in the case of the former, which intended Branch) did little to clarify matters. Moreover, not knowing the students' 'off-duties' until they arrived made it difficult for staff to plan things for them.

CFP allocations - community

Community personnel interviewed in 1992 also reported that CFP allocations were working better now that staff had got to grips with what was required, and various administrative and other difficulties had been addressed. (In some places education and community managers had got together to do this after problems had 'come to a head'.)

Community nurses had also got more used to the idea of constantly having a student with them, although student numbers remained one of the main problems. As in hospital areas, specific agreement had been reached with colleges to limit overlap of placement/supervision requests for CFP, Branch and other students, and to impose a ceiling on the numbers which an area or team would be asked to accommodate at one time. Changes had also been made to the length and order of placements. In one scheme one-day/one-week allocations had been combined into a three-week block which was said to work much better and to provide greater continuity. The practice in most schemes of allocating students as far as possible to the same community teams, if not the same supervisory nurses, on placements at different stages of their course, also provided continuity as well as easing the process of adjustment for students and staff.

The CFP students could still be very demanding, respondents observed, especially where they came to the community at a very early stage of the course (after only three months, for example) and had to be taught basic nursing skills from scratch. In one scheme where this had applied previously, however, these concerns had been 'taken on board', and the students were now said to be receiving more instruction in basic practical skills, like taking blood pressures, in college.

70

The extension of 'observer' placements with different community nursing teams, in one scheme from one to two weeks, was something on which respondents in the different specialisms had divided views. From the viewpoint of a CPN manager, two weeks enabled students to get a better understanding of the services offered by the community psychiatric team. But it was still too short a time for students to participate in activities such as therapy groups. There was, not surprisingly, a good deal of overlap with the views of respondents in acute psychiatric admission areas of hospitals in the reservations expressed in CPN services about the presence of a succession of different students, and the consequent risk of patients feeling like 'exhibits'.

As for the experience of community learning disability residential group homes which had been arranged in that scheme to ease pressures on CMHNs, this had, it seemed been fraught with problems initially. Even visits to the homes by students were viewed as too intrusive and could only be made with residents' consent, which was occasionally withheld. It was felt that the community resettlement nurses responsible for the homes could have put together a 'shorter, more concentrated package' about their work which would have been more beneficial for the CFP students.

In general, it seemed, initial communication difficulties surrounding the CFP community placements had been largely ironed out. Early problems of some students not turning up to placements or turning up 'when they felt like it', also seemed to be a thing of the past in most places, except for the occasional 'rogue', to use the expression of one health visitor! The problem of transport for those students without their own vehicles, especially in the rural Districts, was more intractable. But efforts to address that too had been made in places, for example, by the college providing a bus to pick up and drop off the students at particular points. The onus had been put on the students to make their own arrangements, however, and according to one manager, they 'got better at finding their way around'. But lack of personal transport could still limit the students' experience in such areas since in terms of visiting services and clients independently, they had (in one CMHN's words) their 'wings clipped'.

Supernumerary status

Some respondents in all schemes underlined the point that it was very much up to individual students how much they benefited and learnt from the CFP placements. Some would press to get involved; others preferred 'to hang back'. There was consequently a risk that the quiet, less assertive students 'could miss out'; 'get forgotten'. Their new supernumerary status and the emphasis on their being responsible for and negotiating their own learning made this a greater risk for the Project 2000 students than their predecessors, in very short placements and especially in the very early stages when they did not know what they wanted or needed to learn. A few supervisors detected a definite change in students' attitudes since the start of Project 2000 – giving less of an impression that they 'thought themselves superior', and showing a greater willingness to help and to learn. But there was still mention of some students' lack of interest, mainly in areas other than their chosen Branch specialism, and isolated references to some seeing themselves as observers and not wanting to help or get involved, or thinking they could 'come and go as they pleased'.

Although better understanding of supernumerary status was widely reported in the 1992 interviews, there was still variation in how confident supervisors were or how much they were prepared to let students do. Supernumerary status was 'a big advantage' according to one sister, provided it was 'not taken to the extreme' with staff not letting the students give nursing care: 'They need to be part of the team or they feel they are no use.'

As in the first round interviews, respondents often drew a distinction between students who had previously worked as nursing/care assistants in hospital wards or nursing homes and those coming with no practical skills or experience at all. The former would tend to say what they wanted to do at an early stage. They would also tend to revert to the role of a nursing assistant and get on and do things – 'get stuck in' – if the ward and their supervisor were busy. The students' desire to be 'part of the team' and eagerness to gain practical skills and experience clearly facilitated their use as 'pairs of hands' and, in the case of those with prior experience and/or greater self-confidence, their own tendency to function in that capacity.

Particularly during the CFP, uncertainty about their role and the expectations of their supernumerary status had been experienced by the students, and had been the focus for the widespread misunderstanding and misinformation about Project 2000 which they reported encountering among practice-based staff. Students valued the flexibility to leave placement areas to observe certain practices or events, or to follow through the care of individual patients. They displayed an eagerness to participate and get involved and while there were a few comments indicating an awareness of the protective function supernumeracy could serve, students more commonly expressed relief that it had not obstructed their practice.

The vast majority of staff welcomed the students' supernumerary status for the flexibility it allowed them as supervisors and the opportunities it afforded the students to pursue and achieve educational objectives on and off the wards – opportunities which they themselves had been denied in their training because they had been relied on as providers of basic nursing care. Respondents, without exception, maintained that the students were able to avail themselves of such opportunities, even if they were also making a real contribution to service on the wards at other times. While the CFP students were not included in staffing numbers anywhere officially, about a quarter of hospital-based respondents admitted that students did get used as extra 'pairs of hands' when the wards were busy. None the less, only very few respondents indicated that supernumerary students would actually be included in the numbers for staffing purposes, and then only for brief periods in extreme circumstances (when someone went away suddenly on compassionate leave, for example), with the student's agreement.

Rostered service

The students' rostered allocations had not been under way for very long when the second interviews with practice-based staff took place in 1992, and had not started at all in some areas. Because only a few – often literally just one or two – students had been rostered in their areas at that time, respondents had individual students very much in mind when commenting upon how those particular placements had been working out. Across the six schemes, however, practice-based staff consistently expressed the view that the students' rostered service had generally been going well – indeed, better than some respondents had anticipated. Compared with the short CFP allocations, far fewer problems were reported. Staff much preferred the longer placements and longer hours for the greater continuity – and the time to get to know – and assess – the students better, which they afforded. For the students, the much desired sense of being part of the team was at last realisable.

There was a good deal of variation between the schemes in the way the rostered service was structured. The main differences were in respect of the timing of the students' rostered allocations, the organisation of study days, and the latitude given to service areas as regards the weekend and other 'unsocial' shifts worked by the students. The importance of the stage in the Branch programme at which the rostered service occurred, and of how the allocation was to spread-out over time were emphasised in more than one scheme. Completion of all or most of it well in advance of the end of the course was also something which (it was evident from subsequent student interviews) made quite a difference to the students as they approached final examinations and submission of final projects. The temptation at ward level to put students on weekend shifts now they no longer qualified for extra-duty payments was pointed up by some respondents, and the consequent need to keep the situation under review.

Respondents frequently commented that the rostered Project 2000 students did not have the same practical knowledge and skills – or same confidence – as previous third year students at the same stage, because of their having had less hospital experience earlier in the course. (There was some feeling that it was unfair to draw comparisons but inevitably this still happened.) But most staff referred to the students' considerable theoretical knowledge. 'They can tell me a few things now and then!', one ward sister observed. But she also shared several other respondents' concern about what they perceived to be the students' limited knowledge and exposure to different medical conditions, compared with the previous training – knowledge of conditions of the heart, for example, and of signs and symptoms of illness, physical and mental.

There was a general feeling that the students needed more supervision and guidance and could not be relied upon to the same extent as previous third-year students in terms of service-giving – at least for the first part of their rostered placements. Once they had gained further in skills and confidence and could 'branch out on their own' to a greater extent, there was not perceived to be that much difference. Again, however, respondents stressed that the speed with which students settled into placements – and into service-giving – varied from individual to individual. As with the CFP placements, students with previous experience of auxiliary nursing work would sometimes be singled out for mention.

There was some confusion for students (particularly on one site) about whether being on the roster in terms of the hours worked meant inclusion in the workforce numbers. There was also the point that for them, rostering seemed to be indistinguishable from being a third-year in some schemes, with increased levels of responsibility being attributed to the latter as readily as to the former. Rostering did not herald a dramatic reappraisal of the placement experience, but students could identify features of both supernumeracy and rostering which they felt should be promoted (although the two were not, as stated, always seen as mutually exclusive). Supernumerary status (when accurately practised) meant flexible hours (although not necessarily less) and the freedom to follow patients through or attend relevant sessions or watch key procedures or activities. These gains made it a feature that students wanted to safeguard.

There was a tension evident in the students' responses between what they identified as constructive features of their placements – being there full-time as part of the team, having increasing degrees of responsibility – and their needs, rights and obligations as students. These confused pressures on students emerged from one of their comments that 'rostered experience is a really good idea and essential to build up people's confidence levels. It's the only way you'll get accepted into the system, sadly.'

The rewards that students identified from rostering may be linked with a certain release of tension as it relieved them of the need to stand outside the traditional student nurse pattern – a departure that had caused some difficulties. Not doing the full nursing shift was often an uncomfortable prospect - which focused attention on what was realistic for any individual whose designation included the word nurse as well as student. The need for rostering if you had not been working shifts already was spelt out by the student who felt that 'you should be there at handover time and there is no point in coming at 9am and asking for details when the changeover was at 7.15am'. The emphasis on being part of the workforce rather than a student for whom concessions would be made (because of their other commitments) could be linked to comments such as this.

Staffing in rostered service

Rostered service was the subject of confusion and varying interpretation for staff as well as students. Students may have been rostered on all sites in the sense of their names appearing on the duty roster and working the same hours (37½ hours a week), if still not always the same shifts, as qualified staff. But in many places they were still regarded as extra to established staffing numbers – still supernumerary in effect – for part if not all of their placements. The 20 per cent service contribution allowed for in the complex calculations made for replacing the pre-Project 2000 workforce on the wards was clearly not a reality in many areas.

As had already emerged from the 1992 interviews with senior service and education managers, however, the whole edifice of those calculations had been skewed subsequently by all the changes wrought by the NHS reforms and ubiquitous skill-mix reviews. Rationalisation of services, ward moves and mergers, and changed shift patterns had all brought changes in staffing and confused the replacement picture. The planned programme to replace the traditional students as they left had, it seemed, 'ground to a halt' with the advent of Trust status, the sister in charge of one medical area observed. Although the forecast replacement increase had not materialised in that area, some extra staff had been added to the establishment to take account of a change to 24-hour cover. Eight out of ten sisters/charge nurses in other areas of adult nursing where replacement staff had been appointed considered the provision inadequate. They spoke of the 'dramatic' effects on staffing of the departure of the traditional students (particularly the third-year students who, in one sister's words, were 'very much our back-up system'), and their heavy reliance on bank and agency staff to make up the shortfall.

Although wards did not expect to lose established staff because the Project 2000 students were allocated for rostered service (and the delegation of staffing budgets to ward managers seemed to be making this even less likely), there was clearly an effect on use or non-use of extra bank/ agency staff. Some areas were depicted as normally dependent on 'a fair number of' such staff. When the rostered students were there, that dependence could at least be reduced. But again, this could vary from student to student. A supervisor on an acute medical ward referred to the four students who had been on rostered placements so far, two of whom they could 'count as part of the team', the other two, not. If after two weeks on the placement it was felt they could not really help by way of service-giving, the ward would still book extra staff – unless they were 'light' in terms of patient dependency.

Just as the students' supernumerary status had sometimes been misinterpreted and taken to the extreme, initially, so too, it seems, had their rostered service. A supervisor on a neurological unit spoke of the difficulty students had in adjusting from supernumerary status, but considered that the staff had been at fault also, because: 'The student would come on and staff would say, "Right, you take that side of the ward and get on with it." But once we got used to it, we would supervise the students for so many weeks before they were let off on their own. The students did very well, but initially it was quite hard work for everybody.'

In two areas of Adult Nursing visited (a cardiac ITU and a five-day medical investigation ward) as well as most areas in the other specialisms of Paediatrics, Mental Health and Learning Disabilities, replacement as such was not an issue in the same way. Because students prior to Project 2000 had already been officially regarded as supernumerary, such areas had received no replacement provision or only a minimal amount – a single support worker, perhaps.

But the difficulties, reported in some areas of the other specialisms when the traditional students finished, with the reliance on relief staff and overtime, had been just as great. In three areas (two in Mental Health and one in Learning Disabilities), managers said they had succeeded in negotiating some extra staffing subsequently, but this was due to skill-mix and other changes as well. The blurred picture with regard to replacement everywhere was further obfuscated in these areas by the accelerated run-down of the large institutions necessitating redeployment of established staff.

Branch community placements

Although some of the students' community allocations in their Branch programmes were being classified as rostered experience, the picture across the six schemes was mixed and confusing. Some staff were still uncertain whether the more substantive Branch placements were/would be rostered or not. In one District, the community nurse manager said that the experience had originally been categorised that way but, she added: 'They can't be [rostered], because our district nurse and health visitor students can't be... they're always supernumerary, though they carry case-loads.'

The question of whether students should be able to take on a small case-load of their own patients/clients, and visit them unaccompanied, had also been – and was still – the subject of a good deal of discussion in places. It had again raised questions of transport (particularly in areas where buses were few and far between) and, even more importantly, of accountability. Two Districts in the same scheme were reported not to have been able to agree about this. The policy of one health authority was that only first-level nurses with a district nursing qualification would carry 'a case-load'. RGN staff nurses would simply hold a 'work-load', the ultimate responsibility remaining with the qualified district nurses.

All six schemes offered the first students a Mental Health specialist option, but there was only one where Branch students were already doing case-work with clients at the time of the last interviews. In that scheme, students picked up clients gradually throughout the whole 18-month period, with study days in college (four days a week at the outset) declining as case-load practice increased (to half-a-day a fortnight in the last six months). Elsewhere, Mental Health Branch students would get case-work experience while allocated to CPN teams. Only one of the three schemes with a Learning Disability Branch available to the first intakes offered the students supervised case-work during their (six-week) CMHT placement. As elsewhere, the extent of this depended on the calibre and experience of the individual student – and whether or not the student had transport.

Where the experience of students on Mental Health and Learning Disability Branches was nearly all client-centred, with very little residential experience, respondents expressed considerable reservations about the lack of opportunities for students to acquire the management skills they would need on qualification for work in residential areas. Only one respondent in an acute psychiatric admissions unit was a dissenting voice. He believed that much of ward management involved 'nitty gritty skills' (such as doing duty rosters, ordering) which could easily be picked up when the students qualified. (Arrangements varied from ward to ward anyway, so all the pre-Project 2000 students learnt at the end of three years was that everybody had a different way of doing it!) What the students were learning about 'being a Mental Health Nurse' was more important.

In general, however, it seemed that community nurses saw the students' limited 'hands-on' experience as less of a problem, than their hospital-based colleagues and one outweighed by other attributes they displayed – particularly a greater social awareness and understanding of environmental effects upon health. (It was not that the traditional students did not think that way, one district manager commented, but they were 'not trained to'.) They were not hospital-oriented like previous students tended to be. The influence of a 'stand by your beds, here comes sister' approach was noticeably absent, according to another respondent.

The new students' eagerness to make up any deficiencies in their 'hands-on' skills was frequently commented upon. It also meant, in one manager's view, that they could 'pick up good practice from the beginning', because they were not coming with pre-conceived ideas – or 'bad habits'. As in hospital areas, the students were perceived as questioning and keen to learn, and particularly where individuals were known from earlier placements, their growth in confidence and assertiveness was remarked upon.

Supervision

All six schemes now had staff supervisor systems in place in practice areas. The one exception to this in the first round was the scheme where teacher practitioners (in post in most areas of general nursing) had primary responsibility for supervising and assessing the CFP students, assisted by link tutors. All first-level registered nurses were eligible to act as supervisors after a settling-in period for newly qualified staff, usually of about six months but a lesser or unspecified period in places. There were, however, still variations between schemes as regards the extent to which sisters/charge nurses – and second-level registered nurses – took on this role. In two schemes in particular, sisters/ charge nurses, or at least those of 'G' grade, in 'general' nursing areas would not normally act as supervisors, given all their other (increasing) managerial responsibilities. In the other schemes, they would do so, it seemed, although tending to concentrate on the third- year students needing management experience or to fill in for other staff.

Second-level registered nurses were said to be much involved in student supervision, but where it was not policy for them to take on this role officially, some respondents still felt unease about what was perceived as a slight against staff with often considerable nursing knowledge and experience. Some areas shared out supervision responsibilities according to grade of post rather than level of registration, with, for example, 'D' grade nurses allocated to supervise support staff undergoing training, or the more junior Project 2000 students. However, the situation was becoming more fluid with the increasing trend towards allocating supervisors in pairs to each student, analogous to primary and associate nurses assigned to groups of patients where team or primary nursing systems were in operation.

As was the case prior to Project 2000 as well, all staff in an area would contribute to the supervision of the students, including experienced auxiliary staff, from whom they could 'learn a lot about basic nursing care' (a situation in conflict with guidance from the ENB, 1993b). That was one reason why it was 'so important' for those staff to be well-trained, a surgical ward supervisor pointed out. But with the spread of team and primary nursing, the supervision of the Project 2000 students was being shared in a more formal way too. It was now more common (in some areas of five schemes at least) for students to be allocated to two named supervisors and/or to particular teams, with their supervision effectively shared between the staff nurses in those teams backed up by other members.

Nevertheless, the number of students needing to be supervised at a time, even when shared between two nurses, was still an issue. The ideal of a supervisor having only one student allocated at a time was rarely achieved. About two-thirds of the supervisors interviewed in Adult and Paediatric Nursing areas said they could have two or more students at once – and this was not an infrequent occurrence. In many cases, two was 'usually' the number, excluding support staff working for NVQs and, in one scheme (with teacher-practitioners to help), excluding CFP students.

There were also still difficulties, in the CFP in particular, arranging for student and supervisor shifts to coincide when students were working different hours and not working weekends. Where they could exercise some option in this matter (and as reported previously, early experience had been salutary and students allowed greater flexibility as regards the shifts they worked as a result), individual students' willingness to fit in with the shifts of their supervisors (including late duties, nights or weekends) often drew favourable comment. But it was also recognised that some students could have valid reasons for being reluctant to work unsocial hours – not least because they were not paid for doing so and could have other jobs to supplement their bursaries at those times.

Nevertheless, there were still differences between schemes and areas within schemes as regards the amount of weekend working students would do. In some cases it was limited as a matter of policy to a certain number of weekends (one in two or three, for example) or because staff thought it unfair that students should work weekends when they were not paid extra to do so. The students' own willingness to comply in this matter was, of course, another factor – as the students themselves confirmed. In some specialisms, such as Learning Disabilities, working weekend shifts enabled the students to experience the social side of the residents' lives.

The students presented a very varied and complex picture of the depth and extent of supervision they had received on placements. Staff were said to vary tremendously in what they provided in terms of supervision and support. The students' expectations of a named supervisor were limited and they did not aspire to substantial one-to-one contact. The most positive reflections, throughout the course, reflected an ethos rather than an individual. At each stage, one-third of the students felt that the system had not worked well for them either because no such person(s) had been allocated to them, or they had had minimal contact. There was very little reference to consistently high-quality, inspiring supervision and although there were many overall descriptions of placements that conveyed this, the focus was not on key individuals. Students valued a supportive work environment which may or may not have included a named person(s). They did not report feeling inadequately supported if the supervision system was not particularly comprehensive, provided that alternative support was available to them.

What changed over time was the students' perceptions of what supervision should entail. By the third year there was pride in autonomy and in increasing levels of responsibility, and in only seeking support when two people were necessary for a particular task. Rather than a fairly continuous process of monitoring and practical support, what students welcomed by this stage was a more detached supervisory role, removed from immediate practice and there was relatively little reference to that happening. This student's comments about the form the relationship took was fairly typical in the third year: 'I certainly would not use the word mentor about what I've had because if you are attached to a staff nurse you become her appendage and it's as if she is your boss and you do work for her. I certainly wouldn't say that the people I have been assigned to have been key figures and really they have just been a name I have had to deal with if I need to change my shifts.'

A distinction was drawn between practice-based staff who could supervise the students and those who could assess them. But it was a more clear-cut distinction in some places than in others. In the scheme where teacher-practitioners played a major part, particularly in the CFP placements, staff fulfilling a supervisor role were required to have completed the ENB 998 course in teaching and assessing – or the relevant five-day teaching and assessing module – in order to assess the students. This was said to apply within some areas of other schemes too, but not universally. Requirements in this varied from scheme to scheme, with staff quite commonly able both to supervise and assess students after a lesser period of preparation.

In multi-disciplinary Community Psychiatric and Learning Disability teams it was already established practice for colleagues of other professions such as social workers and occupational therapists to contribute to the student nurses' placements and ease the supervision load for the responsible CPNs/CMHNs, just as the latter would help with the supervision and teaching of students of other professions and a range of other nursing courses (conversion, post-registration) as well as Project 2000. Skill-mix changes were envisaged in those nursing services, too, although these had not progressed very far as yet in the six case-study sites.

Despite the informal sharing of supervision responsibilities among community team members, the fact that no allowance could be made in nurses' case-loads for the considerable work and time commitment supervision entailed was still a 'bone of contention'. A locality manager in one District described it as 'the biggest conflict between the college and ourselves'. 'It's our one big bug-bear', said a health visiting manager in another District. Most hospital ward areas had received at least some extra staffing by way of replacement for the former students' labour, but community areas where students had always been supernumerary, had not done so. Hence, the new and demanding requirements of supervision and assessment of the Project 2000 students were widely seen as 'an extra function for community nurses without the benefit of extra resources'.

Community practice teachers were supposed to have an allowance in their workload for supervising (DN/HV) students but even this could rarely happen in reality, it seemed. Only managers in one scheme said this did in fact apply, although one considered that supervision of the Project 2000 students was just as intensive if done properly, because it needed to be closer and tailored to students with more varying needs. Elsewhere, it seemed, frequently 'just lip-service' was paid to the notion.

Assessment

Staff had needed time to adjust to new systems of practice assessment as to other aspects of the Project 2000 placements, especially where continuous assessment was itself still an unfamiliar process. Revision and simplification of assessment documents and further input from education on their use and interpretation had combined with greater familiarity to ease staff difficulties in this area. There was, however, still quite frequent criticism of assessment tools as being 'long-winded', 'repetitive' or 'broad' with objectives occasionally thought inappropriate for the stage of the course, irrelevant to the area, or dependent on circumstances for fulfilment (for example, dealing with an incidence of challenging behaviour, or the admission of an elderly or psychiatric patient, if none occurred while the student was there).

While it was often acknowledged that practice assessment systems were more thorough and comprehensive than those used prior to Project 2000, they were also extremely time-consuming. The time required to sit down and discuss in detail with each student what s/he had done and needed to do at the start of , end of and midway through a placement was described as time frequently just not there in working hours for many supervisors, except perhaps at staff changeover periods or on night or weekend duties when wards were quieter, if students were there. One supervisor (recently promoted to 'E' grade and often in charge of her care of the elderly ward when on duty) said that 'nine out of ten times' now she would have to stay on after hours to do the students' assessments. Supervision of support staff undertaking training for NVQs added to the burden for many staff, and the forms and format of their assessments were still criticised for being even more complex and time-consuming than in the case of the Project 2000 students.

On short placements of four weeks or less, it was still very difficult to fit in all three interviews, namely, the preliminary, intermediate and final plus the mid-point review (important if students were going to have time to rectify deficiencies), which was omitted in places. Both staff and students were being encouraged to review progress in achieving objectives on an ongoing basis, and ways in which this was working, to mutual benefit, were described. One charge nurse in an acute psychiatric assessment area, for example, would discuss with students at the start of each day which objectives they would aim to achieve and how, and have them feed back to her afterwards. The sister in charge of a medical area in another scheme reported that students were assisting their supervisors in this respect, by, for example, writing up particular aseptic technique procedures after they had done them.

Some respondents still queried the appropriateness of 'self-directed' learning objectives for first- year students who had difficulty identifying their learning needs, when they did not know what they needed to know, or what a placement could offer. For self-assessment, too, there was some feeling that more guidance was needed. According to the supervisor on one psychiatric ward, the college of nursing had told the staff not to provide formal teaching for the students but to 'facilitate' their learning. As the students had only received two days' preparation for the placement, however, that respondent felt she had to teach them something and so would give them handouts on various topics on which to base their learning and reading. In other areas, formal teaching sessions were said to be still very much part of the culture, with, for example, a specific afternoon set aside for that as far as possible.

A sense of needing more concrete evidence of learning applied to some of the students' practical skills too, and the area where respondents most felt the lack of a formal practical assessment was the administration of drugs. In one scheme visited there was still some uncertainty and confusion among staff at the time as to whether the students would be required to have a formal 'drugs assessment'. With the Project 2000 students' system of assessment, competence in drugs procedures did not give the same assurance as that in place for traditional students. For one mental health supervisor, the 'biggest problem' as regards the Branch placements was having students coming at a late stage, never having done a drugs round, and having little knowledge of the drugs they were administering. A student in her final unit, whom she was supervising at the time, had, she said, done her first drugs round on that placement.

In some areas of the Mental Health and Learning Disability specialisms, where students were not ward-based but client-based for some, if not all, of their practice experience, the supervision and assessment system worked rather differently. In one scheme where Learning Disability Branch placements were organised so that the students were only coming to the wards where their clients were resident one day a week, the consequent lack of consistency and contact with their supervisors made building up any kind of relationship with the students, let alone assessing them, very difficult. The matter had been taken up with the college of nursing, however, and subsequently students were being allocated so that they could fit in with their staff supervisors' shifts in a more acceptable way. But practice-based staff continued to have misgivings about the college's selection of (sometimes very difficult) clients for the students, and considered it would be much better if the allocations were done by the staff who knew the clients.

In another scheme where the Mental Health Branch students would each have a small case-load of six or so clients, each student would be allocated a named nurse supervisor for the entire 18-month period. One deputy charge nurse fulfilling that role described how his students would come to him twice a week for supervision and he would liaise as necessary with the key-workers of the students' clients, hospital- or community-based, who were responsible for day-to-day monitoring of the students' work. The key-workers would not necessarily be nurses, but could be other accountable professionals, such as social workers.

The students were aware of the extra burden placed on staff in familiarising themselves with the new procedures and were very appreciative of those staff who made particular efforts to achieve what was required. They also stressed the need for judgements about their work to be made by someone with adequate knowledge of it, and the complexity and inappropriateness of some of the assessment documentation. What was clear was the value students placed on using the assessment process as an opportunity to discuss their progress at length. As they negotiated their learning experiences, and sought to develop areas of competence, this focused exchange (ideally at the beginning, middle and end of each placement) was highly valued.

As regards the documentation, a major concern for students was when what was required did not fit into what was available on the placements (procedures, patient activities or more general approaches such as the nursing process or particular models of care). Some learning opportunities were not there at all, others were infrequent and others required considerable perseverance. The obscurity of some of the language was also commented upon. Where it was unclear or ambiguous, students recalled discussions with their assessor to try to interpret categories.

What emerged forcibly in the third year was students' concerns with the grading of progression. On the sites where marking schemes were designed to show improvement, the rigidity of this superficially logical approach was questioned. As one student expressed it: 'Staff at school said that we **had** to show progression so no matter how good you were at something initially you had to start off at 2 (on the rating scale) and work your way up and I really don't understand this.' It was clear, however, that students' reservations about the rating systems and structures for classification could be overcome if the quality of contact with staff, undertaken as part of the assessment requirements was high. Students were very conscious of the variation in the rigour and care taken by staff in relation to the assessment process.

Preparation

As emerged from the first round of interviews, the extent of formal preparation of practice-based staff for their role as supervisors and assessors of the Project 2000 students was very variable. The length of workshops/courses put on by colleges of nursing for this purpose varied (from one to five days), and so did uptake— and availability – of relevant training (both short courses and the longer ENB 998 or City and Guilds 730 courses). When interviewed in 1991, just over half (18) of the sample of (35) supervisors had attended the latter two courses, but almost a third had not attended any formal preparation sessions at all.

Of 19 supervisors interviewed for the first time in 1992, only seven had undertaken the 998 course, five of them concentrated in the scheme where they had only taken on official supervisor/assessor responsibilities for the Branch students, and where the 998, or the five-day teaching and assessing module, was considered the appropriate qualification for the role within the terms of ENB regulations. Six of the new interviewees – about the same proportion as in the case of the 1991 sample as a whole – had not had any formal preparation for their role. Of the remaining six, one had done an assessor's course (but had not had any update for Project 2000); four had attended (two-day) workshops; and for the other, who had qualified as a RMN a year previously, an accredited teaching and assessing module had been incorporated at the end of his training.

Difficulties in staff getting on the 998 course were reported widely. Long waiting periods (up to a year or more) were the norm and D grade staff nurses, with fewer management responsibilities, and therefore more opportunities to work with the students, would usually be the last in line. Even in the scheme where most of the staff nurses interviewed had undertaken it, ward managers reported that staff turnover/movement continued to create problems – and for the responsible education staff, it was still 'a continuous battle'. (One ward, for example, had prepared three supervisors, but when the college had wanted to allocate students, they had found that there was no one with the 998 qualification there.) But it was envisaged that the process would be speeded up, with the running down of the more protracted old-style 998 of 15 days in length, and its replacement by the new five-day teaching and assessing module. That would be added on to the ten-day core curriculum for the ENB 900 series of courses which was already in place in that scheme.

Only another six of the staff interviewed previously had since attended other courses or study days for Project 2000 supervisors/assessors, although in one scheme where there was a progressive programme of staff preparation corresponding to the various stages of the first students' course, another round of half-day updates was expected shortly. Valuable help given in service areas by individual link tutors (and in the one scheme, teacher practitioners) was also acknowledged in places.

Many community nurses were participating in the formal assessment of pre-registration students for the first time in the Project 2000 Branch programmes, but the preparation they received for that role also differed between the six schemes. As in the case of hospital-based supervisors, some colleges required them to have done the ENB 998 course, or appropriate module; elsewhere shorter courses of preparation sufficed. Moreover, there was no formal obligation upon community personnel trained after a certain date (1981, in the case of district nurses) to undertake any further training in order to assess the students. But according to respondents in the different schemes, opinion was divided upon whether the further preparation available was necessary or appropriate.

Education-service liaison

All six schemes had systems of link tutor liaison in operation, although in each case the perceived effectiveness of the links varied from area to area. Not only the frequency of visits, but also the form of support provided, depended very much upon the individual tutor fulfilling the liaison role. As noted elsewhere, colleges' expectations of the liaison role differed, especially with regard to tutors having any hands-on involvement in the practical work of an area, alongside the students. It was not usual for this to happen in three schemes (except occasionally in the case of a student experiencing particular difficulties). In the other three schemes, practice varied from area to area, and tutor to tutor.

In several areas revisited in 1992, therefore, the situation was viewed quite differently from the previous year solely because the link tutor had changed, although other changes, particularly the relocation of education staff in the course of college rationalisation/amalgamation, had also had an effect in places. A charge nurse in a Learning Disabilities hospital, for example, spoke of missing the 'closeness' which had existed when education staff had been based nearby on site. The increasingly generic nature of the work of tutors in that specialism was another factor mentioned in two schemes.

A majority (roughly 60 per cent) of hospital-based respondents expressed themselves quite happy with the links which existed, with improved support liaison reported in some areas, even if in some respects they shared other respondents' desire for closer contacts of one form or another.

Ward managers were more likely to have access to formal channels of liaison such as curriculum planning or review teams, and/or to have contact with education staff in other contexts. Staff nurse supervisors were more reliant upon contacts with tutors visiting their areas – usually liaison tutors, but occasionally personal tutors also. Regular visits (about once a week or fortnight when students were there) were reported in only approximately a third of areas visited. Otherwise, it was very much up to practice staff to initiate contact by ringing tutors if they had problems with the supervision or assessment of individual students. With exceptions, requests of that kind were said to meet with a swift and helpful response so that staff felt that support was there when they needed it.

The extent of support given to supervisory staff by visiting liaison tutors also seemed to vary considerably. In three schemes in particular, a few respondents spoke highly of the link tutors' role in preparing and updating staff and helping them with student assessment. But other respondents conveyed a feeling of being 'left to get on with it', in terms of the support they received in executing the onerous teaching and assessment responsibilities Project 2000 placed upon them. Most supervisors did not mind – or indeed enjoyed – having the students to teach and assess, despite the added pressures entailed. But many still felt that they did not get enough feedback on their efforts and the placements generally.

Where there were invitations to attend placement evaluation sessions in college, again, it seemed to be ward managers to whom these would be extended in the first instance. About half those interviewed said they had received such invitations, although most found it very difficult to attend, especially if travel to sites some distance away was involved. In two cases, respondents had reservations about the presence of placement staff at such gatherings – whether students would give an honest evaluation, and how any negative criticism would be received if they did. It was rare for staff nurse supervisors to be invited to attend or to get time off to do so. In five instances when staff nurses said they had attended such meetings, however, they had found them useful. According to one RNMH staff nurse, it had made him realise that the students had not necessarily learnt what he had thought they had learnt, or that they could have misunderstood some procedure or incident: 'This has helped both staff and students. It's not just a gripe, it helps you understand more about the learning process.' Written feedback from such evaluations was also mentioned as very helpful by a few respondents.

Apart from the teacher-practitioners, formal involvement of practice staff in the colleges' preparation of students for their placements seemed to be very limited, at least up to the point of the last interviews. Such involvement was only mentioned by four hospital-based respondents, although several said that they would like to contribute in that way. In the scheme where teacher-practitioners were in post, they were seen very much as an embodiment of education-service links in their respective areas, although supervisors in three areas visited without a teacher practitioner at the time also spoke very highly of the input and support provided by their link tutors. Elsewhere, tutors with a base in practice areas were rare. One exception to this was a tutor based in a surgical area who would work alongside the students and their allocated patients (two or three each) for two half days a week.

Community service/education liaison

Formal liaison arrangements between community services and colleges of nursing had continued to evolve in the six schemes, with a number of new structures in place since 1991 reported at both senior management and operational levels. The practice of allocating link tutors to particular localities, reported previously in two schemes, had been extended to a third, although only in one (other) scheme had an additional – and much valued – community coordinator post been created in the college team, relieving the pressure on the one community tutor who had undertaken this task single-handedly hitherto.

In all but one of the six sites, respondents said that links had continued to improve or, as in the scheme cited previously, where support was described as 'first-class', had always been very good. According to one manager in that scheme, it was absolutely 'crucial' to have that kind of support network (i.e. with tutors assigned to each health centre who would visit regularly, participate in tutorials, meetings, etc.) if a new approach like Project 2000 – about which some of her colleagues had been very apprehensive – was going to work.

One of the main ways in which respondents considered links could be strengthened was by greater contact with tutors in placement areas. Although help and support might be readily available when requested if, for example, there was a problem concerning a particular student, there was a desire to see tutors getting out to community localities on a regular basis – for the benefit of both students and staff. This was happening in at least some community services in three schemes, but not, it seemed, elsewhere. As one locality manager put it: 'It seems at the moment a one-way communication, with us doing all the communicating, always going to the college to talk, and not the other way round.' Again, there was appreciation of the pressures college staff were under including, in one scheme in particular, severe financial restrictions upon their movements.

Although community managers would frequently attend or be represented at relevant curriculum management meetings in colleges, it was not common for community nurse supervisors to participate in student placement evaluation sessions and, like their hospital-based counterparts, they wished to have more feedback of this kind. Where this did occur, however, it was evident that the nature and value of such gatherings could vary. One nursing manager, for example, welcomed the opportunity evaluation sessions gave for both staff and students to air any problems – and to iron out any anomalies between what students felt about their experience, and what the staff believed was actually happening. But in another scheme, where an evaluation session, with all district nursing and health visiting as well as some other community-based personnel present, had taken place at the college, at the community managers' own request, this had not proved very successful. Respondents felt that such evaluations should be strictly between students, supervisors and tutors, and that a big impersonal gathering was inappropriate for the discussion of individual students' problems.

Continuing education and support for staff

With the advent of the Higher Award and PREP proposals, the whole question of Continuing Education opportunities for qualified nurses was assuming an added urgency. But amid widespread reports of shrinking budgets and increasing pressures on qualified staff, it was clear that concerns about funding and release for further training were growing apace.

As more units acquired independent trust status, the trend, noted the previous year, towards staff being expected to pay part, if not all, of the costs of such training (50 per cent in one District; 25 per cent in another) and to do it in their own time, was unlikely to be reversed. The same applied to the trend towards the provision of more in-house training (albeit not immune from financial constraints), and increasing restrictions upon more expensive external courses, particularly some of the longer ENB courses.

Although a few areas were able to draw upon trust funds for staff development, the main exceptions to this rather gloomy picture were Learning Disabilities or Mental Health Units, with large institutions in the process of contraction, where a good deal of money was said to be going into training to give staff, facing an uncertain future, the opportunity to develop their careers in other directions. The opportunities had 'never been so good', according to one RNMH nurse who was about to be released for a year to do the ENB 807 course in a neighbouring District, with funding for a temporary staff nurse secondment by way of replacement. In the same District, however, a staff nurse training post in the CPN service was reported to have been frozen because of lack of funds. This 'rotational' post had allowed hospital-based RMNs (three circulating at one time) to gain experience in different specialist areas of the service and then take on a small case-load under supervision.

Secondments of different kinds were part of the quite extensive in-house staff development programmes being developed in these specialisms by (sometimes newly appointed) staff training/development officers. Systems of personal profiling and accreditation of prior learning (APL) proposed for practice staff with the Higher Award and PREP were an area in which several respondents said they would like more help and advice. In the scheme, where teacher-practitioners were in post, this had been formally incorporated in their role and in that of the link tutors. Concern about the likely costs to staff of those systems was expressed as well.

With implementation of the NHS reforms, the delegation of managerial responsibilities was continuing and bringing further changes to the roles of ward managers and staff nurses. Respondents at both levels reported increasing responsibilities and pressures as the tier of senior nurse nursing officer posts above them was being taken out, and (judging from the accounts of staff in one scheme where this had occurred just prior to the 1992 visits) not always with a great deal of sensitivity to, or consideration for, the individuals affected.

Not just G grade nurses were being further removed from direct patient – and student – contact but F and E grade nurses too. In one District, G grade managers in the Mental Health Unit would now cover the whole hospital at night and weekends, whereas in a neighbouring District, F grade nurses in the Learning Disabilities Unit would now be in charge of the hospital there at night for six-month spells of duty. Staff in Acute Units were also assuming wider managerial duties of this kind. In a Medical Unit, where the senior nurse had been replaced by a non-nurse business manager, not only would sisters now have to 'carry the bleep' during the day as well as evening shifts, but E grade staff nurses too.

The students' perspective on their placements

The first student interviews

The first responses (in the Autumn of 1990) of the (77) students to their very varied early placements in the six schemes, conveyed a mixture of elation, confusion, and frustration. They spoke of insights gained, skills developed and demonstrated, and the joy of making contact with patients and clients. In all but one scheme, the students had done ward placements of several weeks duration by that time, and it was clear that the opportunities these had afforded for what they defined as 'real' nursing, and for them to 'fit in' and 'get involved', were what they had found most rewarding. Short, fragmentary experiences (for example, one day a fortnight on the wards) had been for them, as for the staff, difficult and unsatisfying.

Placements of only a few days duration with community nurses had usually been enjoyed and appreciated, but those with previous experience were aware that very brief spells, in mental health and learning disabilities areas in particular, could offer only superficial insights. In some areas (some residential homes, for example), there had only been the opportunity for domestic work. A wide variety of non-nursing placements had been accepted for what they were, but these rarely engendered enthusiasm (placements with police officers in one scheme being an exception!). The rapid sequence of short placements had left many students 'reeling' from the sheer volume of learning experiences and the demands simply of being in so many places.

It was clear that the students' experiences depended to a large degree upon their own approach to staff, with the value of assertiveness both in terms of making requests and of saying 'no' emphasised. Students had to decide whether they would limit themselves to the (very few) practical skills they had been taught in college, or whether they would capitalise on the opportunities practice presented. The former often led to frustration and the latter to uncertainty and anxiety.

The students pointed out that staff concerns about the new training had sometimes been translated into hostility. Nearly a third of them spoke spontaneously of some direct unpleasantness experienced from particular staff members – mainly directed at their level of proficiency and whether or not they were going to be 'real' nurses. A similar proportion spoke of unpleasant encounters with students on traditional courses, although the camaraderie of being a student (whatever the course) often overcame workplace tensions.

The second student interviews

When the students (71 of the original 77) were interviewed again in 1991, they were still in the early phases of their Branch programmes. As they had settled into placements of a longer duration, their reflections on their experiences had also altered. Most of their comments were very positive – 'brilliant', 'rewarding', 'thoroughly enjoyable' were frequently used descriptions. The longer period in practice areas reinforced what they perceived the courses were aiming for, and seemed to increase – or rekindle – morale and enthusiasm.

Being released from the rapid sequence of very short placements meant the students could settle into the host areas and become involved in the work of the ward team – a much sought after outcome. There was, however, still the need to adapt to new areas, and many spoke of the transitional period as a time of stress. Moreover, some students across the six sites had reservations about the benefits of the study days spent in college each week during the course of their placements. Where these were perceived as loosely structured, without clear objectives, they could feel 'removed' from their placement areas for no good reason.

The students conveyed a sense of practice-based staff building up a better understanding of the Project 2000 reforms. Only a few respondents now reported unpleasant encounters in relation to the course. This was mirrored by the comments on contact with peers on traditional courses. Four-fifths of students described relations positively, and the efforts made by third-year colleagues to assist their learning were greatly appreciated. Students could identify why there had been problems and could sympathise with the feelings of being threatened and 'left behind' which some people had harboured initially. The confidence and competence which the third-year traditional students exhibited in the placement areas, particularly with regard to ward management, were a subject of frequent comment among students who were seeing (with apprehension in a few cases) the end of the second year in sharper focus, and the time before registration narrowing.

The third student interviews

The sample of students (68 of the original 77) interviewed for a third time as they approached the end of their placement experiences, were settled into Branch programmes and able to reflect on the courses as a whole. The period between the second and third interviews with students had seen a shift in the form the placements took that extended the trend apparent in the time between the first and second interviews. Placements were longer and consequently there was less variety. In the scheme having the most emphasis on 'tasters' and non-nursing placements, there was a corresponding brevity in the placements under discussion here. (There was just the one ten-week placement here whereas other sites typically had one of four months and others of between two and three months duration.) During the period covered in the third interviews the experiences of those on the Child, Mental Health and Learning Disability Branches took on a rather different pattern to those on the Adult Speciality in that they tended to work on longer placements. The starkest example of this approach to placement organisation was where students worked with individual clients and had contact with institutions and staff only as they featured in the care of those clients.

Students were able to identify precisely what they valued on placements – indeed by this stage of the courses, a framework for good practice emerged. As before, the attitudes and practices of staff *vis-à-vis* the students were crucial. General enquiries about placement experiences did not elicit detailed reflections on the clients or patient – students took it as read that, for them, this contact had been at the very least satisfactory. While there were a few comments about placements that focused on philosophical objections to practice affecting students' levels of satisfaction, it was working colleagues that had the major impact. A placement on an acute medical ward drew the comment: 'I really enjoyed it because the staff are so enthusiastic. They gave me teaching sessions at least once a week and staff there were doing courses which they were keen to involve me in.' This key determinant of how a placement was experienced was summed up by the student who explained that 'the main thing that you need is staff who are open-minded and see themselves as still learning and are happy to help you with your learning without feeling threatened'.

The central theme was of students negotiating their way through a series of experiences that varied in their length, value and appropriateness to what the students perceived as their learning needs. They professed a strong desire to learn and to respond constructively to the ever increasing responsibilities they were meeting on placements. They also expressed an undercurrent of unease and apprehension – the fear of failure or of setbacks to hard-won gains was ever present. As one student embarking on a surgical placement explained: 'I was very nervous about this because, with the ten-week community and the six-week summer break, it meant that I had been quite a long time off the wards and my confidence was very low and it took a while to get back in again. It's a totally different experience being on surgery and takes time to adjust to.'

It was evident that most students had gained a great deal from their placements and their eagerness to learn had, in many situations, been rewarded. One placement that dominated any analysis of the students' placement experiences across the six sites was that of work with community-based nurses (in the Adult Branch), both because of the differing extents to which this featured in the courses, and the way in which they included key features of what students defined as good practice. Community experience ranged from two weeks to ten weeks in this phase of the course (in the latter, students had their own case-load) and it was striking that this experience dominated the students' responses to a general query about recent placements. A typical statement was that: 'It was wonderful to know what I was doing was right and to be given that responsibility. You really felt you had the chance to put that into practice.' The most eloquent comment described this experience as 'heaven on earth' and the placement was rated as 'brilliant, ten out of ten' by another. The crucial features that earned this approbation were the degree of independence, the opportunity to use skills already acquired and the access to community nursing teams.

When the students were asked to take a retrospective overview of their placements to date, the challenges presented in the organisation and planning of such a range of experiences emerged clearly. Students consistently spoke of the optimum length for practice placements – where it had been experienced, 17 weeks was seen as too long and those of five or so weeks could be frustrating. Ten weeks appeared to be widely regarded as a period that would maximise the gains. Given that students expected a great deal from their placements, they were easily disillusioned by the obstacles set in train by current systems.

As well as length and progression (which meant timing placements so that students were neither too inexperienced nor too advanced in their practice to benefit from them), the problem of providing realistic insights was widely discussed. The vast majority of students said that the principle of covering placements in other Branches was sound and they generally felt that what they had done was worthwhile, but the more reflective comments (particularly from those who had previous experience of the relevant client groups) suggested how misleading and potentially unhelpful some placements could be. As one student expressed it: 'The paediatric experience was totally inadequate, hopeless. We had six days in a nursery and six days on a ward. I don't remember anything about it – you can't learn anything in this short time that is going to stay in your mind.'

Perspectives on work in the specialisms of Mental Health or Learning Disability could be unproductively influenced by the three-day placements on offer on some sites. The need for these important attachments to be well organised with clear goals was made forcibly, and concern was expressed that without this there could be considerable time-wasting and confusion. Flexible arrangements could mean, as one student suggested, that 'you get away with a lot more, you could go through the whole placement without learning anything'. The potential value of, and the need for, placements across specialisms were illustrated forcibly by the student who said: 'The mental handicap was enjoyable, but I'm not really sure what I learnt from it although I am surprised when the general nurses come into contact with someone with a mental handicap... and they do think of these people as "loonies".'

Having said that students preferred their substantial placements to be of such a length that there was an opportunity to settle, they also expressed reservations about the short attachments commonly referred to as 'tasters', which varied in their frequency and degree of direct relationship with nursing practice from site to site. A general unease was expressed in the comment that: 'They [the placements] should definitely be longer and we should not have so many "tasters" because you lose sight of what you are trying to achieve.'

On the site where there were shorter placements throughout and more 'non-nursing' attachments than usual, the students did not express appreciation of the breadth of experience on offer and were not supportive of the varied programme they had encountered. What **could** be gained was illustrated by one mature student's unique reflection that: 'You could say that this was a waste of time but the course has given me the opportunity to do so many things that I would never have had otherwise.' School visits to study the 'normal child', sessions in shopping centres and work placements were referred to very negatively in the sites that provided them.

The improvement in relations with practice-based staff identified in the second interviews had been consolidated at this stage. Although this had been a relatively slow process of acceptance, attitudes were said to have changed amongst the qualified staff and there was little reference to bad feeling or animosity in the interviews. The improvement (with undertones of the struggles for acceptance they had encountered) was captured by the student who explained that: Things are a lot better now and they are getting used to us, but they are still not quite sure about how we are going to do. Getting into the third year now means that we get more respect and I have actually heard some positive comments from nurses and doctors about us being good.'

What the evidence the students presented about working relations indicated now was that misunderstandings were still widespread (one-third of students explicitly made this point) and that implementing change of this order challenged fundamental patterns of working and met with varying degrees of resistance. Although there was now little unpleasantness, it was clear that there was still a need for sustained attention to how the new challenges of Project 2000 could be assimilated by practice-based staff. Students again reported high levels of questioning by staff about the courses – they were still left with a sense of providing information about the courses as they progressed.

There was a difference in what staff were expected to facilitate for the Project 2000 (as opposed to the traditional) students, and the extent to which this was understood has already been raised as an issue. Without an adequate level of understanding students could lose out on appropriate responses to their learning. As one student explained it: 'We are doing our management training now at the same time as traditional students and what we need to do is different but staff don't acknowledge that and expect us to do the same and achieve as much even though we have much shorter placements.'

This difference in what was expected could be difficult to incorporate into practice, as some students readily acknowledged. What was apparent was that raising staff's level of knowledge and understanding to a degree that would accommodate students' learning needs, was a long-term process and that this first intake had met with varying degrees of understanding. The pressures this created were captured by one student who explained that: 'I know there were great reservations about our level of skills and as every intake has been structured quite differently to the one before, they've had to cope with changing groups of students which is obviously very confusing for them.'

Staff had clearly been challenged by the learning needs of the Project 2000 student and this continuing reassessment of what was needed may only be fully assimilated when, as one student predicted: 'We will examine the student's learning needs and teach them as best we can in relation to the objectives that they bring.'

86

Students had had limited contact with peers on traditional courses in this part of the course (because these courses were being phased out) but for those who had, again, there was a negligible amount of direct hostility and some constructive working encounters were described. There were still some misunderstandings (as with staff) but generally contact had been constructive and pleasant. The traditional students were said to have expressed mixed views on the changes nurse education was going through, with the only direct animosity relating to fears that Project 2000-educated nurses would be advantaged in finding employment and securing promotion.

Summary of main points

- A fairly positive picture of the students' early placements emerged across the six Districts.

- One of the main problems was the brevity of the CFP placements – both overall and in terms of hours/days worked during the allocation.

- Several problems surrounding student supervision were highlighted: the large number of students; the difficulties of finding enough supervisors and arranging for their shifts to coincide with those of the students; and the demands of teaching and supervising students without basic skills or experience.

- Asked, in 1992, about the CFP placements, practice-based staff almost universally reported continued improvement as staff had become more accustomed to the new students and had a clearer understanding of what was expected of their allocations and assessments.

- Some respondents in all schemes underlined the point that it was very much up to individual students how much they benefited and learnt from the CFP placements. Some would press to get involved; others preferred 'to hang back'.

- The vast majority of staff welcomed the students' supernumerary status for the flexibility it allowed them as supervisors and the opportunities it afforded the students to pursue and achieve educational objectives on and off the wards.

- Across the six schemes, practice-based staff consistently expressed the view that the students' rostered service had generally been going well.

- There was a good deal of variation between the schemes in the way the rostered service was structured. The main differences were in respect of the timing of the students' rostered allocations, the organisation of study days, and the latitude given to service areas as regards the 'unsociable' shifts worked by the students.

- There was some tension for the students between the benefits of rostered service – being part of the team and having responsibility – and their needs, rights and obligations as students.

- Both supernumerary status and rostered practice were the subject of confusion and varying interpretation for staff as well as students.

- The students gave a very varied and complex picture of the depth and extent of supervision on placements. They did not, however, report feeling inadequately supported if the supervision system was not particularly comprehensive, provided that alternative support was available to them.

- Both practice-based staff and students felt that the assessment documentation needed revision.

- The extent of formal preparation for practice-based staff for their role as supervisors and assessors of the Project 2000 students was very variable.

- Staff's concerns about the new course had sometimes been translated into hostility, and this was an issue for students in the early stages. Although it was a relatively slow process of acceptance, attitudes were said to have changed by the third year, when students made little reference to bad feeling or animosity from staff.

- Ten weeks was widely regarded by students as the optimum length for practice placements.

- It was evident that most students had gained a great deal from their placements and their eagerness to learn had, in many situations, been rewarded.

- On the site with the most radical reforms – short placements throughout and more 'non-nursing' attachments than usual – the students did not express appreciation of the breadth of experience on offer and were not supportive of the varied programme they had encountered.

- It was clear that raising practice-based staff's level of knowledge and understanding to a degree that would accommodate students' learning needs was a long-term process and that this first intake had met with varying degrees of understanding.

Discussion

Practice is the crucial testing area for successful implementation of the new paradigm Project 2000 represents. The picture which emerged from the interviews with both practice staff and students in the final year of the first courses was very positive overall. Education managers and staff, interviewed for the last time in 1992, were also greatly heartened by the feedback they were getting from practice areas on students' progress in the Branch programmes. Reports that students were rapidly catching up in the area of skills development were contributing in particular to the growing sense of optimism many respondents expressed.

The students' supernumerary status had allowed curriculum planners scope for innovation and experimentation in the provision of practice experience in the CFP. But operationalising the very concept of a broadly based CFP, aimed at giving students a taste of a wide range of experiences and services for different client groups, had meant shorter, often more fragmented, placements. The resultant lack of continuity for students, staff and patients/clients (particularly in the areas of Mental Health and Learning Disabilities where, potentially, the effects could be most damaging) featured prominently among those aspects of the new practice arrangements disliked by staff and students alike. Interviewed in 1992, practice staff had got used to the CFP placements (which had also been extended and restructured in places to meet some of the objections raised), and had adopted strategies to give the students the best experience they could in the time available. But some inherent tensions remained.

As the students moved into the Branch programmes and a more familiar pattern of longer placements in a chosen specialism, the perceptions of both staff and students changed gear. An increasingly positive tone became apparent and was most marked with respect to the rostered service period and – in one scheme in particular – community experience with students' having of a small case-load under supervision. The longer placements allowed the students time to settle in, become part of the team, and contribute to the work of the area – outcomes which both staff and students viewed as highly desirable. While both staff and students could be said to be using the old frame of reference in expressing such views, this did not necessarily mean that realisation of the concept of the **knowledgeable doer**, fundamental to Project 2000, was being thwarted.

Many respondents were quick to comment on the students' grasp of academic knowledge (if not always of particular clinical conditions/syndromes) and their frequent questioning of practice and procedure. Asked specifically if they considered that Project 2000 had had any effect on the way that care was delivered in their ward/unit, approximately 40 per cent of practice-based staff thought it had, and of the two-thirds of that number who saw the effect as positive, most referred to the new students having made staff reflect more on their practice and look up relevant research. In a few cases, respondents mentioned research-based ideas (on mouth care, for example) which had been cited by the students, and which had actually been implemented on their wards. (The majority of staff who did not think there had been any effect on care mostly said this was because standards of care were already high on their wards, although a few of those respondents, too, hoped there would be a move to more research-based care in future when the Project 2000 students were qualified practitioners. The diplomates' views are recorded in Chapter 7).

In some ways, it seemed the pendulum of reform swung too far initially in the Demonstration Districts. This was evidenced in a number of ways – often bound up with interpretation of student status – which affected the early practice experience: the somewhat *laissez-faire* attitude towards college attendance which seemed to spill over occasionally into practice areas at first; the '9-5' hours of placement attendance initially (in four schemes); and the manner of students' introduction to ward practice generally, which was perhaps **too** gradual and/or too late in places, with an over-emphasis on **observer** placements and 'wellness' at a time when, in some schemes at least, students would be allocated to areas with very ill patients. A reluctance to teach students even basic practical skills in college undermined the confidence which an adult educational approach and greater knowledge should have given them, and increased pressures on both students and staff in the early placements. All were matters fairly quickly addressed by the colleges, and in the case of the misconceptions of the supernumerary student as pure observer, by the eagerness to learn and work demonstrated by most of the first students themselves.

Elkan *et al* (1992), in their study of Project 2000 in one District, highlighted the difficulties of putting the concept of self-directed learning into operation in practice placements. Both staff and students in this research emphasised that what was learnt on a particular placement depended upon the individual student, and the confidence and assertiveness of that person. It was also dependent upon the supervisor, for whom considerations of safety and patients/clients' needs generally were paramount, who decided how much the student was allowed to do. While the onus was now much more upon the students themselves to ensure their learning needs were met, those with no prior nursing/care experience would not necessarily know what they needed to know, and even in the case of those with prior experience, there could be, as Watts (1992) has emphasised, the student 'who does not know, but does not know s/he does not know'.

Self-directed students had a thin line to tread in placement areas. If they were too assertive about their learning needs and expecting staff to meet them, they could appear unappreciative of the demands upon staff and the fact that, for them, patients' needs were their top priority. If they were diffident, this could be interpreted as lack of interest. They could not, especially in the early placements, just slot in and get on with the work, as they did not have the basic skills to do that. With supernumerary status, they **could** stand back if they were unsure or unconfident. It was easy for some students not to get involved – and easy for busy supervisors not to involve them, when doing so could slow down pressing work.

Staff had reservations about the extent to which achievement of often broad placement objectives in fact signified competence to practice. Both among staff and students there were also some concerns about the varying degrees of rigour with which different supervisors approached the assessment task, and about how competent a student shown as achieving a particular objective was in fact, if a procedure had only been performed once or if some event (an incidence of challenging behaviour, for example) had only been talked through and not actually experienced in practice.

Clearly there are still lessons to be learnt from the first students' practice experiences, even though, as some participants in the study pointed out, there were lessons from undergraduate nursing experience (not least about misinterpretation of supernumerary status (for example, Smithers and Bircumshaw, 1988) which seem not to have been borne fully in mind when Project 2000 was implemented, not to mention the more recent ENB pilot schemes which presaged the Project 2000 experience in so many ways (Collins, 1990; Leonard and Jowett, 1990).

All the confusion surrounding the students' formal status – supernumerary and then rostered - has, it seems, been something of a smokescreen clouding – unnecessarily – the essence of the Project 2000 changes. The time needed for staff to understand clearly supernumerary status – and the difference between service and practice – were underlined from the start. A senior nurse manager interviewed in 1990 thought that the term should be replaced by 'supervised practice' for that reason, and in the last round of interviews with practice-based staff, the occasional area visited was said to have dropped use of the term. Although the allocation pattern was radically different, and if a supernumerary student was absent, the ward manager could not say the area was short, it was felt that the colleges had been at fault in overemphasising the differences between supernumerary status and rostering.

Certainly for the students, in their later placements at least, the differences were not very apparent, and practice staff themselves not infrequently spoke of the rostered students still being supernumerary. With services frequently said to be running on minimum staffing levels, capable students, both 'supernumerary' and 'rostered', were boosting numbers and contributing to the nursing workload as extra hands. This did not necessarily mean that their educational needs were being neglected. Students on 'rostered' placements were, for example, often still able to leave their areas for educational reasons if the workload permitted. As `supernumerary' students, they could, in theory at least, not be stopped from doing so, even if their ward **was** busy, although often they would themselves not want to.

The real anomaly was having students on a bursary included in staffing numbers during the rostered period. In cash-strapped times, it was this which left them open to exploitation. In some places restrictions on the numbers of weekends and other unsocial hours worked by the students were imposed by colleges. Elsewhere students and staff themselves agreed what the limitations should be. But that exploitation did happen in some areas was evidenced by students who found they were obliged to work the weekend immediately before their final examination. When students spoke so highly of the value of their rostered experience, it was the value of working full shifts and being regarded as full members of the team which they prized. They could have been 'on the roster', but still 'extra' to staffing numbers for that to happen – as indeed they were in quite a number of areas. Nurse education staff reported that this crucial aspect of the Project 2000 student experience had been going well, although there were some strong reservations about the place of a rostered contribution in an educational course. The importance of good education/service communication about the rostered aspect of the course, as about supernumeracy, was underlined.

Many rostered students could not be 'relied on' in the way previous third-year students could be, because, at least in the early part of their rostered experience, they had not had the opportunity to develop their practice skills sufficiently. In some areas this did mean additional work for the existing staff; in other areas ward managers would still bring in extra bank/agency staff or do so up to the point at which they felt they could rely upon the students in that way.

Wards may not have lost posts when the rostered students were allocated as some managers, particularly in one District, had feared, but there was clearly an effect on the use of extra bank/ agency staff. Managers of most (Adult Branch) hospital placement areas reported receiving some additional staff by way of replacement for the previous student workforce by the final interviews, but many felt it to have been inadequate, especially in the period immediately after the pre-Project 2000 courses ceased. Then and during the peaks and troughs of rostered students' allocations, reliance on bank/agency staff was heavy. Dependence on a transient workforce is, it seems, continuing with Project 2000, despite the constraints that places on the implementation of individualised care, and continuity of care (Procter, 1989).

The question of student numbers and the demands of supervision continues to loom large in the practice areas. In some areas, the situation had eased with cessation of the overlap of students on Project 2000 and previous courses. Elsewhere, with the build-up of both CFP and Branch students, and support staff undertaking NVQ training in many areas, the pressures continued. Other changes taking place in the service areas, including ward closures, were also bringing more stress, and at times additional students, to some areas, despite agreements widely negotiated with colleges about the maximum student numbers which they could sustain at any one time. As qualified staff become an increasingly scarce resource, the risk of saturating community areas is also unlikely to lessen – nor the pressures of supervision for staff, obliged to meet purchasers' targets of performance in which such time-consuming activities do not feature.

Teaching staff were well aware of the burden of student supervision on practice staff and shared their service colleagues' concern about their inability to get out to their 'link' placement areas as frequently as they would like – for the sake of students and staff and their own clinical credibility. The six schemes provided examples of ways in which the still unresolved question of who **should** be teaching students in practice settings is being addressed. As with the advent of PREP proposals and the Higher Award, the ripple effect of the Diploma students' passage through the practice areas becomes more of a tide, the need to give staff the help and support they need, given all that the educational reforms have demanded of them, has also assumed an added urgency.

Chapter Seven
THE PROJECT 2000 STUDENTS

Introduction

The students' views and experiences both during and after their time on the Diploma courses provided a crucial perspective on implementation. Their reflections on the practice-based placements, the contact with HE and aspects of curriculum delivery are presented elsewhere. In this chapter their views on being on the courses and on entering nursing (collected in three interviews conducted during the courses) are explored, as are their experiences as qualified nurses (gathered in one interview at least six months after they completed the courses). For some issues (such as course attendance), the variations over time are presented in some detail, whereas others (such as preparedness for becoming a staff nurse) pertain only to one point in time. The students' employment destinations are presented on page 112.

The questionnaires distributed to students in the early stages of the CFP collected valuable data to be built on in subsequent interviews (Jowett *et al.*, 1992a). The biographical data provided a picture of a group of students who are predominantly female and under the age of 25. Most had five or more GCSE/O- level passes or equivalent qualifications and some had gone on to pursue further academic, professional or vocational qualifications. Most also had experience of previous employment, often in care-related spheres, before applying for their current course. Three-quarters of the students had applied for a traditional course, but most looked forward with enthusiasm to participating in Project 2000 and, in particular, to their clinical placements and the Branch they would be studying in depth. They had been attracted to nursing as a worthwhile profession which would offer them the kind of caring activities they were seeking, and for more than one-third nursing had always been their main career ambition. At this early stage, three-quarters of the students were able to describe definite nursing career plans.

The staff involved in various capacities with the students presented a very positive picture of their experiences of the new recruits to date, and of their expectations of the future. In Chapter Eight, the managers' pleasure, sometimes tinged with surprise, at how well the students were settling in and their optimism about the calibre and practice of this embryonic workforce are recorded. For those in HE, the students were widely regarded as rewarding to teach, providing opportunities for professional development. As with any group, the students' response to the courses was mixed, but where HE staff had risen to the challenge presented by the new courses there were rewards to be had. Issues raised by the students' emphasis on relevance have already been outlined (Jowett *et al.*, 1992b) and the staff's desire for them to suspend judgement and wait for the course to gel was widely expressed (although reservations about the extent to which the courses this first intake experienced did in fact achieve coherence are presented in Chapter Four).

Nurse education staff gave a clear exposition of the positive qualities of the students and of their expectations for them. It was commonly felt that the students had a greater breadth and depth of knowledge in comparison to those on previous training courses. The students were also said to be thinking critically and reflectively about nursing; to be highly motivated, inquiring, assertive, confident, and to have well developed academic skills. Only a handful of nurse teachers felt that students' competence in practical skills was an area of concern as the courses drew to a close (whereas they were divided on this issue mid-course and had been converted by the students' experience on the Branch programmes). With very few exceptions, the nurse teachers saw the Project 2000 students very much as a new breed. Staff were aware of the students' positive response to the more sustained placements, the rostering and the emphasis on pathology brought in with the Branch programmes and anticipated that this enthusiasm would be translated into the progressive, skilled nurse envisaged in the original aims of Project 2000.

Reflections on the courses

During the CFP many students spoke positively of their experience to date. They described the courses as enjoyable and rewarding, frequently linking their comments to aspects of the Project 2000 philosophy or style. A small proportion were negative in their overview, remarking, for example, that the courses 'don't seem to be getting anywhere', and a few took a purely instrumental approach, being prepared to 'stick it out'. The remaining students felt that the courses had a long way to go in their development and were, in a sense, reserving judgement. There was considerable uniformity across sites in these early views, although the least positive group of students was from the scheme with no ward placements for the bulk of the CFP. Here only one student gave a totally positive response, while others were anxious about the 'long wait to see if you want to nurse'. This generally favourable overview across the sample was sustained as the courses progressed, although those in the last group referred to above maintained their reservations about the content of their CFP.

Throughout the courses, the most unease was expressed (across sites) about the academic work and assessments, and this was from students with varying educational backgrounds. One of those with several A-levels reported that: 'The exams were undoubtedly the hardest and the course has been quite supportive in many ways and suddenly you're dropped into it and you really are on your own against this final exam.' There were different emphases to these concerns about the work and, although examinations were a major feature, there were also comments on the less tangible academic difficulties of coping with studying and (from one site) the 'unrelenting' work. Learning study skills and getting to grips with the demands of the courses had been problematic for many. One student described her growing awareness of what was expected as '... we used to have these very difficult lectures and I used to go home knowing that I didn't need to bother because we'd go over it again and I should have actually spent that time reading-up on things myself and of course all that time is lost now. So it actually seemed like a cushy time but it was a misuse.' O'Neill *et al.* (1993), in their study of the CFP in Northern Ireland, similarly found that 'Project 2000 students identify issues relating to coursework in general and self-directed learning in particular as principal causes for concern'.

Looking back over their time as students, the qualified nurses identified a wide variety of strengths and weaknesses of the course. The most frequently stated positive feature (from half the respondents) was the opportunity to gain academic knowledge and skills. This strength was elaborated on by one student who explained: 'The course is up to date and it does make you question and I know now that I've got to look things up and follow things through and it's very good because it prepares you professionally to carry on learning.' One in six Project 2000 staff nurses referred to supernumerary status as a strength, allowing you to visit a range of areas and follow patients through, and the same number welcomed the wide variety of placements. A few said that they appreciated having a Diploma level qualification, especially now that there was an expectation that nurses would gain such qualifications, and a few also said that the inclusion of work in the community had been a distinct advantage.

The most frequently mentioned weakness (by about one-third of respondents) was of insufficient practical skills development. This view was typified in the statement that 'you didn't do enough clinical experience and you really panicked about skills and it was up to **you** to go out and locate your weaknesses and try and remedy them'. The next most commonly mentioned deficiency (by rather fewer) was the poor organisation of the courses which had caused confusion and frustration. Other references were to the too short placements, subject matter that was not related adequately to nursing and not spending enough time on the Branch programmes (because of the 18-month CFP).

A desire to leave a course is one expression of discontent, and there was a fairly even split mid-course across sites between those who had never considered discontinuing (38 people) and those who had given it serious thought at some stage (33 individuals). Towards the end of the courses less than one-quarter said that they had considered leaving in the interim. In the earlier stages of the courses it was a general sense of dissatisfaction or unsettledness that precipitated a desire to go. A few students referred to a feeling of 'not getting anywhere' on the courses that had made them consider such an action, and there were students intending to take the numerically smaller Branch programmes who had felt frustrated by the Adult bias of the CFP to the extent that they had considered discontinuing. Only a few students mentioned personal circumstances or crises that had prompted a desire to leave. Towards the end of the courses where students had considered resigning it was mostly the stresses of the academic work that had precipitated it, although a few spoke of poor placement experiences or of particular members of practice-based staff contributing to their desire to leave.

There were rich data here, revealing the demands courses like these make and the turmoil students may be going through to reach an appropriate standard. There was a great deal invested in these courses for many of them and their self-esteem, indeed feelings of self-worth, were vulnerable. For several people who had not considered leaving, for example, the depth of their personal investment should not be overlooked. One mature student explained: 'It has taken me 20 years to get here'; and another that 'This is my last chance'. The sense of being challenged was captured by a student who had not seriously considered leaving the course but explained that: '... in that two weeks before the exams it really crossed my mind that I would have to go if I didn't pass them, and we all felt so depressed and tired and it's only been the fact that we've helped each other through that phase that has got us through the last three months.' Towards the end of the course, maintaining a sense of momentum was difficult for several students. This was expressed as 'just keeping going' or 'trying to keep up your enthusiasm'.

When interviewed towards the end of their course, nearly 90 per cent of the students said that they would recommend it to a friend. When asked what they would emphasise to someone thinking about embarking on Project 2000, the demands of the courses emerged again. Most students would advise their friends that this was a taxing three years, not to be undertaken lightly, that could be extremely rewarding if approached realistically. Recurring points were summed up in the statement that: 'I'd tell them that it's hard so that they were aware of it. There's an awful lot to do and nursing itself is hard and there is a lot more to it than you realise when you come in. I'd try to give them a realistic picture so that they don't come in blindly like I did. It certainly isn't an easy course.' There were warnings about not embarking on such courses if your personal life was 'shaky' because of the strain it could impose on one's relationships. While those who **would** provide a recommendation focused on the rigours and challenges of courses of this kind, those who would not said so either because it was unwise to embark on still rapidly developing courses, the degree route seemed a preferable option or because nursing *per se* was not an option to be recommended.

Students were also asked about Branch choices, and the extent to which there had been any changes was recorded. Very few students had contemplated any change of direction and choice was not an issue at this stage – only two students in the sample were now on different Branches from those originally intended. On one site, one had changed from Mental Health to Adult Nursing and on another, one in the opposite direction. There were 14 students currently on the Adult Branch who reported seriously considering a move to Mental Health or Learning Disability Nursing (for some this was still a possibility after qualifying). Only one student said that they had asked to transfer (from Learning Disability to Mental Health) and been refused.

Benefits from the courses

The students described a mixture of vocational and personal gains they had made, with considerable overlap between the two. They spoke of the satisfaction from their work with patients or clients and their growing sense of professional competence. The feeling of doing something worthwhile and the consequent sense of accomplishment were frequently expressed rewards. All students had experienced gains, and an extremely positive set of data emerged. Even the man who maintained a cynical, detached view of his course, at times presenting very strong criticisms of its content and direction, saw overall gains for himself. He reported developing 'as a better human being and that's been very rewarding'. For many there had been a re-evaluation of attitudes and values resulting in a certain moral openness. One student described herself as 'less rigid, more open. It sometimes felt like time-wasting but it was getting us to look at ourselves and our prejudices. I am not as self-righteous as I was.' Another said that frequent discussions of dignity and related issues 'had a big impact on me'.

Other people focused on the liberating impact the courses had had on their lives. One student's experience illustrated this process and highlighted the demands such a transition can make. She reported having '...a lot more confidence. There is tremendous satisfaction in learning that I am not as thick as I thought I was. It's nice to stretch your brain. I think I must have been very defensive and scared when I came onto this course.' Another student applauded her own academic development, highlighting again the potentially destabilising effect of personal growth by pointing out that 'once you actually try to achieve, you realise your own insecurities... you wonder if you will be able to achieve and you are expected to expose your own views.' In these elaborations of personal growth it was the mature students who used the most vivid language, but such development was not confined to them. One young woman described life at home as like 'being wrapped up in cotton-wool' so that the courses had 'opened up the world to me' and enabled her to grow up. However painful they may have been, all the changes described above were presented enthusiastically. One student summed it up: 'The course has broadened me. I feel capable and that I am as good as anyone else.'

The central themes outlined above, of an increase in confidence and self-awareness, were sustained throughout the courses. There was a strong sense of optimism and buoyancy in these answers. The key words used were 'confidence', 'awareness', 'tolerance' and 'assertiveness'. These comments sound an optimistic note for the realisation of Hooper's (1989) aspirations for Project 2000 offering 'the chance to provide educational processes for nursing students in a way that has never been done before in this country – to organise the curriculum in such a way that students are able to increase their knowledge and skills in the art and science of nursing while attending to their personal growth as students and supporting them in the examination of their values and attitudes'. There was only a handful of people who had found the courses so demanding that their confidence had been undermined. One of them spoke of her difficulties in coping and said that it was 'demoralising to have to keep on proving myself'.

When the now qualified nurses looked back over the courses, the main benefit they identified for themselves was personal growth and development. (Approaching half of them made this point.) A typical comment was that: 'I'm a better person, more open and understanding, I accept people as they are. It made me push myself a bit and pace myself.' Nearly one-third of them focused on the development of their academic potential as in: 'I'm now more likely to push on academically. I have the incentive to do things.' Other comments referred to the benefits of friendships made and to the general experience for life that the courses had provided. There was real enthusiasm running through these recollections. One staff nurse, who had originally had to be persuaded to do the RN rather than EN course, epitomised this when he explained that: 'I have matured a great deal and there was a great whoosh from being a student and I developed academically to a degree that I couldn't believe.'

Student feedback

Continuous monitoring of the courses, utilising the reactions of the consumers, was built into the programme on each site. The students' reflections on the opportunities to provide feedback to staff consistently stressed dissatisfaction with both the process and outcome. From the early stages regular feedback sessions when the results would only be of benefit to subsequent intakes were wearisome, and there was a feeling, even then, of saturation summed up in the comment that: 'I think people now have so much to do personally that they don't feel they can make a further contribution.' There was increasing frustration expressed about feedback being one-way with no overview being provided of the corporate views of their peers. As a few students explained, 'You don't get feedback on your feedback!' Specific concerns were the way in which discussions so readily turned into 'moaning' sessions, with the consequent lowering of morale and the inhibitions evoked in group sessions or when written feedback was not given anonymously.

What was increasingly clear was that if the course ethos promoted feedback from students and debate, students expected both an overview and 'results' and where these were lacking they were aware of a contradictory message in relation to openness and communication. As one student expressed it: 'I'm not sure if they are changing things because I seem to hear from other people of things that are the same, and I find this quite annoying because they shouldn't keep asking us if they don't want to know.' The feeling of criticisms not being perceived constructively by staff was fairly widespread.

Views on the system of elected student representatives varied across the sites, although the majority of students had had some contact with their peers who had taken on this function (there were two schemes where a substantial minority had not had any contact). Whilst the value of the system obviously depended to some extent on the individuals involved (the commitment and usefulness of some representatives were particularly commended), opportunities to meet as a group with the representatives were limited and a few students suggested building in such sessions to the timetable. It was acknowledged that taking on this responsibility presented a challenge, but students valued having 'reps' although where there were few opportunities to meet as a student body, concerns were expressed about how representative they could be. Where the representatives had produced newsletters or other forms of feedback on staff contact, these were much appreciated.

Student or student nurse?

The commitment to student status that features in Project 2000 represented a fundamental shift in thinking about the nature and intent of nurse education. Beckett (1984) described student status as 'not just a dignity, nor a status symbol to be granted to someone preparing for a "certificate of competence in nursing practice". It is a necessity as part of the process of growth implying much more than supernumerary status.' The UKCC explained the need for change in that 'today the twin features of student labour and constant replacement appear as a system inefficient, ineffective, unjust and in severe need of overhaul' (1986). The ambiguities expressed by students in this sample about their role highlighted the tensions that surfaced when this move was put into practice. In the early stages, more than half of the students identified themselves clearly as student nurses and several were unclear about their position on the student/student nurse divide. The remaining 19 described themselves as students, with 8 of the 13 from the site with no ward placements at that time awarding themselves this designation.

As the courses progressed, there were shifts in that, while a similar proportion described themselves as student nurses, there was an increase in the number of students who were unclear about their position on this divide and a decrease in those who described themselves as students (down to eight respondents). This ambiguity was most clearly illustrated on the site where there had been no ward placements at the time of the first-stage interviews. Of the 12 remaining in the sample for the second interviews, only one described herself as a student. (A breakdown into categories has been used here to convey a sense of the prevalence of different views. It should not be taken to imply exclusive groupings – the confusion and uncertainty about roles outlined below were expressed by students whose responses fell into each of the categories.)

Confusion about what their role was created varying degrees of concern across five sites towards the end of the courses (in one where students were now hospital-based all were emphatically student nurses) that were illustrated by a student from the 'no early ward placements' site above. She explained that: 'For the first 18 months I think I did feel like a student but now all of a sudden you are expected to be a student nurse. They start going on about punctuality and dress and they do seem to be jumping on us. It has all changed now. We've had to stand around like lemons and now they seem to be making this dramatic change.' The pockets of resentment this situation encouraged were illustrated by the statement that: 'On a placement you are an employee under a disciplinary code. However if you want extra duty payments you suddenly become a student. You are a student when **they** want you to be one.'

Not having the time to do justice to the set work was quoted by several students as indicative of their not being 'real' students. A student who came to the course with an honours degree explained that:

> *Since we've been rostered it's been difficult to do the academic work and it's incredible the amount of things that we have had to fit in. The build-up to the exams was awful and people were very fraught and stressed. We had lectures in school just before the exams and these were on quality standards (this was seen as irrelevant to the exams) and the atmosphere was extremely tense because people just didn't want to be there and they wanted to be studying. Unless you were lucky, you could be actually working on the night before the exams and it was purely up to the ward area whether you were allowed to relax and revise before the exams.*

Towards the end of the courses there had been a considerable shift in views about student status. Now, only two students identified themselves as students and the same number were confused about which would be the most appropriate designation. The overwhelming majority now saw themselves as student nurses. Obviously they were now much more fully engaged in the workplace and there was negligible contact with HE and only sporadic visits (varying across sites) to the college of nursing. This sense of distance was captured by the student who explained that 'at the moment it is as though the school is inconsequential and the only reason we feel like students at all is because we don't get paid'. Students could identify quite clearly the factors that identified them as student nurses rather than students. They had heavy workloads in the placements areas, which meant that they were unable to study full-time and they had nothing approaching what they defined as a student lifestyle. The comparison for them was between traditional views of students in HE and themselves. They did not (unlike many staff) see the introduction of supernumerary status or other changes within nurse education as indicative of student status *per se*. This could lead to a sense of frustration and of being cheated. Where they identified financial losses in comparison with traditional students (because of no additional payments for the hours worked) they felt used.

Attendance

The delivery of courses with a tightly prescribed number of hours (4,600 divided evenly overall into practice-based and academic work) raised issues about the underlying principles and the learning opportunities provided, and the students' shifting perspectives on the monitoring of attendance are of interest. In the early stages, more than two-thirds of the students were of the opinion that attendance at all course sessions should be both compulsory and monitored, although there was uncertainty about how this should be achieved. As the courses progressed, there was a shift in that fewer students (half of them) felt that there should be a rigid system for monitoring attendance, a few were unsure and the remainder felt that such a system should not be in place. Towards the end of the courses only a handful of students felt that a system of registration should be in place. Systems for monitoring attendance had been tightened up across sites and this increase in the number of students resistant to such a practice may be a response to this as well as to an emerging questioning of the nature of the learning experience to be achieved. (There were differences among the sites on this issue – in one, 11 of the 14 students were in favour of a system of registration; in two, all students but one were **not** in favour and the other sites produced mixed reactions.)

As the practical implications of a rigid system had become clearer over time, this had fuelled students' resistance. The realisation that there was a maximum of 15 days, sick leave for the duration of the course was felt as a particular unfairness. For the few students who had met with what they regarded as unsympathetic responses to requests for compassionate leave or a period of extended sick leave, the structure was seen as unjust. A mature student who had made a substantial commitment to doing well on the course expressed her frustration at having been 'caught out' (and subsequently reprimanded) by random registers. She had '... only actually missed two hours but there were things at home that were really pressing and just having that time really helped me out'.

The students' comments on this aspect of course organisation indicated the complex issues underpinning what could appear at first sight to be an administrative procedure. For some there was an educational dilemma – that such a system was not conducive to adult education. As one student expressed it, 'the whole point is that we are being **taught** nursing rather than studying nursing. The forms we have to fill in (detailing how time is spent each day) just don't fit in with the notion of studying and absorbing a subject.' The main theme to emerge from the responses of those who were not in favour of a rigid system of monitoring, however, was of frustration about the value of such a practice when it could be abused so easily and proved nothing anyway. Detailed registers (particularly when they had been introduced at a relatively late stage of the course) were regarded by this group as 'heavy-handed and limiting'. Students did not expect a 'free-for-all' approach but experienced current arrangements as unsatisfactory. One suggested that 'there should be proper guidelines about what is expected but it should then be left up to the individual student'. Persistent non-involvement with the courses was not sanctioned but several students made the point that recalcitrants should be dealt with as appropriate. One explained the contradiction here in that staff 'tell us to look at people as individuals and yet they look at us as a group'.

For many nurse teachers attendance was still an issue which had to be addressed, even as the first intake came near to completing the courses. There was frustration at having to enforce rigid and complex systems of registers and timekeeping, mixed with concern for the academic progress of the non-attenders. There was a feeling from some nurse teachers, across sites, of impatience with the lack of clarity about the position from college management and educational bodies. There was a sense that once a decision was made either way, discussion and debate could give way to more important educational and curricular issues. As one member of staff expressed it: 'I think nursing has got to make its mind up whether it's teaching adults or not.'

Taken together, these concerns highlighted areas for discussion. Where does the responsibility for learning lie and how is the contradiction between a theory of individual self-development and the well-defined end-product of an educational programme (Burnard, 1990) to be resolved? At its starkest, the issue is one of vocational competence – will these diplomates be safe practitioners if they have not attended certain sessions? Confusion about the interpretation of EC guidelines on course requirements compounded the issue. This school of thought was illustrated by the student who expressed annoyance that 'you just don't get credit for being there. If they (students) are not putting in the hours they are not getting the instruction that they should.' This vocational frustration was clear in the comment that 'it's not fair that people who are absent all the time will get the same qualification as those who come along every day'.

Entering nursing

Having reached the mid-point of the courses, only a few students felt that their views on what nursing encompasses remained unchanged. The least detailed responses came from the scheme with no ward placements during the bulk of the CFP, where students had had limited exposure to nursing practice. For the majority there had been a re-evaluation of what nurses do, focusing on the nature of the work (mainly the high levels of responsibility and autonomy) or a broadened view of the role. Nearly half of the students who had changed their views made the first point, and slightly fewer the second. Four students in the former group who had been NAs expressed their surprise that even with their background they had not realised the responsibilities and managerial functions of a staff nurse. The broadened perspective on nursing included a new awareness of work in the community and of the holistic approach to patient care.

As the time for qualification approached, just over half of the students said that their major reaction to entering nursing was apprehension (this contrasts with one-third of them presenting this at the mid-point of the course). What the students were expressing was not a debilitating anxiety about working as a qualified member of staff but rather a reflection of their desire to reach an appropriate standard. They were aware of the responsibilities and challenge of the work they would be embarking on and expressed a constructive apprehension about meeting these demands. Several students commented on their hopes for a supportive environment in which to start practising.

Very few students displayed any sense of panic, and most of this apprehensive group were reasonably confident about their potential. As one of them explained: 'It's frightening, but you do realise the responsibility and, of course, the goal is to register. Registering isn't the finality that you thought it was at the start but it's just the point at which you learn from and the point at which you become responsible for so much. I suppose there is fear but it's not a real nervousness, it's just hoping that I'll be able to cope with what is required of me as a nurse'.

For just over one-quarter of the students about to qualify (rather less than in the mid-course interviews) the overriding response when they considered becoming a nurse was of great enthusiasm. One of them, for example, described herself as 'raring to go', adding that 'I think it will be really good when there are five or six sets of us (Project 2000 diplomates) in jobs and we'll be recognised for what we contribute. For the moment I have a lot to give and I can't wait to get out there and give it.' For the remaining individuals, their responses focused on either a mixture of emotions ('half and half, scary and excited'), anxieties about obtaining a job and feelings of not knowing enough.

Once qualified, only a handful of the respondents said that they had real doubts about coping with a staff nurse post. (One of them had been frequently left in charge of a ward in a private hospital, which she had subsequently left.) Overall, one-third said that their transition to qualified nursing had been unproblematic and two-thirds that there had been initial doubts and insecurities on their part that had gradually abated. Becoming a staff nurse meant acknowledging the extent of the responsibilities now carried and realising that people (nursing and other colleagues and patients) would be relating to you as such. This breakthrough was summed up by one student as: 'I wasn't confident at all and I did find it really difficult to adjust and it was very difficult to break the habit of knowing that there was someone to help you and that you didn't have to do everything perfectly because it wasn't your responsibility and suddenly you qualify and you are out on your own.' These nurses were well aware of their accountability and of the expectations of others (particularly doctors) now that they were qualified. Many of these newly qualified nurses referred spontaneously to the impact immediate colleagues had on this process of acclimatisation. As one of them explained it: 'The staff were very supportive and the sister is very easy-going and I do think that's got a lot to do with it because if you have a good ward manager then it affects the whole attitude of the staff.'

With regard to the levels of responsibility placed on these newly qualified staff nurses (which varied to some extent in terms of being the person in charge at any given time), only one had found the expectation unworkable (the staff nurse who had left the private hospital), and of the others a little more than one-third had felt daunted by the realisation of what they were responsible for and rather less than two-thirds had experienced no difficulties. Again the attitude and actions of colleagues were seen as crucial. As one who had had problems explained: 'I found the responsibility overwhelming in the first couple of months and the senior sister put me in charge of a whole row of rather heavy patients who needed a lot of care and I didn't have those skills and I was out of my depth. It came to a head after a couple of months and I said how hard I was finding it but now it has settled down.' In a more positive environment, a typical response was that 'the responsibility is overwhelming sometimes because of the nature of the ward situation [Acute Medicine], but the support is so good you can cope'.

A period of preceptorship for newly qualified staff nurses has been widely discussed (UKCC, 1993) and those taking part in this study who had been appointed to a nursing post were asked for their experience. Three-fifths of them had not been allocated any such support, although some had had induction days or felt that other staff had eased them in. One-fifth had had this type of individual support to good effect and the remaining fifth had been told that such a system was in place but could not identify any impact on their functioning. (There were frustrations expressed by several staff nurses who had been told that such a system was in operation but who had seen no evidence of it.) There were mentors (the term most commonly used by respondents) who had only been seen a handful of times and the words 'farce' and 'ineffective' described the reactions of the fifth who had experienced these arrangements. Of the fifth who had had some degree of constructive mentoring, three were degree students who had been allocated a keyworker and the others experienced a range of practices to ease their early months. At its best, the system was described as: 'excellent. During the first week I was supernumerary and I visited placements, then I had three days induction and then I was given a preceptor for three to six months and we worked out a programme with objectives. It was just the way this Unit does it and was not because I was from Project 2000.' The staff nurses described what they had been given as established standard practice for the Unit they worked on and not as a recent development.

When the qualified nurses were asked whether they were glad that they had come into this line of work, it was clear that the vocational motivation they brought to the course was sustained. The overwhelming response was that they were pleased to have taken this route and the expression 'no regrets' was voiced repeatedly. The job satisfaction available shone through their comments but so too did some of the difficulties faced. As one staff nurse outlined: 'In nursing you get no thanks for what you do. You work long hours and have a lot of responsibility for not very much (money) but it's still for me! I don't know what else I would do.' There was a sense of vocation evident in these responses, starkly illustrated by the mature entrant who, although on a short-term contract, felt that: 'It's certainly right that I did it and there's no question of that because I'm so happy and so settled and I am very much a different person doing a job I thoroughly enjoy. The money isn't good and there aren't any prospects at the time but that doesn't affect the validity of the original decision.'

When asked whether they would recommend nursing to a friend only a handful of these nurses said a definite 'no' and the rest divided evenly into three groups. One was an unequivocal 'yes', another was 'yes' with clear reservations and another that it would need to be spelt out precisely what was involved so that unsuitable applicants were deterred. The reservations centred on the uncertain climate of a rapidly changing NHS, although there were a few references to the demands of the high levels of responsibility carried by nurses. As one staff nurse explained: 'I would recommend nursing and nursing care but the wider picture of nursing in Britain at the moment really does concern me and it wouldn't be fair not to point those things out to people. You certainly aren't guaranteed a job at the end and there's a lot of uncertainty around.' The other 'yes, but' group emphasised that an applicant would have to really **want** to nurse and should only be encouraged to apply if they had the necessary levels of commitment, flexibility and drive.

Preparation for nursing

The students were asked directly whether they felt prepared to take on a staff nurse post and to identify any particular areas which they felt needed developing. More than two-thirds of the students unreservedly said that they felt prepared. They also displayed a realistic expectation of what preparedness could mean at this stage which fitted with the UKCC's (1986) call for an end to the 'old tradition of a once and for all training, encyclopaedic in its objectives'. The students showed a substantial degree of confidence in their ability to rise to the challenge and were expecting to learn a great deal and to feel comfortable about asking in the workplace. As one of them elaborated: 'I think that Project 2000 people may be less afraid of saying that they don't know something but a lot of it is experience and it does depend on what area you get a job. If you went to Oncology you would be at sea but if you went to Orthopaedics you'd have completely different things to learn and even experienced staff nurses couldn't transfer from those departments.' This approach fits in with Robinson's (1986) elaboration of 'the need to prepare practitioners who will be able to cope with uncertainty, certain only in the knowledge that however sophisticated forward planning may become there can be no precise prediction of the needs and associated nursing tasks which may be required in 20 years' time'.

Only one in seven of the students stated that they felt unprepared for taking on a staff nurse post and the remainder said that they were unsure about their degree of preparedness at this stage. The feelings of not being prepared stemmed from a lack of personal confidence and a feeling that staff nurses should know 'everything'. Such students reported needing 'constant reassurance that I am right'. (Nurse managers' reservations about whether the students would be competent and confident to fulfil a staff nurse role when qualified and the potential of a period of preceptorship are reported in the chapter on reflections on implementation.)

Focusing on where students felt they needed to develop revealed a small range of skills and areas of experience, namely management, drug administration and certain procedures such as catheters and injections. (This may be unrelated to the Diploma courses' structure. Lathlean (1987) found that 98 per cent of traditionally trained newly qualified staff nurses in her questionnaire study felt that they needed to know more about ward management, with one-third of these stating that they needed to learn a great deal.) However, in the present study there was again a measured response to these 'deficiencies'. Students were keen to develop competence, and ward management was obviously an area of potential difficulty if there were unrealistic expectations of them once qualified. Drug administration was also a threatening area to feel unprepared for. (It is of interest to note that concerns have been expressed about the competence of traditionally trained newly qualified staff nurses in management and drugs administration (Shand, 1987) and that such nurses 'were confronted with many situations for which they felt ill-prepared, often with no one more experienced available to advise them', (Gerrish, 1990). For the majority of students in the current study, there was an optimistic eagerness in their comments. This underlying confidence was captured in the statement that 'I am only worried about the management. I think I will need help and support from somebody when I am in charge of the ward. Otherwise there are always little things you haven't done before, but it's just a case of being shown them once or twice and then you can go and do it. All those little things you pick up very quickly.'

Narrowing the discussion to practical skills, the majority of students felt that their level of achievement was satisfactory and only one-sixth said that they felt inadequately prepared, mainly because the opportunities to do what they saw as appropriate had not been available on their placements. The widely held sense of achievement was clear in the student who stated that 'I am happy with my practical skills. I have come to the realisation that no one ever knows how to do everything. You are always going to be learning, even when you are a sister you are still learning. No one expects a newly qualified nurse to be a super-nurse.' French's (1989) observation that 'whilst examination performance generally improves and can be achieved in a shorter period of time, performance in tests of practical skills was the same for students on experimental courses when compared to students on the traditional course' reinforces these findings.

Where students were uneasy about their level of skills acquisition, this reflected either an expectation of newly qualified staff having a skill 'omnipotence', or a perception of the courses as having a finality in terms of preparation for practice. On the first point, one student lamented: 'I don't think my practical skills are brilliant. I have only just learnt how to do drip pumps properly on this ward. The problem is **exposure** to things is limited. For example, I couldn't just walk onto a surgical ward and do a gastric lavage. I've never even seen one being done.' On the second, another student explained that: 'In practical terms I've still got three months, so if I get good supervision there'll be more that I know and less that I'm anxious about not knowing but there certainly are practical techniques that I'm not happy with and you go on these short placements and get established so they know you're reliable and then you go, so you don't get the repetition that you need to be able to do things instinctively.'

Once practising as qualified nurses, only one respondent said that there had been insurmountable difficulties with regards to using their practical skills (the person who had left the private hospital) and of the rest, nearly three-quarters said that they felt their level of practical skills to be satisfactory and just over one-quarter had experienced some difficulties. For this group there were problems because they had had to settle into an unfamiliar speciality (working on a surgical ward after only five weeks on a general surgery placement) or because they had struggled to put relatively unknown skills into practice. For the majority, qualified work had provided a confidence- boosting opportunity to practise.

When asked how they had developed in their posts all but four of the staff nurses gave enthusiastic accounts of progress. A handful focused on the confidence they had acquired, and slightly more emphasised specific practical skills accomplished, but for the majority of respondents there was all-round growth that may have included these two specific points. As one student outlined it, this comprehensive development over several months meant that:

> *What I've learnt is a great deal of surgical knowledge and how to care for very poorly people. I've also learnt how to manage the ward and to order things and there's an awful lot that I just didn't know before. You have time to build up relationships when you are working and before that you are flying around everywhere, but I've been there long enough to be able to develop working relationships with doctors and other staff and that's quite an achievement.*

The rostered practice element of the Branch programmes gave students an opportunity to work the same patterns as their qualified colleagues (although this was not a radical departure from what they had already been doing for some students) and, once qualified, the respondents were clear about the value of this feature of their course. Only one in seven of them did not feel there should be a rostered part to the course and of those in favour, one-quarter were emphatic about the need for such practice. On a related point, several students pointed out that not being paid for the extra hours and unsocial shifts was unfair and led to a feeling of being used as cheap labour particularly at weekends. The responses to this question highlighted the key features of placements from the students' perspective. They spoke of belonging, of being part of the team and of gaining insights into the reality of nursing. As one newly qualified staff nurse reflected: 'If we had not had that our confidence would have flagged badly. It was the time when we could consolidate what we had learnt and have continuity. It was very important.'

Those who would not retain the rostered element of the course emphasised the value of being supernumerary and being able to visit other areas and put one's need to learn and study first. One Project 2000 qualifier's lengthy elaboration is quoted in full here because she highlighted both the pressures on staff and the demands for the rostered student. She explained that:

> *When we get students, they are rostered and I know that there are certain things I want to do with them but I am not able to do them because there's work that needs to be done. To do the drugs round with a student for instance can take you an hour and a half and it would be much easier to just do it yourself and send them off to do some work. I've just done one with a student who didn't know any of the drugs and it took ages but I didn't*

want to put her off and make her feel inadequate because I had to get on quickly without her. That used to happen to me and I can understand why people do it.

A different preparation?

When asked directly whether they thought that Project 2000 courses would result in a different type of nurse, nearly three-quarters of the students answered in the affirmative, only a handful thought that this was not the case and the rest were unsure. A belief that the outcome would be different was often couched in terms of the course being such a radical departure that this was inevitable. Being on the Project 2000 route had given a boost to students' confidence in that they believed the new course ethos to have promoted a certain awareness, a depth of knowledge and an enhanced insight into their work. They perceived themselves as more patient-centred, more 'holistic' in their approach and less prepared to perpetuate routines without a rationale. The strength of this optimism was expressed by the student who predicted that 'they will be more questioning – kinder even, if I dare say that. They will respect people a bit more and think things through before they do them. I think we are going to be nurses that stand together and give nursing a say.'

What also emerged very strongly from the students' projections was a concern that the espoused benefits to nurses and nursing might not be realised if the system was not prepared to adapt. As one student, who felt that nurses from Project 2000 would definitely be different, explained it: 'We'll want to change things ... I hope that they don't end up feeling that they're banging their heads against brick walls. People might just cop out and I'm certainly thinking of joining the paramedics which will be a way of working in the NHS but not having to cope with the nursing system.' Students were aware of the contradictions they faced when qualified if they sought to be part of the team (a much valued outcome) whilst at the same time attempting to influence current practice. As one of them explained: '... I hope we are able to work with others whilst maintaining the things about us that are different.' (Horsburgh's (1989) work on newly qualified graduate nurses' transition to work was pessimistic about the extent to which they could act as agents of change without parallel developments in management structures and widespread deliberations about the nature of desirable nursing practice.)

Students spoke of the pioneering nature of their position, realising that it would take several years before the steady influx of Project 2000 diplomates would mean that they were able to make an impact. It was acknowledged that it would be '... hard as a lone Project 2000 nurse out there'. Students believed themselves to have absorbed and to be strongly influenced by the principles underpinning the Project 2000 reforms and used the language of these modifications – 'academic nurse', 'research and practice', 'patients' advocate' – to make their case. An insight into the forceful nature of this culture was provided by the student who questioned the extent of the difference and identified dogmatic adherence to a belief in the change. She stated that:

> *It's hard to say, but we'll soon know. Maybe we have been getting a bit more theoretical input or maybe not. The thing is while we've been out in practice we have been taught by traditional nurses, so perhaps we will not be so different – perhaps we have had an input from Project 2000 <u>and</u> the traditional way. I was in a meeting once with my personal tutor and she said I had the attitude of a traditional student. She was quite put out that she wasn't producing this ideal Project 2000 student that they had dreamt of in their heads.*

Once working as qualified nurses, the respondents were almost evenly divided into those for whom having qualified on a Project 2000 course was not an issue in the workplace and those for whom it featured in their working lives. There was a theme running through the responses of these newly qualified staff of wanting to be judged 'as seen' rather than as the personification of a new development. The responses conveyed a desire to minimise any reactions to their course by limiting discussion of it. There were a handful of these newly qualified nurses who recalled colleagues' surprise when they learnt of their background and a few back-handed compliments were recalled where people had not immediately realised that new staff were from Project 2000. One respondent experienced 'a bit of amazement that I can get 20 patients up and do what they need'. Of those who would describe Project 2000 as an issue at work, half reported positive responses and half negative ones. The positive outcomes were because these staff were seen as being particularly conversant with aspects of practice such as standard setting and quality assurance. One respondent had been appointed team leader for care plan development with explicit acknowledgement of the strengths she brought from her Diploma course.

The negative encounters were sometimes 'just an excuse to air some prejudices' and little of substance was conveyed. One respondent who had gone on to the 'top-up' degree had 'two new features to carry' as there were reservations about both her diploma and forthcoming degree preparing her to practise competently. Although the majority of these newly qualified staff nurses did not feel impeded by reaction to their preparation, the negative encounters of about one-quarter of them indicate pockets of suspicion and unease that will presumably linger until mediated by successive 'generations' of Project 2000 diplomates.

The students were reluctant to commit themselves on the impact of Project 2000 on the health promotion role of the nurse. (The students on the Mental Health or Learning Disability Branch felt distanced from this as an issue in their work.) More than half of them were unsure how this might be influenced by Project 2000 and those who answered in the affirmative or the negative frequently qualified their answer to such an extent that categorising it would lead to a misleading overview. Students differed in their awareness of the complexity of the issue of health promotion *per se* which obviously influenced how readily they felt they would be playing a significant role – their views on this being the major determinant of how they felt nurses could contribute. A superficial view of the issue could lead to a very optimistic statement of their future role.

Students with this optimism as well as those with a more considered perspective on what health promotion involves were clear about the major influence of different working environments and on the appropriateness and feasibility of different approaches to promoting health. The commitment to change some students espoused was illustrated by the one who said: 'I think we'll definitely be different in health promotion and the only real health promotion you see at the moment is in cardiology because heart attacks are such an issue, but I think we're more well-equipped and that's given us confidence. I think that health promotion has been seen as something for specialist nurses and I think that we'll make it much more part of the role of general nurses.'

When the newly qualified staff were asked to reflect back on the health orientation of the CFP, the vast majority of them said that this had been a useful approach to take although some reservations were expressed about the CFP being too long and the fact that placements were frequently with unwell people at this stage meant that 'there was a massive contradiction and you need to make it quite clear from the start **why** you are doing this'. Two-thirds of the staff nurses felt that this early orientation had an impact on their practice. At this point in their career these nurses attempted to relate patients' illness to the spectrum of health. Some of the key points were summed up in the comment that 'I don't know about the health promotion because you have to face it that most people are not very well that you come across and I think it's important to realise that there is a well person there and not to lose sight of that. At the time it seems very silly and a waste of time and I don't think it warrants 18 months. I don't consciously think about the well person but I think it probably does make some difference.'

Reflecting on students' perceptions of how they viewed themselves as different from traditionally trained staff and saw Project 2000 as heralding a new era for nursing, it is interesting to consider the extent to which it was factors associated with Project 2000 that were emerging or whether it was just the ubiquitous zeal of students approaching qualification. Students' alarm at incidents or attitudes that suggested a lack of respect for patients or a willingness to laugh at their expense were the clearest illustration of this. Where staff were said to have 'forgotten what it might be like if **they** were patients', this could reflect both the ethos of Project 2000 and the potentially unrealistically high standards students in any discipline can impose on those already practising. Having raised this caveat, it was also clear that students quite categorically saw positive differences between themselves and traditionally trained nurses, taking them as a whole. Their emphasis was not on practical skills (which on the whole they saw as adequate and readily improvable) but on a type of approach and set of attitudes and values which had given them confidence in their potential.

This belief in the course outcomes was illustrated clearly by students' responses to being asked whether they felt they were more questioning as a group than their traditionally trained colleagues. The vast majority of them felt that this was so, with a further one in ten expressing uncertainty and only a handful stating that they did not believe this to be the case. Students across sites were adamant that they had been wholeheartedly encouraged to question staff, but they expressed varying degrees of willingness to do so and differing views on what form these questions would take. There was a clear acknowledgement that caution needed to be exercised in when and where questions were asked, but students did believe that the courses had inculcated an analytical perspective on current practice. The caution was because 'you do have to be careful and make sure that there are going to be benefits in raising these issues. There's certainly a lot you have to conform to and you do have to be careful on the wards.'

The zeal of students approaching qualification has already been noted and needs to be taken into account when students' descriptions of practice are analysed, but the extent to which they were critical of routine practices for which no rationale other than tradition could be found was striking. (A contrast was apparent with Lathlean's (1987) finding that the newly qualified staff in her study tended 'to accept established clinical procedures uncritically and to demonstrate a very limited knowledge of research, which throws into question some practices'.) A few examples of these practices surfaced repeatedly in the present study (notably patients being told to eat and drink nothing for a considerable period of time before an operation which is not substantiated by research and regular 'observations' of temperature and other physical indicators for patients irrespective of their condition). As one student explained: 'We have been told to question and ask by the school of nursing but people on the wards are threatened by it ... This is because things on the ward are not generally rationalised. Staff often don't know why things are done that way. It's a case of having always done it that way. Then you come along and ask why and people don't know because they have always done it. Therefore, they feel threatened.' A more sympathetic view was presented by several students who explained that nursing was changing anyway and staff were less willing to 'take everything for granted' so that the Project 2000 ideas about practice were not totally new.

Once qualified, there was a slight shift in the proportion of respondents who felt that their course of preparation would produce significantly 'different' nurses. At this point, two-thirds answered in the affirmative and one-third felt that this was not the case. For those who identified differences, the emphasis was on individual, holistic approaches to care, a challenge to ritualised practice and the incorporation of their social science input into their work. As one of them explained it: 'We had the latest training and it is only now that I realise how radical it was.' There were a few references to principles being 'drummed' in during the course, and certainly at this early stage of their working lives the recipients had these ideals clearly in mind.

Where it was not felt that Project 2000 would necessarily produce any difference, it tended to be because those newly qualified staff were comparing themselves with current colleagues and their working environment was one based on the principles they wanted to adhere to. There were a few who said that it was the individual nurse not the course that was crucial, but the majority in this group were in situations they found conducive. As one of them explained: 'The staff are very tuned in here and think a lot about how to work with people who are so sick so I don't think there are those sorts of differences.' These new staff were aware of the fortunate position they were in. One of them emphasised the point that 'it's not the sort of place you'd be frustrated because when I asked sister how they did a particular thing she said they don't have set ways of doing things so there is this openness there'.

Where there was what these staff nurses identified as good practice, the reasons they gave for this designation emphasised again a desire to put their principles into practice. One respondent explained that 'the whole team are like that, open to question and to change' and his next comment illustrated the ripple effect innovation may have. He believed that 'Project 2000 has had an impact on established staff because they **think** we will question so they change their attitude and try to get ready for us'. As with other responses, the vital importance of one's colleagues in determining what was acceptable or feasible emerged clearly from the data. There was a good deal of elaboration of principles from these newly qualified staff but it was against their colleagues that they measured what they would be able to do in practice. As well as this need for a conducive atmosphere, the issue of sustaining momentum was raised in this staff nurse's reflection that 'there are definitely things from the course that I've learnt that I would like to put into practice but I am doing a full shift and I just don't get the opportunity to do the more creative things and it's difficult to think about doing them in your own time'.

The students resisted formal procedures for reflective practice. Where there was a written journal, only one student had praise for the document. There was a good deal of support expressed for the principle of thinking retrospectively about what one had done but it was something to be done casually ('I think that reflecting on practice on the way home from work is a natural human process') or informally with peers. As one student explained: 'I think that the journals are a waste of time and I think that people do reflect on their own practice on a day-to-day basis and a journal just makes it a paper exercise. I think that people just fill it in as a shopping list. I certainly reflect without even thinking on what I've been doing and how I've handled things.' The students, on the whole, saw talking to their colleagues or friends as a wholly spontaneous activity from which they could gain the relief of sharing their experiences and some support from others who were '... all in the same boat and having the same problems'.

Where there were sessions set aside in the colleges of nursing to reflect on practice, these did not, on the whole, generate useful discussion. Many students saw a need to reflect but what they wanted from staff was an acknowledgement that they were thinking things through on a continuing basis and an attempt to build on this, rather than set sessions to do so. These placed an unsatisfactory structure on what had to be an *ad hoc* exercise. This perspective was provided by the student who said that:

> *Having a session about it [reflective practice] in school is inappropriate because you have already worked out these things, already talked to someone. It's a waste of time. It would be better used in a personal tutorial, but not to be put on the spot in a group of ten people to think up something. I think you have to deal with these issues much more quickly as they happen, or you'll have high blood pressure by the time you are 25.*

Four-fifths of the newly qualified nurses had had contact with Project 2000 students coming to their workplace on placements (indeed a few had been mentors or key workers for them). The main point from their comments on these encounters was the pleasure with which they were viewed by those still to qualify. The respondents were aware that they provided for subsequent intakes something they had been denied – a qualified role model – and they took on this task with enthusiasm. (This contact was mutually beneficial. As one newly qualified staff nurse explained: 'I realised how much my confidence has grown when I see how scared the students are and it's not that long ago that I was scared by the same things as well.') It was said to be different for subsequent students in that they did not meet hostility to the extent that the first intake had and both college of nursing and practice-based staff were more familiar with what was required.

There were lingering concerns, however, about the assessment documentation for placements, which was said to be still misunderstood, and about the structure of the course placements. As one staff nurse explained it: 'You still get staff complaining about students who can't do bed baths but that placement might be their very first time with adults so of course they can't do them and they need a sympathetic response rather than a writing-off of their course.' The key points were summed up by the staff nurse who explained that 'they feel overwhelmed by all the assessments and the ones who started now seem to have the same sort of blues that we did. Students still come up to borrow my assessments and assignments and word gets round that there is a Project 2000 qualified nurse whom you can talk to.' The point about the need for there to be several intakes of students through into the system before they make an effective presence was reinforced by the staff nurse's comment that 'I enjoy working with them because I know what it's like and we can relate better to them because we've been there and the others aren't always sympathetic but we know what it's like with all the studying'.

Future plans

As they approached the end of the courses, the students were asked whether they had any plans for further study, and all but three of them were beginning to formulate these (the three felt 'drained' by the demands of their current course). The vast majority of students assumed that they would go on to gain further qualifications, with three-fifths of them referring specifically to a degree as their goal. (There were three people who stated categorically that they did not want to do a 'top up' nursing degree but wanted one with more 'depth', and one graduate was already following a course that would result in an MSc as well as the Diploma. Students referred to a variety of specialist qualifications they would be seeking (sometimes in addition to a degree). Of those who were specific at this stage, eight wanted to pursue midwifery and six aspired to qualifications in district nursing. The UKCC's proposal for 'a lifelong progression of professional learning' (1986) was supported by these projections.

When the newly qualified staff were asked about further study, again the vast majority (all but five) expressed a firm intention to develop in this way. As one of them expressed it: 'I am fearful of getting stale. I don't want to be like people I see who haven't done anything for 30 years. I'm not sure what I will do but I am determined to keep up my skills professionally.' Two-thirds of them had specific plans at this stage, a few had done a short course in their workplace and a handful had secured places on ENB courses. What these staff wanted was courses to develop their area of specialty, so there was variety in their aspirations. What surfaced at this stage was the realisation that course places and funding would necessarily be rationed (this was particularly acute for those not on permanent contracts). As one staff nurse expressed it: 'You have to be so careful because there are so few opportunities that you shouldn't set your heart on something.'

There was also some frustration with the limited guidance on options they had had from either the colleges or their employers. What was becoming apparent at this stage was a realisation that a desire for further study and development was not sufficient. The pitfalls diplomates from Project 2000 could face were epitomised by one respondent who had been unable to find a nursing post and was working as a bank nurse. Being unable to secure employment, she had enquired about a humanities degree locally, only to be told that her bursary counted as three years of public funds, making her ineligible for a mandatory award (although able to apply for a discretionary one). She had also made enquires about a health service management course but was unable to apply because her bank shifts were not predictable enough to guarantee her the necessary placement experiences. Her reaction is quoted in full because of the insights it provides. She felt that:

> *They do set up these expectations on Project 2000 for further study but then it's just so frustrating... You don't get any guidance at all on what you could go on to and I feel this is difficult because they build up your expectations and then just leave you to it and you find out things like the shortage of grants. If I did get a job and there wasn't any promise of further study, then that job could only be temporary because I'm determined to keep up the study and I'd very much like to do a management course and I do want to use this potential that Project 2000 has shown me I have.*

Once qualified, rather more respondents (two-thirds) had aspirations to degree-level study (in addition to the staff nurse completing her MSc and the three doing the 'top-up' degree). There was considerable variation across sites in the options available to students, although the desire to move on in this way was spread across them. In one area it was reported that nothing had been said (even during the final consolidation block in college) about degree options, whereas in another of the six sites three staff nurses in the sample were entering the final phase of their 'top-up' degree studies. At this stage, several people pointed out the need for part-time study because of financial constraints. Those who did not want to pursue a degree were not opposed to further study, but wanted to stay firmly in their practice base and did not feel that degree studies were the appropriate way ahead.

As they approached qualification, students were asked what they hoped to be moving on to immediately, and all but one of them (a student who had consistently been ambivalent about taking up nursing) hoped to go on to a practice-based post immediately (apart from the handful who either had or were hopeful of securing a place to complete a degree and **then** move on to practice). They wanted to develop their expertise in nursing and whilst many had clearly formulated preferences for certain specialties, they were mindful of their potentially very limited choice. The interviews were undertaken sufficiently prior to the end of the course for students to still be optimistic about obtaining employment, although only one student had been appointed to a post (with several others awaiting interviews). They spoke of jobs they would 'love to' do and what they would 'ideally' hope to achieve.

The students' plans for specialisation covered a wide range, with only three individuals aspiring to go straight into a community post (several students commented that an institutional post was a necessary precursor to work in a community setting). A couple of students had applied specifically to London (other than those based there) but most intended to stay locally or hoped to find a post near partners or family.

In five years' time the students still intended to be practice-based with almost half of them hoping to have obtained posts in the community (mainly as district nurses for Adult Branch students and group home managers for those in the Learning Disability and Mental Health fields). Just over one-quarter of the whole group spontaneously said that they hoped to have achieved a promotion during this period. This was usually couched in fairly cautious terms and there was no 'fast track' ambition revealed. The few innovative goals were a tropical diseases course with a view to work in Africa, an autonomous consultant job, a PhD (on mental health) and starting a crèche or residential home. The main thrust of their plans was to gain relevant, practice-based experience to assist them in building a steady career in a nursing specialty of their choice.

Looking ahead another five years, the same patterns emerged. There was still a desire for practice-based nursing expressed by the vast majority of students (by now one hoped to be raising children, one to be engaged in research and/or writing, another to be in management or tutoring in HE and another to tutor on Project 2000). A similar proportion hoped to be working in community settings (there was a little movement here in that some hoped to have moved to community in the last five years and others hoped to have moved on to other nursing-related work). Again, there was little emphasis on ambition, with only a few students referring to it at this stage (indeed several explicitly stated that they would be happy to stay as practice-based staff nurses). Again, there were a few aspirants to innovative posts – working abroad, setting up a residential establishment, etc. There was more emphasis by this stage (though only from a few students) on working in some areas for which students expressed a principled preference – women's health and HIV/AIDS being the clearest examples of areas where students hoped to be experienced enough to be working. There was also the emergence of some general achievement targets such as 'to have done something useful for the care of elderly people in the NHS'. There was little desire expressed for work outside the mainstream NHS route; indeed there was sometimes a spontaneous, forthright assertion of the desire to stay in practice.

When qualified, the nurses still displayed the same level of commitment to practice-based care and, for those not in permanent posts, job security was the immediate goal. Nearly one-third of respondents hoped to be working in the community at some point. Where they were settled, it was common to feel that another 12 or 18 months in that post would be valuable in consolidating skills, and a few had their sights set on promotion to an E grade in the near future. Plans to travel abroad were largely sustained and one person who had been keen on general management as a career had secured a place on this training. Seven staff nurses had already decided that they did not want to nurse in the longer term, five because they wanted some breadth ('nursing is all I have ever done') and two because of poor experiences they had had ('I feel confused and lost. Poor morale does rub off on you').

Summary of main points

- The staff involved in various capacities with the students presented a very positive picture of their experiences of the new recruits to date, and of their expectations of the future.

- Only a handful of nurse teachers felt that students' competence in practical skills was an area of concern as the courses drew to a close (whereas they were divided on this issue mid-course and had been converted by the students' experience on the Branch programmes).

- Throughout the courses, the most unease was expressed (across sites) about the academic work and assessments, and this was from students with varying educational backgrounds. Learning study skills and getting to grips with the demands of the courses had been difficult for many.

- There was a fairly even split mid-course between students who had never considered discontinuing and those who had given it serious thought at some stage. It was a general sense of dissatisfaction or unsettledness that precipitated a desire to go.

- There was a great deal invested in these courses for many students, and their self-esteem, indeed feelings of self-worth, were vulnerable.

- Most students would recommend Project 2000 to a friend, although they would advise anyone that this was a taxing three years, not to be undertaken lightly, that could be extremely rewarding if approached realistically.

- All the students had experienced gains from the courses and when asked to reflect upon them, an extremely positive set of data emerged.

- The central themes of the students' reflections of an increase in their confidence and self-awareness were sustained throughout.

- As the courses progressed, uncertainties about what student status was, surfaced and students were confused, and sometimes disillusioned, by the designation.

- The delivery of courses with a tightly prescribed number of hours raised concerns about the underlying principles and the learning opportunities provided.

- Once qualified, only a handful of the respondents said that they had any real doubts about coping with a staff nurse post.

- The vocational motivation respondents had brought to the courses was sustained and, once qualified, the overwhelming response from them was that they were pleased to have taken this route.

- Two-thirds of the diplomates thought that Project 2000 courses would result in a different type of nurse. They perceived themselves as more patient-centred, more 'holistic' in their approach and less prepared to perpetuate routines without a rationale.

- The vast majority of students assumed that they would go on to gain further qualifications, with three-fifths of them referring specifically to a degree as their goal.

- As students and nurses, these respondents displayed a high level of commitment to practice-based nursing. Nearly one-third of them hoped to be working in the community at some point.

Discussion

The information collected from these respondents was optimistic in terms of the outcomes of the Project 2000 reforms. The challenge for the courses is, it must be said, considerable. Owen (1988) summarised the anticipated 'product' of Project 2000 as 'a mature confident practitioner, willing to accept responsibility, able to think analytically and flexibly, to recognise a need for further preparation and willing to engage in self-development .... a doer – but a knowledgeable doer, able to marshal relevant information, assess need .... devise and plan care .... implement, monitor and evaluate it'. The data presented here offer an insight into how feasible and realistic such aims are, and the inevitable flaws exposed must be set in context. This was a time of ambitious development which was examined in detail. These students wanted to 'fit in' on a personal level (whatever their aspirations for becoming a different type of practitioner) and very few revelled in the stimulation of their uniqueness as the first intake. Most were pleased to see the spotlight gradually disappear over time. Once qualified, they wanted to be respected for doing a job competently and there was still a sense of a Project 2000 background being something to be overcome – presumably a hangover from the early hostility the course generated.

When speaking of gains from the courses there were references to skills and knowledge, and a sense of the release of academic potential was conveyed. The courses had been demanding academically for many of the respondents, but the efforts expended had been worthwhile. However, the emphasis was on personal growth and development. Increased confidence and an appreciation of their access to life-enhancing experiences were paramount. The students' comments hinted at one dimension of such significant shifts – the destabilising impact on individuals experiencing change. Students saw their transition as individual rather than as a fundamental course goal, and this hidden curriculum could potentially benefit from wider articulation. In moving into their vocational identity, students were re-establishing key facets of their personal functioning (for some profoundly) and may benefit from sustained acknowledgement of and support in this.

When asked directly about what they had gained from the courses the depth and impact of the personal growth was evident. People **were** different as a result of the courses – highlighting the forceful impact an intensive vocational preparation can have. Such change was not without cost, which emphasised the need both to anticipate and provide support for students' periods of unease and threat. The extent of the ripple effect into students' personal lives should not be underestimated.

One dilemma that the students had to contend with was the contradiction produced in any new form of preparation by the need to be 'different' (the product of the new regime) and to be 'the same' (a competent practitioner). Students were themselves ambivalent about their role in the process of change and the extent to which they could or should act as the personification of the principles underlying Project 2000. They were aware that caution needed to be exercised but were also committed to expressing their difference where it was feasible.

The material collected on the students' role in influencing course development and on being consulted on decision-making on course-related matters indicated further gaps between a truly consultative approach to course management and the practice. Students were disillusioned by the response to their feedback and did not feel part of the process of change. The student representative role has not been fully exploited and there were still instances of staff decisions or actions that appeared to have been taken in isolation from any consideration of the impact on students.

The students' changing perceptions on their position on the student/student nurse continuum illustrated the complexity of this key dimension of change. In the document establishing the fundamental tenets of Project 2000 (UKCC, 1986), there was said to be 'a degree of unity and determination on the student status issue as there is around no other in this complex debate'. What emerged at this stage suggests that there are different criteria used to judge student status which will inevitably cause conflict. The students' criteria are study time, 'free' weekends and extended non-term time, on which they saw their courses as deficient. Staff appear to see the designation as referring to supernumeracy and their comparison is with pre-Project 2000 courses, whereas for the students it is their peers on parallel courses in HE. The notion of those on Project 2000 having student status received a resounding challenge from the evidence presented here. Indeed, the designation seemed increasingly an irrelevance to these respondents. The conflicts inherent in the student nurse role were evident from their elaborations on the demands the courses had made.

Reflecting on entering nursing and influences on their desire to do so, the students' profound sense of vocationalism emerged. There was apprehension certainly, but a good deal of enthusiasm and eager anticipation was displayed – most potently reinforced by time spent in placement areas. They did not expect to have learnt 'everything' and had a realistic perspective on how they would develop their practice. The reservations expressed as Project 2000 was being developed about potential deficiencies in students' practical skills under the new system would appear to be unfounded from the students' (apparently balanced) perspective and from their experience as qualified staff. There were some concerns about the courses providing insufficient practical skills development, but this was not a major deficiency.

The students qualifying from Project 2000 courses clearly foresaw their new form of preparation as having an impact on nursing practice. They were expecting to be different. Given a congenial working environment, they hoped to be able to influence and inform. Once qualified, they still appeared well-versed in the principles of Project 2000. They spoke forcibly of continually emphasising the needs of individual patients and used the vocabulary of health, striving to take patients back to wellness. They wanted to work by Project 2000 principles, which were already current practice in some of the settings in which they had obtained employment.

Health promotion and reflective practice were aspects of the new approach that need to be continually reviewed. Students varied considerably in their understanding of the potential and complexity of these concepts and in their perceptions of how these might be incorporated into their practice. Prefaced again by the need to be working in a supportive environment, students saw themselves as bringing a more questioning stance into the culture and practice of nursing with a view to influencing the current situation. The Project 2000 ideal of an analytical, questioning practitioner appeared to have been realised in the students' perceptions at least.

The qualified nurses' responses made it clear that the potential for job satisfaction was there in the work, and any concerns expressed were about the need for supportive colleagues, and the broader political context of nursing practice. The transition to a staff nurse had been difficult for some but overall the data conveyed an emergent confidence and preparedness and most had experienced substantial all-round development in their place of work (for the majority without the support of a preceptor). Their sense of achievement was heightened through contact with students from subsequent intakes, as they realised how much these people appreciated seeing qualifiers from their course. It is to the respondents' credit that they gave priority to providing the type of placement support that had not always been available to them, because they were the first set through.

The data on respondents' future plans were positive in terms of the nursing workforce, which should allay any fears about their value to service. The students wanted to further their qualifications and expertise and to build up careers in practice-based nursing, for the foreseeable future at least (a finding that mirrors the evidence on graduate nurses from Bircumshaw and Chapman (1988), Reid *et al.*(1987), Sinclair (1987) and Howard and Brooking (1987). There was no evidence of them wanting to pursue tangential jobs or of seeing themselves as bypassing the current procedures for promotion. Indeed there may well be a **lack** of ambition that causes concern. Once in employment, they were still eager to pursue further studies (the degree route sustained an enthusiastic following) but uncertainties about what options and funding would be available to them had surfaced. The emphasis was still on practice-based nursing, although there were signs of flight, with seven qualified nurses planning to leave.

Employment Destinations

68 students in sample

60   contractually employed (four part-time)

3   doing top-up degree (in addition to the one who was continuing with an MSc as well as working)

4   agency or bank staff (one as a HCA whilst going through an appeals procedure having failed some assessments)

1   unemployed

60 students on contracts

49   permanent

11   short-term

67 students employed

53   in NHS

8   in private institutions

4   nursing in the Navy

2   in Social Services

54 from the Adult Branch

44   D grade staff nurses

1   HCA

4   leading naval nurses

2   sisters in private residential homes

1   E grade in private residential home

1   E grade school nurse

1   E grade in NHS residential home

— — — — — — — — — — — —

45   working in hospitals

6   working in residential community establishments

3   working in community services

7 from the Mental Health Branch

6   D grade staff nurses

1   E grade in private hospital

— — — — — — — — — — — —

5   working in hospitals

2   working in residential community establishments

5 from the Learning Disabilities Branch

1   Grade 3 Social Work post

1   E grade staff nurse

1   D grade staff nurse

1   Day Services 1 designation

1   unemployed

— — — — — — — — — — —

1   working in hospital

2   working in residential community homes

1   working in a day centre

1   unemployed

2 from the Child Branch

2   D grade staff nurses

— — — — — — — —

2   working in hospitals

There was only one respondent working outside the specialty followed - an Adult Branch diplomate working on permanent nights with children with learning disabilities. Twenty three staff nurses were employed in settings where they had previously had a practice placement (and one somewhere she had worked unqualified before the course).

Chapter Eight
REFLECTIONS ON IMPLEMENTATION

Introduction

In the final round of interviews with service managers and nurse education and HE staff in 1992, respondents were asked to reflect upon those aspects of implementing Project 2000 in their Districts which they viewed as most – and least – successful. The many and varied responses to these open-ended questions convey something of the pleasures and the pains experienced by those who were the first in the United Kingdom to be involved in the major change process which Project 2000 entailed. It should be remembered that interviews with senior managers, nurse teachers and HE staff only took place in the six case-study sites. Principals and course leaders were interviewed in all 13 Demonstration Districts.

The service management perspective

Since the first interviews with senior managers in 1990, the NHS reforms implemented with effect from 1 April 1991 had wrought radical changes in the world of health service management. Three of the six 'case-study' Districts had Units which were among the first to become independent Trusts, and Units in two other Districts were about to become independent Trusts in the 'second wave' with effect from 1 April 1992. As explained in Chapter 1, managers saw Project 2000 as just one factor in the multiplicity of changes with which they – and front-line service staff – were having to grapple simultaneously. The difficulty of singling out effects directly attributable to Project 2000 implementation, and the danger of any adverse effects being wrongly attributed to the initiative, have already been underlined.

In 1992, reflecting on the process of implementation, managers tended to see Project 2000 as adding to or compounding difficulties and pressures rather than creating them. In the words of one manager, it had 'put extra stress on the nursing service at a time of maximum change'. For another chief nurse, with no reservations about the educational approach of Project 2000 or the future benefits for the profession, the fact that there had been such 'a lot of change for service staff to implement over a very short period of time ... so much for practitioners to get used to' had been the main problem.

General views on Project 2000 implementation

Asked about aspects of Project 2000 implementation which had been a particular cause for satisfaction, the most frequent response – by approximately half the senior managers interviewed – was one of reaffirmation of the basic aims of the Project and the 'health' and 'holistic care' model on which it was based. They believed that it was creating nurses who were more questioning and assertive and would be better equipped intellectually and professionally to hold their own with other disciplines. In a few cases, people expressed themselves more optimistic about that than they had been two years previously. Several managers were particularly pleased about the `knock on' effect there had been on existing staff, making them reflect more on current practices and keen to update their own knowledge.

A number had been pleased – and surprised – how well the Branch students had settled and become integrated into ward teams. In a District where students had only had very limited hospital experience until they commenced the Branch, one respondent said that the surprise among service staff at the calibre and motivation of the students had been 'almost tangible'. The Acute Services manager in the scheme had in fact written formally to the college principal commenting upon the very favourable impression the students had made when they commenced rostered service. Despite the particular difficulties reported for ward staff during the transition phase when the pre-Project 2000 students were being phased out and rostered service not yet established, senior managers frequently referred to the situation on the wards as having 'gone quiet' or 'settled down'. Project 2000 was 'simply part of their working life' now. It was just 'there'. In one first-wave Trust, it 'just went on while everything else changed about it'.

The students' supernumerary status was another aspect particularly welcomed by some managers – 'one of the best things done for nursing' in one person's judgement – as was the greater stability of staffing replacement of the student labour force permitted, also seen as 'a major benefit', and enabling 'some wards to move from reacting to issues to being proactive'. When 50-60 per cent of the staffing was on the move every ten weeks, they could 'only do fire-fighting', as one Unit head of nursing put it.

Although there were references to continuing staff anxieties – about the strain of providing supervision at peak times etc – staff were widely report not to feel as threatened by the new students now. The latter sentiment was not universal, however. In one Mental Health Unit, for example, the manager said that although nurses in the Acute division saw the Project 2000 students as 'delightful', in other divisions where resources were very scarce, he had still encountered jealousy and resentment because 'they are overloaded at present; they said they couldn't cope with having to teach these people new skills and also displayed this inverted snobbery towards them as academic people'.

Reservations

As for continuing reservations, by far the most frequent were about the amount of practical experience the new students were getting and whether or not they would be competent and confident to fulfil a staff nurse role when qualified. It was felt that a period of preceptorship as envisaged in PREP (UKCC, 1993) should rectify any deficits in practical or managerial skills, although there were some worries about how that would be resourced. In one Trust hospital, the head of nursing thought that 'serious consideration' could be given to a training grade of salary to enable extra qualified staff to be employed if the Project 2000 students could not be left in charge. However, a decision on that (rumoured elsewhere too) would not be taken until the first students qualified. She and other respondents acknowledged that such worries about the students were purely an assumption: they could prove to be unfounded.

Mental Health Unit managers still had some concerns that CFP students might be getting a distorted picture of the specialism and/or that Branch students might not be equipped with the skills they would need in future services. One manager was also worried about the expectations students had of their future role: 'They seem to expect that psychiatric nursing will be all counselling and psycho-analytical approaches whereas in fact there is a vast amount of continuing care work at present – work with long-term chronically ill patients with dementia, for example, from whom there would be a lack of feedback.'

Optimism

A manager in a Learning Disabilities Unit expressed the sense of greater optimism about Project 2000 which was echoed in several of the second round interviews. He said he had been impressed by the manner of its introduction in his District on the part of both education and service staff. It had not caused major disruption in the Unit and, he felt, it had been done 'very sensitively and very well': five years previously they had thought it would be 'disastrous'.

The Acute Unit manager elsewhere who had formally commended the calibre of the students doing rostered service for the first time – and who cited instances of the students' questioning of established practice having led to that practice being changed – thought that it was **now** when they had been through many of the problems and were beginning to reap positive benefits that their experience would be of particular value to other Districts. He very much wished to see some form of peer group of DNS-level managers like himself where they could share their experience and help others to deal with all the practical issues of implementation, 'because it was all very negative at first, it was very difficult to help people. All we could do was to get our heads down.' Now he said, when they were seeing positive benefits, they could encourage others by telling them that, despite the problems, it was 'worth it in the end'.

The education perspective

The nurse teachers' views

When asked how they viewed the Diploma courses, responses among nurse teachers in 1992 differed from those of the previous interviews. Generally, the feelings of excitement and enthusiasm as staff rose to the initial challenges of Project 2000 had been replaced by a new realism arising from the experience of obstacles and problems which implementation had brought. A member of staff articulated the change in attitude thus: '... I was so taken up with the excitement of it all in the beginning, and Project 2000 was something which seemed full of promise .... Since then I seem to have undergone a period of cynicism – a watershed of adapting. So much water has gone under the bridge since then.'

It was evident across the board that staff still felt they were involved in something which was innovative, unique and worthwhile, but their initial orientation to the changes had been moderated by subsequent experience.

Looking back over the process of Project 2000 implementation, there was a perception amongst many teaching staff that it had been a difficult period of change to manage, and that colleges of nursing had by and large performed well in the circumstances, primarily as a consequence of the tenacity and commitment of staff at all levels. There were some comments pertaining to the rushed timescale of implementation (although to a far lesser extent than prevailed in previous stages of the research), the repercussions of which continued to affect the courses. As one senior member of staff put it: 'We suffered from lack of planning and foresight all the way through it, and this is still going on. They are tinkering with something that won't quite work.'

Nurse teachers were positive about Project 2000 and the progress which had been made so far, but many respondents felt that there was still some way to go. Some members of staff were concerned that the organisational structures evolving in colleges of nursing were not always appropriate. One teacher remarked: '.. the senior managers here still don't know what it is to deliver this course and therefore they are managing something which doesn't exist .. in that respect it causes considerable difficulties for those of us at the bottom.' In one scheme which had repeatedly reorganised over the implementation period, staff felt this had not been helpful. Nurse teachers in two schemes where developmental work for degree schemes and the ENB Higher Award was under way felt that staff's time and attention were being diverted from the Project 2000 issues which would need to be addressed before revalidation.

Speaking on the successes of Project 2000, an often quoted advancement was the opportunity for both teaching and service staff to take their knowledge base further and to advance their educational and professional development. Improved working relationships were remarked upon, between nurse teachers themselves, with colleagues in HE and service, and with students. Teachers welcomed the broader academic base and enhanced academic standards which the Diploma courses offered. They were witnessing the students' progressing through the courses in a different way from those on the old style courses and 'blossoming' in a new educational environment.

116

In terms of areas for development, staff identified a number of issues for Project 2000 courses which remain unresolved. The most common concern was the large student intakes and the difficulties which they posed to the organisation and teaching of the courses as they were currently resourced, and to service. A number of staff referred to problems with CFP: that it did not meet the needs of Mental Health and Learning Disability students; that it was inflexible; and it was too long. One less frequently stated issue was that the absence of a national curriculum and national guidelines on academic standards had produced localised difficulties which could have been avoided, and could lead to a lack of rigour.

Other areas still causing teachers concern were that students were not integrating with HE as had been intended, and that service seemed to be under-resourced in terms of providing adequate systems of supervision. Moreover, in some areas, practice-based staff were still not perceived to be in tune with the Project 2000 philosophy, with the result that the students' practice experience suffered. One senior member of staff was very concerned about this matter: 'When I validated the '82 syllabus the ENB said to me, "Unless you change the attitudes of clinical staff you won't be able to implement this course." And now they've been so careless about this issue with the '92 syllabus.'

In contrast to the interim stage of the research, nurse teachers made far fewer spontaneous comments concerning communication problems. The small number of staff who made points on this topic were reacting to lack of communication about structural changes; the organisation of teaching; and between specific college of nursing or HE sites. Overall, however, communication no longer appeared to feature as an issue for teaching staff respondents in the final interviews.

Reflections of HE staff

HE staff interviewed for a third time in 1992 were also asked to reflect upon the positive outcomes and problems of Project 2000 implementation from their perspective. As would be expected, their responses were, for the most part, focused specifically upon the links with colleges of nursing and, as such, their views are covered in greater depth in Chapter 3. Nevertheless, the general observations of HE staff are included here too, permitting some direct comparison, and occasional contrast, with the perceptions of their nurse education counterparts.

Obviously, the whole perspective from which respondents looked back over the process of implementation differed in the six schemes, depending upon the current state of the links with colleges of nursing, which ranged from full integration to the prospect of complete severance of relations. In the latter case, the HE institution's association with the college of nursing was to be discontinued (and a new HE link established) as a consequence of the continuing rationalisation of nurse education in the region. Inevitably respondents closely involved in the Project 2000 scheme expressed feelings of disappointment and some bitterness about this turn of events, and referred to its demotivating effect on staff generally. The most senior HE respondent, however, looked back on Project 2000 as very interesting, challenging work. He did not believe it had been wasted time, although he shared his staff's sadness that they would not see the fruit of their labours.

Of the five other schemes, full integration of colleges of nursing into HE had already occurred at the time of the final HE interviews in one case and was imminent in another. Moves closer together and better understanding between institutions were also a source of satisfaction to respondents in the other three schemes. This was particularly marked on the site where HE/college senior management relations had been at a very low point and the links generally attenuated almost to breaking point. Although there were still many uncertainties, there had been a dramatic change for the better in relations and there was optimism that the situation was now 'back on the rails'. It was, in one respondent's words, like 'starting again'. In these five schemes, respondents felt that courses were working quite well or, in one site, were satisfied just that it was working, given the huge size of the programme. There was satisfaction that overall, standards were quite good. Even where the link was being discontinued, the courses were seen as 'a good model': the rigorous CNAA validation process had ensured that.

HE staff across the six schemes were very positive about relations with nurse teacher colleagues at grassroots level. Some were pleased about the development opportunities Project 2000 afforded individuals and the academic credibility it gave the nursing profession. There was also acknowledgement of the benefits for HE from contact with enthusiastic nurse teachers who valued academic qualifications – opportunities for collaborative research were mentioned as especially welcome in three schemes – and students who were particularly enjoyable to teach. One (social sciences) lecturer saw it as a very positive development that they, as academics, should extend their knowledge and insights to other more vocationally oriented groups, and learn in turn from the latter's practical application of that knowledge: 'It is useful for them to have academic knowledge brought to bear on the issues they confront, and useful for us to lecture to people who apply themselves practically in the world and can use that knowledge to inform us.'

Asked about the less satisfactory aspects of implementation, respondents in HE, as in colleges of nursing, referred most frequently to the speed of implementation and its consequences. With the exception of the scheme where HE links had been evolving for some years before Project 2000 (the head of the RNMH programme holding a joint appointment based at the HE institution since 1986), respondents in all the other case-study sites had found themselves having to contend with what one person termed 'the legacy of the rush'.

Having had 'to force the pace' of implementation meant that some aspects had not been thought through, and HE respondents in these first schemes reiterated their regrets about not having been involved in the planning process soon enough to influence the structure and content of curricula. One senior HE respondent felt that, in designing and teaching the curriculum, college staff were 'too influenced by educational models': there was 'a lot of unnecessary jargon' which 'precludes thinking in a clear straightforward way'. Respondents looked forward to participation in the process of curriculum review for revalidation. In one of the two largest schemes there was particular concern that, because of the rush, the true costs – and the hidden costs – of implementation to the HE institution, in terms of the staff numbers and staff time required, had not been foreseen.

As for the student numbers, HE respondents in both of the very large schemes shared their college of nursing colleagues' views about all the accommodation and other organisational difficulties these had created. When things went wrong, a respondent in one site said, they were so much more 'visible' when there were so many students. 'The infrastructure is groaning,' a lecturer in the other site observed. There was no educational rationale for teaching a hundred students together, a colleague commented.

Across the six case-study sites, HE staff, like college of nursing staff, referred to the difficulties of bringing together two institutions with two different cultures and two different ways of working, evidenced in both concrete ways (different teaching days and years) and in general approach and philosophy. The management style in colleges of nursing was perceived as more hierarchical. Yet, where college management structures had become 'flatter' and respondents found themselves dealing with several heads of department rather than a single course leader (highly respected individuals with whom they had liaised from the outset), they had felt the loss.

As regards the different teaching hours/terms, there was some appreciation of the pressures nurse teachers were under facing a constant succession of intakes without a break, and in the scheme where integration was imminent, a respondent was pleased that the move would 'liberate them from that drudgery'. In the HE institution where the college of nursing had already integrated, however, the fact that some nurse teachers now appreciated that the HE teaching day (9.0 a.m. - 9.0 p.m.) was not a 'soft number' either was also welcomed.

As for differences in approach and understanding, some were seen as 'teething problems' which had already been worked through or would be in time. Other differences could, it seems, be more deep-seated, for example, differences perceived in ideas about knowledge (the college's apparent tendency to favour pedagogy rather than the free expression of ideas was cited by one HE lecturer) and understanding of research. In one (research-based) institution, research and teaching went 'hand in hand', whereas in the college of nursing, they were perceived to be separate. Nurse teachers' research skills, it was felt, were 'not being fully utilised' or 'built into the curriculum'. Differences in approach to curriculum development were also cited, with respondents in two schemes expressing some unhappiness about curricula being or becoming thematic and nurse-related rather than discipline-based.

Although in two schemes in particular there were references to the 'wariness' or 'mistrust' there had been on both sides for political or historical reasons, the overriding impression conveyed by the HE respondents' reflections on implementation there, as elsewhere, was of satisfaction about the better understanding – and better relations generally – which had been achieved by the third year of the first courses.

The views of principals and course leaders

Principals and course leaders, interviewed in 1991 in all the Demonstration sites, were asked what they perceived as the most and least successful aspects of Project 2000 implementation in their Districts up to that point – roughly the mid-point of the first courses – approaching or shortly after the end of the CFPs (Jowett et al., 1992b). In the final (1992) interviews, they, like service managers and teachers, were posed the same question. But they were also asked if there had been any 'surprises'/unexpected outcomes, and what they felt were the main lessons they had learnt from implementation, from which Districts just embarking upon Project 2000 might benefit.

For respondents in nine schemes (including four of the six case-study sites), the fact that they had succeeded in delivering the new and complex course and 'survived' all the difficulties and demands of the transition period was cited as a major achievement in itself. Some people expressed surprise that their programme was working as well as it was, and satisfaction at the way they had been able to address and resolve problems as they arose in order to achieve that.

But, echoing the 1991 responses, the academic and personal development of both teaching staff and students witnessed in the course of implementation was the particular source of satisfaction mentioned most frequently (in approximately two-thirds of all the interviews). For two principals in case-study sites, another of the most rewarding aspects was the 'spin-off' effect of Project 2000 on service staff development, although there were fewer references to this than was the case in the senior service manager interviews.

The 'huge learning curve' teaching staff had gone through and their growth in confidence as teachers and individuals were widely acknowledged; as was the tremendous amount of work and commitment required of them to mount and deliver the courses altogether. 'They believed they could do it and they have' was one course leader's comment. But it was acknowledged in places that there had been some 'casualties' along the way. For the education staff in some schemes, as for their service colleagues, the amount of change with which they had had to contend had been 'overwhelming'. There were also references to the sense of loss or detachment which some teaching staff had experienced with the large Project 2000 intakes when they no longer had groups of students whom they knew well and followed right through the courses.

Respondents' sense of satisfaction about the students' growth and development – and belief that at the end of three years they would have the 'knowledgeable doers'/'reflective practitioners' Project 2000 aimed to produce – had been reinforced by the positive feedback which they were receiving about the rostered service placements. For the principal in one case-study site, it was 'like music to my ears' because 'the frustrations and irritations are minute, infinitesimal, compared with having new practitioners liberating themselves and liberating their profession in doing so'.

For other respondents too, the calibre of the new students was seen as good for nursing, as it would 'put nursing on the map again'. In one site, the feedback from service was said to be particularly gratifying because it had 'taken so long to come'. With previous student groups who were out nursing straightaway, they had got that kind of response immediately. 'They are a different practitioner', another principal observed, 'and there is growing evidence that the vision of Project 2000 has been achieved.' In that scheme, as elsewhere, the positive response from service about the students' performance had included comments about their ability to see patients in a holistic way, to communicate with them and to be sensitive to their anxieties.

Feedback about the students' community placements was mentioned as a particular source of satisfaction in one case-study site. During their ten weeks based in health centres the students carried a small case-load of up to six carefully selected clients, and letters of praise for the students which the college had received from some of those clients were referred to with pride. Some respondents felt that Project 2000's 'vision' had been achieved in other ways, too: that there was now 'general acknowledgement of the theoretical basis of nursing'; and that the level of the students – and hence the profession – was now accepted as academically credible.

The less satisfactory aspects of implementation cited were many and various. Frequently issues touched upon in these responses overlapped with areas where respondents saw lessons to be learnt and/or matters which they would seek to address on resubmission of their curricula, if they had not already done so (assessment, for example). Some were wider resource or workforce issues discussed elsewhere, such as replacement and funding of rostered service, HE, or other areas, and reducing student numbers and employment opportunities.

The course attendance issue, which was particularly exercising principals and course leaders at the end of the CFP, was mentioned spontaneously far less frequently, reflecting the improved situation widely reported in the Branch. But there were still references in six schemes to the difficulties experienced in realising the concept of student status and striking the right balance 'between getting people to conform and accept responsibility but also allowing them to be students'. Three principals spoke of education staff having initially gone 'overboard' on the HE ethos in the CFP and having been rather '*laissez-faire*' in their approach to attendance. In one case-study site the principal described how they had tried to adopt a full adult model of education with the students from the start (negotiating contracts and the like). But in retrospect, she wondered how many nurse educators themselves were capable of the degree of 'self-actualisation' that had been required.

As at the end of the CFP, there were references across the schemes to all the problems of organisation, logistics and communication (travel and information dissemination/exchange) arising from having large groups of students in multi-site colleges and a multitude of increasingly widespread placement areas. The pressures on accommodation – as well as on teaching staff – of the sheer numbers of students had been felt particularly badly in those schemes with intakes of 100 or more. The principal of one of the two case-study schemes in this category thought that the scale of the room pressures and other practical organisational problems such numbers had created could not have been predicted. The principal of the other such scheme similarly saw accommodation as a major problem area which had not been thought through. Existing premises – multi-sited college bases – had been 'totally wrong for Project 2000'. They had militated against cohesion among students and staff and caused major difficulties for tutors. Even finding somewhere to see their students privately was problematic when offices were shared and there were no small interview rooms.

The organisation and coordination of placements, a huge and complex exercise with such large groups, was also cited as 'a major headache' in several schemes, although computerisation of allocations (as of room bookings) had begun to ease the situation in places. The need for

120

strong administrative support was underlined, such as the senior academic registrar posts created or planned in some sites.

Lessons learnt

When asked about the main lessons learnt from implementation, there was one resounding message from nearly all the Demonstration Districts (all six case-study sites and five of the 'other seven'). Respondents repeatedly emphasised that the **time** needed to plan and to prepare staff – both teaching and practice-based staff – should not be under-estimated. They also acknowledged, with regret, that, because of the rushed start, it was time they in the Demonstration Districts did not have. A typical comment from one course leader was: 'The outstanding lesson for me is, that in order to implement major change, you need to prepare well and you need time to do that – more time than we had.' One principal spoke of the staff sickness rate from 'burnout' having been 'dramatic' during the first year, although since 1991 that had fallen and staff were actually 'smiling again'.

Stressing the need to be very well organised in advance, especially given the numbers of students, another course leader advised: 'Tie up every knot you can see because they will always unravel, and when things go wrong it is very visible because of all these students around.' Everything would take a great deal longer than expected, another principal observed: 'You really unearth an awful lot of unknowns once you start making change.' Principals in two case-study schemes stressed the need for precision as well as time in negotiating with service management about funding and delivering the courses: 'You must be very attentive in working out details ... not take anything for granted.' Respondents felt that the Demonstration Districts' extremely tight time-scale for implementation had particularly put them at a disadvantage in the sense of the limited time they had for preparing and involving everyone concerned – HE staff, practice staff, and nurse teachers.

HE

As described elsewhere, HE input into the planning of the first courses had frequently not been possible in the Demonstration Districts. The need to plan and prepare the ground for the links from the very early stages was stressed. The benefits perceived in terms of having had time to iron out many of the 'senior management culture problems' – and the smoothness generally of the subsequent process of full integration – were reiterated in the case-study site where work on the links had begun as early as 1984.

A general message which principals in two case-study sites wanted to convey to others was not to be frightened of HE, because their anxieties were probably unfounded. They should approach negotiations in a positive way and, in the words of one, 'take risks because at the end of the day they will pay off'. A respondent in the case-study college which had already integrated fully into HE, emphasised the need for nurse educators to negotiate their position clearly both prior to going into HE and afterwards, and to maintain their own 'identity, integrity and autonomy'. For integration to be successful, there had also to be a real need and will for it to happen on both sides.

Practice

Respondents across the schemes re-emphasised that it was crucial for nurse educators to get out to service areas and prepare practice staff thoroughly -preferably **before** the students started. There was acknowledgement that in the Demonstration sites, despite as great an effort as possible having been made in the time available, much of this preparation had to be done as the course went along. One principal spoke of the 'very difficult legacy' schemes could be left with if all the issues of staff development were not sorted out before courses started.

The 'enormous challenge' Project 2000 presented for practice staff could not be underestimated. It was not just for initial preparation that time was needed, but for the continual updating and repetition required because staff changed, failed to retain or understand what they already had been told, and partly because, according to one principal, 'the reality is actually different from what you've told them'. The same principal said that she had learnt from Australian experience that 'you've really got to build in a tremendous amount of time to go back and back', an approach validated by the management of change literature, (e.g. Fullan, 1982).

Some respondents expressed themselves surprised by the amount of misunderstanding there had been among practice-based staff at first, particularly about the concept of supernumeracy, and, occasionally, by the entrenched attitudes still encountered at times. One principal observed: 'It's amazing how long it's taken people to understand what's happening. We mounted the biggest education programme we could, but it still took ages to get through to the profession.' A course leader elsewhere was of the opinion that although there was not actual resistance to Project 2000 within the profession any more, 'people have not actually internalised it' – something he still saw as 'a major issue'. In another view, this would not be overcome altogether until the first Project 2000 qualified nurses were working in practice areas.

Advice respondents proffered to other schemes included recommendations that they 'keep links with service open and honest' and 'invest in supporting the clinical areas'. 'Put in for more tutors than a ratio of 1:15 if you possibly can', one principal said, 'or you won't be able to provide the clinical backup.' A major worry for one respondent was that in the students' third year, when they should be operating at Diploma level, there could be real difficulties in practice-based staff supporting them, both in terms of their own theoretical level and the work pressures they were under – including the demands of HCA training and supervision. He referred to the resentment this could cause among practice-based staff and the attitude: 'I came here to nurse, I didn't come here to teach people'. Yet opportunities for staff development were still limited both financially and in terms of time.

Particular concern was expressed in three schemes about community support and liaison and about what was perceived as the under-resourcing of this area from the outset because of the official view that since students in the community were supernumerary already, extra staff were not needed for Project 2000. One principal's advice was: 'Make sure you have a clear idea about what you're going to do about the community as they are not resourced to cope as a hospital is.' Even in the scheme where the case-load work undertaken by the first students (under supervision) was described as 'a great success', there was still concern about the longer term impact of all the pressures on community services.

The teaching team

Time for teaching staff preparation and development was also considered crucial across the Demonstration sites. There were not only the pressures on nurse teachers to attain degree or higher degree status but the CFP placed 'very great demands' on them to be constantly updating themselves in their specialist areas. One thing a course leader said she had learnt was just how demanding it was academically for staff to be ahead of the students all the time. Yet for another respondent, one of the lessons of Project 2000 implementation was the need to challenge 'the traditional assumption in nurse education that the teacher **should** know more than the students ... because this sits very uneasily with the philosophy of the new course'.

The importance of consulting and involving all staff from the start was also frequently stressed. The principal in one case-study site saw the fact that time pressures had precluded them getting everyone involved as 'a major failure'. While acknowledging the time factor, another respondent was critical of nurse education's record in this respect generally: 'The degree of success of change is influenced by the sense of ownership that people have of the **idea** and the **project**. Colleges of nurse education handle change very badly and I think they are going to do the same thing in relation to going into HE. They are all bound by history, hierarchy and power.'

In one site, however, the course leader attributed what he perceived as the college's successful management of the very difficult transition period to 'the incredible ownership of the course' there had been as a result of managerial delegation of responsibility for the course down to the teaching staff. But elsewhere, both principal and course leader acknowledged independently that they had not got the management of their course right yet in that respect. They were still operating on a traditional `top down' model, whereas they wanted staff to feel able to sort out issues and make changes themselves: 'If they can do it in HE when they have courses with 300 students on them, there is no reason why nurses can't do it.'

Other aspects of good management/leadership necessary to smooth the path of implementation were mentioned also. One principal saw it as essential for college heads to be 'visible' – accessible to support students and staff, with 'a finger on the pulse' and a listening ear attuned to picking up potential sources of friction at an early stage. According to another respondent, good course leadership meant knowing the teaching staff's needs as well as those of the students. It also meant to 'give credit – as you go along'. Without that, overworked staff could become very demotivated and easily 'sink' beneath their load.

Planned changes

The Demonstration Districts' Project 2000 courses had evolved considerably by the time of the final research interviews. It was, in one principal's words, very much 'a living curriculum'. Important changes had been made in such areas as college structures, timetabling and the college day, the length and timing of allocations, and the assessment system. Assessment had presented particular problems, and moves to reduce the number of summative assessments and restructure their timing (to allow adequate time for retakes etc.) had been widely effected or were planned. (As noted elsewhere, schemes differed in the extent to which they had been able to make substantive changes to their assessment procedures in advance of resubmission.)

Asked about the main changes they would make when submitting their curricula for revalidation, respondents not only spoke of addressing problem areas like assessment, but also of making major structural changes to the whole course. Most frequently mentioned were moves towards a greater degree of, or even complete, modularisation of courses within the CATS system, fitting in with the Higher Award. There was felt to be a need to give more emphasis to the adult education approach and to make the course more flexible and student centred via greater use of profiling and individual learning packages. Several respondents saw their present courses as 'over-taught' as well as over-assessed. Other major changes mentioned would be aimed at equalising the time devoted to the Branch specialisms, and the amount of theory time in the CFP and Branch. (One course leader considered the current pattern of 42 teaching weeks in the CFP and only 21 weeks in the Branch to get the students actually up to Diploma level as 'an absolute farce'.)

One message from respondents in several Districts was the need to remember Project 2000 was a **nursing** course. According to one principal, a mistake easily made with new courses (and one made in nursing degree courses too) was to give too much time and emphasis to established academic subjects such as sociology and psychology, and too little to the crux areas of nursing. A desire to see the courses more nursing-related from the outset and 'make the integration of theory and practice more immediate' was expressed in that and other schemes. Otherwise, another principal emphasised, there was a real danger of 'fragmentation' – of ending up with the high-level **separate** courses in sociology, psychology and other subjects, which **added** up to a nursing course, rather than a course which was relevant and integrated from the start.

The question of the timing of the CFP students' first clinical experiences (a contentious subject in places in the early days of implementation) was touched upon in two of the case-study sites. In one case, the course leader was adamant that the students would not be allocated to the clinical areas any earlier in the CFP (as some people had advocated), although greater emphasis would be placed from the start on physiological measurement skills (temperatures, urine analysis and the like) so that the students could relate those to 'health'. In the scheme where the CFP students did not have ward allocations until approximately a year into the course, however, the course leader said that they would now wish to bring in some clinical practice earlier in order to increase the relevance of the theory in the CFP. If students had previously worked as nursing assistants, that was not a problem. But if they came straight from college, they had 'nothing to hang concepts on'. The course leader still felt it was right to have kept the students away from the wards until there was time to prepare the staff and get them used to the students being supernumerary. 'Now attitudes have changed we can probably afford to put them in earlier without going back to the old 'pairs of hands' era ... It was crucial in the beginning to change the culture.'

These final interviews with senior education managers (like the 1992 interviews with service managers) provided evidence that for them Project 2000 was no longer considered something new, but had become an accepted part of life. Other issues – mergers with other colleges and HE and the Higher Award – were now far more pressing. Project 2000 (a term some colleges were not even using any more) was now the established 'norm'. In the concluding words of the principal in one of the case-study sites: 'I can't imagine anything else now.' Across the Demonstration sites there was also evidence of the undiminished enthusiasm of many respondents for the Project 2000 changes and the continuing belief in them, despite the difficulties and the acknowledged mistakes of the early implementation phase. One principal described 1990 as the most difficult year of his career. But the general mood was one of optimism as the first students approached the end of their courses. Typical advice to staff in later schemes was to 'be positive and assume that the course will work, because it does seem to do so'. Or in more eulogistic vein: 'Above all, do what you want to do, make the course what you want it to be. At the end of the day, Project 2000 will be the saviour of the profession.'

Chapter Nine
ISSUES IN IMPLEMENTATION

Introduction

Project 2000 offered an opportunity to reformulate the future of nurse education and nursing practice. It was highly innovative in nature and was the biggest change in nurse education for decades. This research has involved both the documentation of that process of change and the analysis of what has been achieved and how further progress might be made. As stated in Chapter 1, Project 2000 was implemented in a period of massive and continued development in the NHS and was just one factor in the multiplicity of changes with which many of the respondents were having to wrestle. Implementing reform of this magnitude has obviously involved 'teething problems' and the discussion of these, as well as of more substantive points, has peppered the text. This chapter will outline some key findings and then focus on broader issues, many of which are currently under discussion, that need to be addressed as the innovation proceeds. The points are made succinctly here, with further detail provided in the discussion sections in Chapters 3 to 7. The reader is also referred to previous publications which contain both data and analysis from this research and are listed in Appendix 2.

Key findings from the data on the implementation of Project 2000

- There is good cause for optimism, particularly from the perspectives of students *vis-_-vis* their role as qualified staff and of staff whose professional development has been significantly enhanced by the changes. A great many individuals have benefited from the opportunities Project 2000 offers, with clear implications for their enhanced performance as practitioners and educators. Students gained a good deal personally from the course and were eager to utilise their skills in the context of work. There were many instances of academic growth, and a good deal of enthusiasm for further study was expressed by the diplomates. The nurse teachers had, in many instances, gained significantly from their involvement in course development and delivery, and their academic confidence was developing.

- The early data from Project 2000 qualifiers suggest that the principles of the courses have been translated into practice, so that they feel well prepared and are able to identify the advantages of their course.

- It is important to acknowledge the force of change. Nurse education staff, for example, spoke of sessions toward the end of the course, as it had evolved, that bore no relation to those at the start. They were adamant that the students' expectations and behaviour on the course were different from those on previous courses.

- Nurse teachers were put under tremendous pressure to develop and deliver the courses, in situations characterised by poor communication and uncertainty. Their academic credibility was questioned, with many needing to acquire further qualifications within a specified time and there were concerns about their practice-based role. They found their practice liaison duties hard to fulfil, with or without any 'hands on' teaching input (a component of the role about which both education and service continued to have divided views).

- Where links had worked satisfactorily, staff in both HE and nurse education spoke enthusiastically of gains in terms of their professional development, and of the constructive team work that had resulted from collaboration. There was, however, considerable variation across sites, and the experience of some highlighted the potential complexities of such arrangements.

- The speed of implementation undoubtedly affected adversely the quality of the courses, the working environment of many staff and students, and working relationships. The starkest example is of students being removed from courses after failing assessments, the structure and timing of which have since been revised radically.

- Nurse preparation courses, with their explicitly vocational aims, have developed rigid structures with occupational goals paramount. The change to Project 2000, with the potential for an adult-centred focus on learning, and flexibility, required a considerable shift that continues to be developed as implementation progresses. For many staff there is still much room for development.

- The wholesale shift to supernumerary status for Project 2000 students in all areas of nursing for the major part of the three-year courses, and the workforce implications of replacing the former students' substantial contribution to service for that time, represented a massive organisational task for service managers. The 20 per cent rostered service contribution, conceded by the profession as part of the Project 2000 approval agreement, may have cut the costs of replacement, but it clearly did not reduce the amount of work – and upheaval – involved in organisational terms. Effected as it was in the context of the new market economy philosophy in the NHS and the split between purchasers and providers of both services and education, it required new accounting mechanisms and, for managers in some Districts at least, where replacement staff had to be withdrawn and/or replacement monies repaid for the rostered service periods, the performance of financial and workforce 'acrobatics'. Moreover, amid all the changes resulting from the NHS reforms, the whole of the replacement picture had become blurred and confused.

- The assumption that replacement staff who would be permanent would be more efficient than students constantly rotating through practice placements was clearly being called into question. A second assumption (both formed the basis for the Demonstration Districts' replacement staff calculations) that the 20 per cent service contribution of the Project 2000 students would be less efficient than that of their predecessors was being borne out in practice.

- Nurse education staff had strong reservations about the place of the rostered service contribution in an educationally led course, although they acknowledged the benefits of easing the transition from a student to employee. The students themselves underlined the value of those benefits.

- Who would be primarily responsible for the linking and the teaching in practice areas, and how that might best be organised since the phasing out of the clinical teacher has never really been spelled out, and the implementation of Project 2000 has brought this whole issue to the fore again. In the event, most of the practice teaching **was** left to staff in the service areas, although the time for such teaching was much reduced in hospital areas, where placements were short and fragmented and supervisory staff nurses, as well as sisters/charge nurses, assumed increasing managerial responsibilities. In community areas, too, staff were being asked to have a much greater input to pre-registration education at a time when resources were stretched.

- Most hospital areas had obtained some extra staffing by way of replacement for the former students' labour, although little heed was taken of the UKCC's original reminder that 'in calculating the number of qualified staff required ... recognition will need to be given to the time to be spent in teaching' (UKCC, 1986). Community areas had not had

126

any 'replacement' provision, and it is perhaps significant that in the one case-study District which had negotiated some extra community staff and tutor support, the students' community placements, involving supervised case-load work, were seen as a particular 'success story' of Project 2000 implementation.

● There undoubtedly was initial unease (particularly amongst practice-based staff) about what Project 2000 involved, which had an impact on the climate of innovation. Some of the difficulties encountered (particularly of students in the practice areas) highlight the consequences of targeting innovation at the entrants to an occupational group, with only a very limited input to the existing practitioners.

● Although practice-based staff had mostly enjoyed having the students on placement and had developed strategies for sharing the teaching and supervision load, Project 2000 had demanded a great deal of them, particularly of staff nurses, whose role in the, potentially anxiety-provoking, area of formal assessment was greatly enhanced. Not surprisingly some respondents, expecting or already doing Diploma courses in their own time and at their own expense, displayed some resentment of the amount of time they were being asked to put into their 'supervisor' role, when by implication at least, their own level of qualification was not deemed high enough.

Issues and progress

The establishment of an academic framework for nurse education

The Project 2000 reforms were heralded by many within nursing on the grounds that they would have an effect on the status and academic credibility of nursing, and the ways which this has taken place emerged from the current work. While much has been achieved on this dimension of change, pointers for the future include:

● The need to build on diplomates' enthusiasm and commitment. For those with ambitions to undertake further study, the great majority, concerns about the opportunities they would have in reality were expressed.

● The need to address the tensions between the two conflicting course aims, the personal and the vocational. The limited options, in real terms, of both placement and academic experience emphasised the pervasive dominance of 'the course' rather that the individual student.

● The need to encourage the academic achievements and development of nurse education staff, by a variety of means.

● The need to establish what HE could and should provide in the longer term and the extent to which links have been a transitional phase.

The creation of a successful Diploma-level course (Chapter 4)

Again, there is much cause for commendation, although consideration could be given to:

● The rationale for, and system of, monitoring student attendance. There was widespread and troublesome confusion over the meaning of the 4,600 hours laid down for the courses.

● The meaning in practice of student status, with its wider possibilities than just supernumerary placements.

- Different rulings on administrative matters, such as secondment, which resulted in frustration and animosity for students.

- The provision of teaching and study accommodation of the appropriate size and type for students and education staff.

- The course content and structure. There was widespread acknowledgement that it was over-taught and over-assessed. The calls for a more unified course structure, and a clearer elaboration of the principles underpinning it, and the rationale for the chosen content, were pronounced.

- The need to address the very varied educational backgrounds and life experiences of the student intakes so that aspirations for student-centred learning can be realised. Some attempts at 'top-up' sessions or grouping students by educational background in particular subjects have been instituted on some sites but such efforts fell short of what is required of a programme whose focus is individual need and progress.

- The frequently *ad hoc* personal support system for students currently in place. The limited development of sustained academic encounters with staff in the third year suggested that students' potential may not be being realised in that aspect of the courses. Given that named mentors played such a limited role in ensuring that students' placement experiences were satisfactory (they were largely only valued as a 'safety net' when problems arose), the lack of any rigorous scrutiny of their individual learning path is worthy of consideration.

- The need to have **a common** foundation rather than one that was so **Adult** nursing-focused.

- Where to locate skills-based work, a dilemma that reflects the contradictions between the principles of the course in the early stages and the practicalities of students being out on placements where the ability to lift patients or measure blood pressures, for example, would smooth their placement experience

- The need to clarify both the personal tuition and practice-based roles of nurse teachers (as discussed by the RCN, 1993).

Student nurse replacement (Chapter 6)

Managing the service personnel element of implementation was a formidable task, and the future debate will need to address:

- The significant use of bank and agency staff as replacement for student labour, even (in some areas) when Project 2000 students were rostered.

- The reality that the aspects of rostered service most prized (longer, more substantial placements, on which students worked full shifts and were part of the team) could – and did – exist without the students' official inclusion in the staffing numbers.

- The option of making students supernumerary to staffing establishments throughout the three years of their preparation, which would give *de facto* recognition to a situation already obtaining in many areas of the Demonstration sites. Were this to happen, it would not mean that they would – or would want to – contribute less, just as conversely, their inclusion in staffing numbers, when rostered, did not have to mean neglect of their educational objectives. Nor would this necessarily prove more expensive, given the costs of the continuing use of extra bank/agency staff, and of cumbersome recharge mechanisms and accounting procedures in the students' third year.

Responsibility for student supervision (Chapter 6)

Although there was much positive feedback from staff and students about the practice placements, areas of (sometimes considerable) concern included:

- The substantial pressures on practice-based staff to gain further qualifications, supervise students, increase their management responsibilities and deliver patient care in a changing service, mean that they too need a sound, facilitative support structure and a source of educational help and advice readily available in the practice areas. Models for such support roles already exist in the teacher-practitioner posts or other change agent/nurse consultant-type posts combining practical and educational expertise, or indeed in the specialist/advanced practitioner roles integral to both Project 2000 (UKCC, 1986) and PREP (UKCC, 1990) proposals. With the disappearance of senior nurses from uniprofessional management posts, the need is even greater. It seems increasingly unrealistic to regard student supervision and assessment as an activity to be 'tagged on' to the existing full-time workload of already over-stretched practitioners. Some recognition should be made in resource terms, of the time needed for supervision and assessment, and for the preparation and continuing support of supervisors themselves.

- The realisation of the magnitude of the task of community liaison with all the costs and complexities of negotiating, preparing and monitoring placements (NHS and non-NHS). For education staff, like service staff, it was unrealistic to expect such liaison to be done by (often sole) tutors, just as an 'add on' to all their other responsibilities. Special 'coordinator' posts, where funded, are reported to have proved their worth. The appointment of community-trained staff to college establishments has also contributed to liaison and understanding, and the allocation of community 'link' tutors to specific localities/health centres has been another valued innovation.

- The need for innovatory structures to promote greater sharing of scarce supervision and training resources. Orr (1988) suggested practice/research centres linking schools of nursing, HE and FE and community services as a way of operationalising community nursing experience within a Project 2000 framework.

Numbers of nursing staff

College principals interviewed in 1992 reported healthy recruitment, with more, and better qualified, applicants for Project 2000 courses or at least for Adult and Child Branches. Mental Health and Learning Disability Branches were traditionally slower to recruit. But at the same time, decreases in staff turnover, attributed mainly to the combined effects of the recession and clinical grading, had resulted in reduced intakes in all but the Child Branch, where regional and national shortages of RSCN nurses had dictated increases. In contracting Mental Health and Learning Disabilities hospital services, the need for redeployment of existing staff was also becoming more pressing. Reservations remained about:

- The reliability – and short-sightedness – of the annual demand forecasts of Trusts and directly managed Units on which regional workforce requirements were based. There was concern that the implications of the three-year time delay built into nurse education were not being taken fully into account; nor the growing demands for qualified nurses within the private sector – the destination of eight of the 68 newly qualified nurses in the study sample. The National Audit Office (1992) drew attention to the need for regions to develop links with the private sector in making their contracting arrangements.

- Reductions in the numbers of Learning Disability Branch students, raising questions which it is hoped will be resolved, though the process initiated as a consequence of the Department of Health's recent consultation with the profession about the future form this specialty's preparation should take.

Project 2000 aimed to produce skilled flexible practitioners able to adapt to the changing demands of the health service in the 1990s and beyond. In the spirit of the NHS reforms, it also offered a means of 'making maximum use of a decreasing level of resources in the most efficient and cost-effective way and where possible without expensive retraining' (James and Jones, 1992). While it is widely accepted that the valuable resource of registered nurses will need to be used more effectively in future, there are still different conceptions of how this should be realised, and of the role of support staff (many also qualified, vocationally, for the first time), with which the question is intertwined. As Robinson et al. (1989) observed before Project 2000 got under way, 'the debate about the health care assistant disguises a debate about the future of nursing itself'.

One vision is of registered nurses freed by auxiliary staff to concentrate on delivering patient care, with ward managers having key responsibility for defining and delimiting support roles. Recent research evidence of the effectiveness of qualified nursing care in the Acute sector has been welcomed by the profession as supporting this view (Carr-Hill et al., 1992). The other prospect envisioned is of an increasingly highly educated but dwindling cadre of registered nurses becoming the managers of care delivered primarily by support staff. Most senior managers in the study, both nurse and non-nurse managers, saw the future in the latter terms, and evidence from the 1992 practice-based staff interviews of the continuing downward delegation of managerial responsibilities, removing both ward managers and staff nurses further from direct patient (and student) contact, confirmed it. Most respondents regretted the changes, however, and certainly there was little evidence among the newly qualified Project 2000 nurses of any desire to move away from a direct patient care role.

The undoubted successes of the Diploma course were evident from this study of the very first intake. Although it was widely accepted that considerable problems had been encountered, there was also broad agreement about the viability and desirability of the changes Project 2000 promised. There have been extensive staff development and academic growth, major changes in thinking about students' needs and responsibilities, and sustained commitment to addressing the deficiencies acknowledged to exist in previous forms of nurse preparation. The enthusiasm and optimism of many of the new diplomates should not be underestimated, and it is largely through their efforts that the aspirations for Project 2000 will be realised. They need to work in a system where their enthusiasm for change will be fostered and their plans for sustained development will be encouraged.

References

ADELMAN, C. and ALEXANDER, R.J. (1982). *The Self-Evaluating Institution – Practice and Principles in the Management of Educational Change.* London: Methuen.

ATHLONE REPORT. MINISTRY OF HEALTH (1938). *Interim Report of the Inter-departmental Committee Nursing Services.* London: Ministry of Health.

AUDIT COMMISSION (1991). *The Virtue of Patients: Making Best Use of Ward Nursing Resources.* London: HMSO

BECKETT, C. (1984). 'Student status in nursing – a discussion of the status and how it affects training', *Journal of Advanced Nursing,* **9**, 363-74.

BIRCUMSHAW, D. and CHAPMAN, C.M. (1988). 'A follow-up of the graduates of the three-year post-registration Bachelor of Nursing degree course of the University of Wales', *Journal of Advanced Nursing,* **13**, 4, 520-24.

BOND, M. (1992). *Nurse Training for Mothers.* Health Services Research Unit, Occasional Paper No. 3. Warwick: University of Warwick.

BRION, M. (1989). 'Evaluation - help or hindrance?', *NAFTHE Journal,* May/June, 24-5.

BURNARD, P. (1990). 'The student experience: adult learning and mentorship revisited', *Nurse Education Today,* **10**, 349-54.

CAHOON, M.C. (Ed) (1987). *Recent Advances in Nursing – Research Methodology.* London: Longman.

CARR-HILL, R., DIXON, P., GIBBS, I., GRIFFITHS, M., HIGGINS, M., McCAUGHAN, D. AND WRIGHT, K. (1992). *Skill Mix and the Effectiveness of Nursing Care.* York: University of York, Centre for Health Economics.

CHARLWOOD, J. (1993). 'The challenge of higher education.' In: DOLAN, B. (Ed) *Project 2000 – Reflection and Celebration.* London: Scutari Press.

CICOUREL, A.V. (1964). *Method and Measurement in Sociology.* New York: Free Press.

COUNCIL FOR NATIONAL ACADEMIC AWARDS/ENGLISH NATIONAL BOARD FOR NURSING, MIDWIFERY AND HEALTH VISITING (1992). *Additional Guidelines for the Development of Pre-registration Nursing Courses Leading to Parts 12-15 of the Professional Register and the DipHE.* London: CNAA/ENB.

COLLINS, S. (1990). 'The ENB Pilot Schemes: how plans have become reality' (Occasional Paper), *Nursing Times,* **86**, 31, 30-3.

CROWTHER REPORT. MINISTRY OF EDUCATION. CENTRAL ADVISORY COUNCIL FOR EDUCATION. (1959). *Fifteen to Eighteen.* London: HMSO.

DAVIS, F. (1975). 'Professional socialisation as subjective experience: the process of doctrinal conversion among student nurses.' In: COX, C. and MEAD, A. (Eds) *A Sociology of Medical Practice.* London: Collier-MacMillan

DAVIES, B., KEYSER, D. and PHILLIPS, R. (1992). Draft Interim Report - The Practitioner - Teacher: a study in the Introduction of Project 2000 in Wales. Report prepared for Advisory Group and Department of Health.

DEPARTMENT OF HEALTH (1989a). 'Personnel, Project 2000, Student Bursaries' Health Notice', HN (**89**)11, June. London: DoH.

DEPARTMENT OF HEALTH (1989b). 'Project 2000, Student Bursaries.' Letter to General Managers, EL (**89**) P/165, 5 October. London: DoH.

DEPARTMENT OF HEALTH (1989c). *Project 2000 – Checklist of Issues to be Considered in Drawing Up Implementation Plans.* London: DoH.

DEPARTMENT OF HEALTH (1990). *National Health Service and Community Care Act.* Chapter 19. London: HMSO.

DEPARTMENT OF HEALTH AND SOCIAL SECURITY (1988). Letter to the UKCC from John Moore, Secretary of State for Health and Social Security, 20 May.

DODD, A.N. (1973). Towards an understanding of nursing. Unpublished PhD thesis, University of London.

DOLAN, B. (1993). 'Reflection and celebration.' In DOLAN, B. (Ed) *Project 2000 – Reflection and Celebration.* London: Scutari Press.

ELKAN, R. and ROBINSON, J. (1991). *The Implementation of Project 2000 in a District Health Authority: the Effect on the Nursing Service.* An interim report. Nottingham: University of Nottingham, Department of Nursing and Midwifery Studies.

ELKAN, R., HILLMAN, R. and ROBINSON, J. (1992). *The implementation of Project 2000 in a District Health Authority: the Effect on the Nursing Service.* A second interim report. Nottingham: University of Nottingham, Department of Nursing and Midwifery Studies.

ENGLISH NATIONAL BOARD FOR NURSING, MIDWIFERY AND HEALTH VISITING (1988). *Changes in the Organisational Arrangements, within or between Health Authorities and Centres of Higher and Advanced Further Education.* Circular, 13/APS. London: ENB.

ENGLISH NATIONAL BOARD FOR NURSING, MIDWIFERY AND HEALTH VISITING (1989). *Preparation of Teachers, Practitioners/Teachers, Mentors and Supervisors in the Context of Project 2000.* London:ENB.

ENGLISH NATIONAL BOARD FOR NURSING, MIDWIFERY AND HEALTH VISITING (1992/93). *Annual Report.* London: ENB.

ENGLISH NATIONAL BOARD FOR NURSING, MIDWIFERY AND HEALTH VISITING (1993a). *Framework and Higher Award for Continuing Professional Education for Nurses, Midwives and Health Visitors.* London: ENB.

ENGLISH NATIONAL BOARD FOR NURSING, MIDWIFERY AND HEALTH VISITING (1993b). *Regulations and Guidelines for the Approval of Institutions and Courses April 1993.* London: ENB.

FIELD, P.A. and MORSE, J.M. (1985). *Nursing Research – the Application of Qualitiative Approaches.* London: Croom Helm.

FINCH, J. (1986). *Research and Policy – the Uses of Qualitative Methods in Social and Educatonal Research.* London: Falmer.

FRENCH, P. (1989). An assessment of the pre-registration preparation of nurses as an educational experience. Unpublished PhD thesis, University of Durham.

FRETWELL, J.E. (1985). *Freedom to Change - the Creation of a Ward Learning Environment.* London: Royal College of Nursing.

FULLAN, M. G. (1982). *The Meaning of Educational Change.* New York: Teacher's College Press.

FULLAN, M. G. (1991). *The New Meaning of Educational Change.* London: Cassell.

GERRISH, C. (1990). 'Fumbling along', *Nursing Times,* **86**, 30, 35-7.

GIBBS, I. and RUSH, B. (1987). 'Higher education: the coping stone of nursing education?' *Journal of Advanced Nursing,* 12, 1-11.

GREAT BRITAIN. STATUTES (1992). *Further and Higher Education Act 1992.* Chapter 13. London: HMSO.

HAMILTON, D. (Ed) (1977). *Beyond the Numbers Game.* London: Macmillan.

HOOPER, J. (1989). 'The future beckons', *Nursing Standard,* **20**, 3, 25-8.

HORSBURGH, M. (1989). 'Graduate nurses' adjustment to initial employment: natural fieldwork', *Journal of Advanced Nursing,* **14**, 610-17.

HOWARD, J.M. and BROOKING, J.I. (1987). 'The career paths of nursing graduates from Chelsea College, University of London', *Int. J. Nurs. Stnd.,* **24**, 3, 181-9.

JAMES, J. and JONES, D. (1992). 'Education for the future: meeting changing needs.' In: SLEVIN, O. and BUCKENHAM, M. (Eds) *Project 2000: The Teachers Speak.* Edinburgh: Campion Press.

JOWETT, S., WALTON, I. and PAYNE, S. (1991). *The NFER Project 2000 Research – an Introduction and some Interim Issues.* Interim Paper 2. Slough: National Foundation for Educational Research in England and Wales.

JOWETT, S. (1992). 'Project 2000 – research on its implementation', *Nursing Times.* (Occasional Paper), **88**, 26, 40-3.

JOWETT, S., WALTON, I. and PAYNE, S. (1992a). *Early Perspectives from the Students.* Interim Paper 5. Slough: National Foundation for Educational Research in England and Wales.

JOWETT, S., WALTON, I. and PAYNE, S. (1992b). *Implementing Project 2000 – an Interim Report.* Slough: National Foundation for Educational Research in England and Wales.

JUDGE REPORT. ROYAL COLLEGE OF NURSING (1985). *The Education of Nurses: a New Dispensation.* London: RCN.

JUDGE, H. (1986) 'A college education?' *Nursing Times,* **82**, 29, 31-2.

133

KERSHAW, B. (1993). Foreword in DOLAN, B. (Ed) *Project 2000 – Reflection and Celebration.* London: Scutari Press.

KIRKPATRICK, D. (1985). *How to Manage Change Effectively.* London: Jossey-Bass.

LATHLEAN, J. (1987). 'Are you prepared to be a staff nurse?' *Nursing Times,* **83**, 36, 25-7.

LATHLEAN, J. (1989). *Policy Making in Nurse Education.* Oxford: Ashdale Press.

LEININGER, M.M. (1987). 'Importance and use of ethno methods: ethnography and ethnonursing research.' In: CAHOON, M.C. (Ed) *Recent Advances in Nursing – Research Methodology,* (12-36). London: Longman.

LEONARD, A. and JOWETT, S. (1990). *Charting the Course: a Study of the Six ENB Pilot Schemes in Pre-registration Nurse Education.* Slough: National Foundation for Educational Research in England and Wales.

Le VAR, R. (1988). 'Vital Links' *Nursing Times,* **84**, 45, 73-4.

LINDOP, E. (1989). 'Industrial stress and its relationship to termination of nurse training' *Nurse Education Today,* **9**, 172-9.

LUKER, K., CARLISLE, C. and KIRK, S. (1993). *The Evolving Role of the Nurse Teacher in the Light of Educational Reforms.* Second Interim Report prepared for the ENB. Liverpool: University of Liverpool, Department of Nursing.

MELIA, K. (1981). Students nurses' accounts of their work and training: a qualitative analysis. Unpublished PhD thesis, University of Edinburgh.

MELIA, K. (1982). ' "Tell it as it is" – qualitative methodology and nursing research: understanding the student nurse's world', *Journal of Advanced Nursing,* **7**, 327-35.

MURNAGHAN, T. and MURNAGHAN, P. (1990). 'Teaching for change', *Nursing Times,* **86**, 24, 40-1.

NATIONAL AUDIT OFFICE (1992). *Nursing Education: Implementation of Project 2000 in England.* London: HMSO.

NHS MANAGEMENT BOARD (1988). 'Project 2000 Implementation.' Chief Executive Letter to General Managers, 6 October, EL **(99)**MB /166. London: Department of Health.

NHS MANAGEMENT EXECUTIVE (1989). *Education and Training. Working Paper 10.* London: Department of Health.

NHS MANAGEMENT EXECUTIVE (1990). 'Health Care Assistants.' Chief Executive letter to General Managers, EL(MB)**90/5**, 10 January. London: Department of Health.

NHS MANAGEMENT EXECUTIVE (1991a). 'Project 2000 Implementation – 1991/92.' Letter, 3 September. London: Department of Health.

NHS MANAGEMENT EXECUTIVE (1991b). 'Project 2000.' Letter to General Managers, EL(**91**)83, June. London: Department of Health.

NHS MANAGEMENT EXECUTIVE (1993). Letter to Regional General Managers, EL (93) 9, 26 January, London: Department of Health.

NATIONAL BOARD FOR NURSING, MIDWIFERY AND HEALTH VISITING FOR NORTHERN IRELAND (1990). *Supervision of Students*. Occasional Paper, OP/NB/2/90. Belfast: NINB.

O'NEILL, E., MORRISON, H. and McEWEN, A. (1993). *Professional Socialisation and Nurse Education: an Evaluation*. Belfast: School of Education.

ORR, J. (1988) 'Project 2000: designing the way forward', *Nursing Times*, **84**, 37, 46-7.

ORR, J. and HALLETT, C. (1991). *The Provision of Community Experience for Project 2000 Students*. An Interim Report for the ENB. University of Manchester: Department of Nursing.

OWEN, G.M. (1988). 'For better, for worse: nursing in higher education', *Journal of Advanced Nursing*, **13**, 3-13.

PARLETT, M. (1972). 'Evaluating innovations in teaching.' In: BUTCHER, H.J. and RUDD, E. (Eds) *Contemporary Problems in Higher Education*. London: McGraw Hill.

PARLETT, M. and HAMILTON, D. (1972). *Evaluation as illumination: a New Approach to the Study of Innovatory Programs*. Occasional Paper 9, Edinburgh: Centre for Research in the Educational Sciences, University of Edinburgh.

PLATT REPORT. ROYAL COLLEGE OF NURSING. COMMITTEE ON NURSE EDUCATION (1964). *A Reform Of Nursing Education*. London: RCN.

POLIT, D.F. and HUNGLER, B.P. (1987). *Nursing Research: Principles and Methods*. Philadelphia: Lippincott.

THE POLYTECHNICS AND COLLEGES FUNDING COUNCIL (1992). *Widening Participation in Higher Education*. Information Document. Bristol: PCFC.

PROCTER, S. (1989). 'The functioning of nursing routines in the management of a transient workforce', *Journal of Advanced Nursing*, **14**, 180-9.

PROJECT 2000 IMPLEMENTATION GROUP (1989). *Project 2000 – a Guide to Implementation*. London: Department of Health.

REID, N.G., NELLIS, P. and BOORE, J. (1987). 'Graduate nurses in Northern Ireland: their career paths, aspirations and problems', *Int. J. Nurs. Stnd.*, **24**, 3, 215-25.

REINKEMEYER, M.H. (1966). The limited impact of basic university programs in nursing. Unpublished Ph.D thesis, University of Berkeley, California.

ROBINSON, J. (1986). 'Through the minefield and into the sun?', *Senior Nurse*, **4**, 6, 7-9.

ROBINSON, J. (1991). *The First Year: Experiences of a Project 2000 Demonstration District*. Suffolk: The Suffolk and Great Yarmouth College of Nursing and Midwifery/The Suffolk College.

ROBINSON, J., STILWELL, J., HAWLEY, C. and HEMPSTEAD, N. (1989). *The Role of the Support Worker in the Ward Health Care Team*. Warwick: University of Warwick, Nursing Policies Studies Centre.

ROGERS, C. (1983). *Freedom to Learn for the 80's*. Ohio: Charles E. Merrill.

ROYAL COLLEGE OF NURSING (1993). *Teaching in a Different World: an RCN Discussion Document*. London: RCN.

SCHATZMAN, L. and STRAUSS, A.L. (1973). *Field Research: Strategies for a Natural Sociology.* Englewood Cliffs NJ: Prentice-Hall.

SHAND, M. (1987). 'Unreasonable expectations?', *Nursing Times,* **83**, 36, 28-30.

SHEEHAN, J. (1986). 'The education connection: the higher education provision for nursing', *Nurse Education Today*, **6**, 145-51.

SINCLAIR, H.C. (1987). 'Graduate nurses in the United Kingdom: myth and reality', *Nurse Education Today,* **7**, 24-29.

SMITHERS, K. and BIRCUMSHAW, D. (1988). 'The student experience of undergraduate education: the relationship between academic and clinical learning environments', *Nurse Education Today,* **8**, 347-53.

UNITED KINGDOM CENTRAL COUNCIL FOR NURSING, MIDWIFERY AND HEALTH VISITING. (1985). *Project 2000, Facing the Future,* Educational Policy Advisory Committee, Project Paper 6. London: UKCC.

UNITED KINGDOM CENTRAL COUNCIL FOR NURSING, MIDWIFERY AND HEALTH VISITING. (1986). *Project 2000: a New Preparation for Practice.* London: UKCC.

UNITED KINGDOM CENTRAL COUNCIL FOR NURSING, MIDWIFERY AND HEALTH VISITING. (1987). *Project 2000 – the Final Proposals.* Project Paper 9. London: UKCC.

UNITED KINGDOM CENTRAL COUNCIL FOR NURSING, MIDWIFERY AND HEALTH VISITING. (1990). *The Report of the Post-Registration Education and Practice Project.* London: UKCC.

UNITED KINGDON CENTRAL COUNCIL FOR NURSING, MIDWIFERY AND HEALTH VISITING. (1993). Registrar's Letter 1/1993 CJR/MJW/CJA, 4 January, London: UKCC.

WATTS, G. (1992). 'Implementing Project 2000: the need for evaluation and review.' In: SLEVIN, O. and BUCKENHAM, M. (Eds) *Project 2000: the Teachers Speak.* Edinburgh: Campion Press.

WELSH NATIONAL BOARD FOR NURSING, MIDWIFERY AND HEALTH VISITING. (1991). *Mentors, Preceptors and Supervisors: their place in Nursing, Midwifery and Health Visitor Education.* Cardiff: WNB.

WHITE, E., RILEY, E., DAVIES, S. and TWINN, S. (1993). *A Detailed Study of the Relationship between Teaching, Support, Supervision and Role Modelling in Clinical Areas, within the Context of Project 2000 Course.* Report presented to the ENB by King's College, London and University of Manchester.

WHITE, M., and COBURN, D. (1977). 'The trials, tribulations and triumphs of curriculum change', *Nursing Outlook,* October, 644-9.

WOOD REPORT. MINISTRY OF HEALTH (1947). *Report of the Interdepartmental Working Party on the Recruitment and Training of Nurses.* London: HMSO.

YIN, R. (1984). *Case Study Research – Design and Methods.* Beverly Hills: Sage.

SCHEME		A	B	C	D	E	F
GEOGRAPHICAL LOCATION		South East	North East	South East	South West	South East (Inner city)	North West
QUALIFICATION OFFERED		First level nursing qualification and Diploma in Higher Education (Nursing Studies)	First level nursing qualification and Diploma in Higher Education	First level nursing qualification and Diploma in Nursing Studies	First level nursing qualification and Diploma of Higher Education in Nursing Studies	First level nursing qualification and Diploma of Nursing in Higher Education	First level nursing qualification and Diploma in Higher Education (Nursing Studies)
BRANCHES OFFERED	Adult	✓	✓	✓	✓	✓	✓
	Child	—	✓	✓	✓	✓	—
	Learning Disability	Offered with one annual intake from first intake (October) onwards	—	Offered with one annual intake from second intake (April) onwards	Offered with one annual intake from second intake (April) onwards	Offered with one annual intake from third intake (September) onwards	Up to Jan 1991
	Mental Health	✓	✓	✓	✓	✓	✓
DATE OF FIRST INTAKE OF THE PROJECT 2000 COURSE		October 1989	January 1990	October 1989	September 1989	September 1989	January 1990
ANNUAL NUMBER OF INTAKES		3	3	2 (From October 1990, one of the two intakes includes 14 students taking a 4-year part-time course)	2	2	2

SCHEME	A	B	C	D	E	F
MONTHS OF ANNUAL INTAKES	February June October	January May September	April October	April September	January September	March September
NUMBER OF STUDENTS IN FIRST INTAKE BY BRANCH (NUMBER OF PLACES AVAILABLE IN BRACKETS) — Adult	42 (42)	73 (75)	48 (48)	93 (96)	45 (45)	46 (45)
Child	—	12 (12)	9 (12)	—	15 (15)	—
Mental Handicap	7 (7)	—	—	—	—	10 (15)
Mental Health	9 (9)	15 (13)	10 (12)	14 (14)	—	16 (15)
TOTAL	58 (58)	100 (100)	67 (72)	107 (110)	60 (60)	72 (75)
CHARACTERISTICS OF FIRST STUDENT INTAKE — % Entrants on DC Test	34	2	37	8	0	38
% Aged 26 and over	17	18	36	22	8	31
% Male Students	20	12	12	8	7	21
% Afro-Caribbean/Asian Origin	1	0	3	0	7	4
TYPE OF INSTITUTION OF HIGHER EDUCATION (in 1989)	College of Higher Education	Polytechnic	University	Polytechnic	Polytechnic	College of Higher Education

SCHEME	A	B	C	D	E	F
FORMAL STATUS OF COLLEGE OF NURSING IN RELATION TO INSTITUTION OF HIGHER EDUCATION	1989 Associate Department status 1991/2 Two schools within Faculty of Health and Social Studies.	1991/2 Associate College	1989 Associate Department status 1991/2 Accredited Institute	1989 Associate Department status 1991/2 A School within the Faculty of Humanities and Social Science	Under negotiation	1989 Associate Department status. All CFP teaching carried out in College Campus buildings Links ceased September 1992
QUANTITY OF HIGHER EDUCATION TEACHING INPUT TO CFP FOR FIRST INTAKE	364 hours	8 hours Information Technology (IT) plus occasional lectures	200 hours	613 hours	Occasional lectures (precise number not available)	One whole term teaching equivalent
ORGANISATION AND SITE OF HIGHER EDUCATION TEACHING INPUT IN CFP FOR FIRST INTAKE	Normally one day per week at College of Higher Education	IT at Polytechnic. Occasional lectures at College of Nursing	Bulk of input at University for three days per week in first six months	Normally one day per week at Polytechnic	Occasional lectures usually at College of Nursing	15-18 hours weekly on a sessional basis. All course teaching (including nurse teachers input) carried out at College of Higher Education
HIGHER EDUCATION STAFF'S MAIN TEACHING INPUT IN CFP FOR FIRST INTAKE	Social science Biological science Information Technology Management	Biological Science Social science Information Technology Law Research	Social science Biological science Law Behavioural science	Social science Biological science Behavioural science	Biological science	Social science Biological science Behavioural science

139

SCHEME	A	B	C	D	E	F

COMPONENTS OF THE CFP	1. Individual in society.
	2. Systematic care.
	3. Health promotion.
	4. Research.
	5. Professional development
	6. Management.
		1. Health.
		2. Ill Health.
		3. Maternity.
		4. Child Care.
		5. Mental handicap
		6. Mental health
		7. Adult care
		  a) Critical care
		  b) Acute care
		  c) Continuing care
		8. Consolidation
			1. Introductory component and lifestyles.
			2. Maintaining health and preventing ill health.
			3. Learning to care.
				1. Nursing studies
				2. Nursing practice
				3. Applied health studies
				4. Science applied to nursing
				5. Behavioural science
				6. Social science
				7. Information technology in nursing
					1. The art and science of nursing
					2. Development and function of the individual
					3. The individual and society
					4. Ethics and politics
						1. Life science
						2. Psychology
						3. Sociology
						4. Health studies
						5. Nursing

SUMMATIVE ASSESSMENT DURING THE CFP — **Second Quarter**	Environmental study Unseen exam on themes covered so far		Lifestyles project. Unseen exam in biological, social and behavioural aspects of course	Laboratory reports. Neighbourhood study. Behavioural and social science assignments. Nursing studies and nursing practice exams	Unseen exam in biological science. Seen essay on parts 1,3 and 4 of CFP	Nursing studies essay. Unseen exam in biological sciences.
Third Quarter	Child-centred study Micro-teaching package	Unseen exam in maternity, child care, mental health and mental handicap.	Health network seminar paper		Health Education project	Social and behavioural sciences essays. Health studies seminar paper
Fourth Quarter	Nursing care study Psycho-social study	Neighbourhood study. Open book type exam in multi-perspective concepts of health and ill-health	Nursing models essay	Nursing Health Assessment Open Exam	Neighbourhood study. Unseen exam in all components of CFP	Written assignments in all 5 CFP subjects. Unseen exam in nursing studies. Unseen exam in the 4 other CFP components.

SCHEME	A	B	C	D	E	F
First Quarter	BONDY* assessment used throughout	Formative assessment of skills on all placements		Summative assessment of skills	Summative assessment of communication, comforting and assessing skills	Formative assessment of early development of skills
Second Quarter						Summative assessment of early development of skills
Third Quarter			Formative and summative assessment of inter-personal, assessment, planning, implementing and evaluating skills		Formative assessment of developing skills	Formative assessment of developing skills
Fourth Quarter	*BONDY, K.N. (1983) 'Criterion-referenced definitions for rating scales in clinical evaluation.' *Journal of Nursing Education*, 22, 9, 376-382.	Formative assessment of skills on critical care placements. Summative assessment of skills on acute and continuing care placements		Summative assessment of skills	Summative assessment of communication, comforting, assessing, planning, implementing and evaluating skills	Summative assessment of developing skills

ASSESSMENT OF PRACTICE DURING THE CFP

141

SCHEME	QUANTITY OF HIGHER EDUCATION TEACHING INPUT TO BRANCH FOR FIRST INTAKE	ORGANISATION AND SITE OF HIGHER EDUCATION TEACHING INPUT IN BRANCH FOR FIRST INTAKE	HIGHER EDUCATION STAFF'S MAIN TEACHING INPUT IN BRANCH FOR FIRST INTAKE
A	119 hours	One week preparation on 'old' HE site. Input into the one day a week in college throughout. Various sites	Information Technology Management Social science
B	5 hours for Adult Branch Occasional sessions for other Branches	College of nursing sites	Employment Law
C	None for Adult Branch Mental Health - 15 hours Mental Handicap - 12 hours	College of nursing site	Social sciences Life sciences (bio-chemistry and physiology top-ups)
D	189 hours	Input into 4 week block at start of Branch and then 1 or 2 days in the college of nursing each week for the first 9 months. All on college of nursing sites.	Life sciences Behavioural science Social science
E	None	–	–
F	None	–	–

COMPONENTS OF THE BRANCH PROGRAMMES (FOR FIRST INTAKES)

SCHEME	A	B	C	D	E	F
	Adult, Mental Health and Learning Disability 1. Individual in society 2. Promotion of Health 3. Systematic care 4. Management in Nursing 5. Nursing Research 6. Professional Development in Nursing	**Adult** 1. Theory and Practice of Nursing 2. Biological science 3. Psychology 4. Communication 5. Health and Health Service Studies 6. Professional and Educational Studies **Mental Health** 1. Patient care 2. Elderly clients 3. Aetiology 4. Management of Care 5. Consolidation **Child** 1. Biosocial and Biological Sciences 2. Psychology 3. Sociology 4. Theory and Practice of Nursing 5. Communication Studies 6. Health and Health Science Studies 7. Professional and Educational Studies	**Adult** 1. Approaches to care across the Lifespan 2. The Process of Nursing 3. Managing Care **Mental Health** 1. Potentials 2. Crises 3. Interventions **Learning Disability** 1. Supporting valued lifestyles within the Community 2. Towards Developing Independence 3. Management of Change - self, client, service	**Adult** 1. Models of Methodology in Adult Nursing 2. Health Promotion 3. Nursing People as they grow older 4. Rehabilitation and Continuity of Care 5. Law and Ethics 6. Quality, Standards and Evaluation 7. Research application in Adult nursing 8. Psychology of Adult health and illness 9. Adult health and society 10. Social Policy 11. Nature, cause and remediation of disease 12. Nutrition **Mental Health** 1. Self and Psyche 2. Psyche under Threat 3. Conceptual Framework 4. Discriminatory Models 5. Clinical Case-work	**Adult** 1. The art and science of nursing 2. Development and function of the individual 3. The individual and society 4. Ethos and Politics in Nursing **Child** As above, with the focus on the specialist client group - children	**Adult** 1. Life science 2. Psychology 3. Sociology 4. Health Studies 5. Nursing **Mental Health** 1. Nursing 2. Psychology 3. Sociology 4. Health Studies 5. Life Sciences **Learning Disability** 1. Nursing 2. Sociology 3. Health Studies 4. Life Sciences - biology and psychology

	A	B	C	D	E	F
SUMMATIVE ASSESSMENT DURING THE BRANCH — Second Quarter	**Adult, Mental Health and Learning Disability** Client centred nursing care study (2,000 words)	**Adult, Mental Health and Child** Unseen 3 hour examination	**Adult, Mental Health and Learning Disability** Specialist related project (3,500 words)	**Adult** Life science, 2,000 word assignment; Nursing Theory, 2,000 word assignment; Health Promotion, 2,000 word assignment. **Mental Health** Behavioural/Social Science 2,000 word assignment	—	**Adult, Mental Health and Learning Disability** Integrative care study (3–5,000 words) on particular client(s)
Third Quarter	Teaching package focussing on acute health problem (2,000 words)	12–1,800 word research critique	Patient/client centred care study	(Mental Health Branch students maintain Portfolios throughout the Branch that are regularly assessed) **Mental Health** Life Science / Psychiatry 2,000 word assignment. 2 hour examination	**Adult** Nursing care study (3–5,000 words); Seminar on critical nursing care (2,500 words/1 hour); Diary. **Child** Nursing care study (3–5,000 words); 3 hour essay; Diary	Case study highlighting factors affecting nursing care (3–5,000 words); Unseen 3 hour examination
Fourth Quarter	3 hour broadly based examination; 1½ hour case study examination; Management Study	— ; Elective Study (5–6,000 words); Unseen 3 hour examination	Unseen 2 hour essay; Dissertation (6,000 words)	**Adult** Unseen 3 hour examination in Life Sciences/Nursing Studies and Behavioural/Social Science; Care Study (5,000 words). **Mental Health** Behavioural/Social Science/Nursing Theory 3,000 word assignment; 2 hour examination	**Adult** 3 hour essay; Course portfolio. **Child** Seminar on critique of research study or government report (2,500 words/1 hour); Course portfolio	

SCHEME

ASSESSMENT OF PRACTICE DURING THE BRANCH PROGRAMMES

F = formative assessment

S = summative assessment

*BONDY, K.N. (1983) 'Criterion - referenced definitions for rating scales in clinical evaluation.' *Journal of Nursing Education*, 22, 9, 376-382

	A	B	C	D	E	F
First quarter	BONDY* assessment used throughout	**Adult** 4 week placement **F**, 4 week placement **S**; **Child** 6 week placement **F**, 10 week placement **S**; **Mental Health** 11 week placement **F**	At the end of each placement the student and practice supervisor negotiate a grade which reflects the students' standards of achievement overall. Specific skills based outcomes are identified which must be satisfactorily achieved by the student by the 5th month of each 6 month unit.	**Mental Health** 1 assessment at level 1 **S**	All placements other than below are short and are monitored but not assessed. **Adult** 7 week placement **S**	**Adult, Mental Health and Learning Disability** 7 week placement **F**
Second quarter		**Adult** 4 week placement **S**, 11 week placement **F**; **Child** 13 week placement **S**; **Mental Health** 10 week placement **S**		**Adult** Throughout the Branch each placement is continuously assessed and scored. All assessments are summative and designed to ensure satisfactory levels of competence	**Adult** 7 week placement **S**; **Child** 10 week placement **S**	8 week placement **S**; 8 week placement **F**
Third quarter		**Adult** 11 week placement **S**; **Child** 9 week placement **F**, 9 week placement **S**; **Mental Health** 12 week placement **F**		**Mental Health** 2 assessments at level 2 **S**	**Adult** 27 week placement **S**; **Child** 10 week placement **S**	10 week placement **F**
Fourth quarter		**Adult** 11 week placement **S**; **Child** 10 week placement **S**; **Mental Health** 12 week placement **S**, 11 week placement **S**; **Child** 10 week placement **S**		**Mental Health** 2 assessments at level 3 **S**	**Child** 14 week placement **S**	10 week placement **S** **S**; 10 week placement

Appendix 2

PREVIOUS PUBLICATIONS

LEONARD, A. AND JOWETT, S. (1990). *Charting the Course: a Study of the Six ENB Pilot Schemes in Pre-registration Nurse Education.* Slough: National Foundation for Educational Research in England and Wales.

JOWETT, S., WALTON, I. and PAYNE, S. (1991). *The NFER Project 2000 Research – an Introduction and Some Interim Issues. Interim Paper 2.* Slough: National Foundation for Educational Research in England and Wales.

PAYNE, S., JOWETT, S. and WALTON, I. (1991). *Nurse Teachers in Project 2000 – the Experience of Planning and Initial Implementation. Interim Paper 3.* Slough: National Foundation for Educational Research in England and Wales.

JOWETT, S., WALTON, I. and PAYNE, S. (1992). *Early Perspectives from Higher Education. Interim Paper 4.* Slough: National Foundation for Educational Research in England and Wales.

JOWETT, S., WALTON, I. and PAYNE, S. (1992). *Early Perspectives from the Students. Interim Paper 5.* Slough: National Foundation for Educational Research in England and Wales,

JOWETT, S. (1992). '*Project 2000 - Research on its implementation*', Nursing Times (Occasional Paper), 88, 26, 40-3.

JOWETT, S., WALTON, I. and PAYNE, S. (1992) *Implementing Project 2000 – an Interim Report.* Slough: National Foundation for Educational Research in England and Wales.

Appendix 3

SAMPLING THE STUDENTS

A questionnaire was sent to all students in the first intake of six of the Demonstration Districts several months into the CFP (the 420 individuals remaining from the 463 who started), and 317 were returned, giving a response rate of 72 per cent (Jowett *et al.*, 1992a). Given the heterogeneity of the intakes, a systematic sample was drawn in an attempt to reflect key characteristics of the population in those approached for interview. Every fourth questionnaire returned from each of the six sites was selected and the sample thus drawn was checked against the total on the characteristics of age, gender, educational qualifications on entry and Branch programme undertaken. This sampling produced a representative group and all but two of the 79 students approached agreed to take part in the first round interviews. Of the nine students leaving the sample, five left the course, two moved to subsequent intakes and it was not possible to contact two.

CHARACTERISTICS OF THE STUDENTS WHO RETURNED A QUESTIONNAIRE, THE SAMPLE SELECTED FROM THEM AND THOSE LEAVING THE SAMPLE

STUDENTS RETURNING QUESTIONNAIRE n = 317

Female/Male		Age on entry n = 302			Educational Qualifications on entry								Branch n = 310		
no	%		no	%	Entry on UKCC DC Test no	%	Entry on 5 or more GCSEs/ 'O' levels (or equivalent) no	%	A-level(s), Degree (Additional qualifications) no. / %		Pre-vocational, vocational, other qualifications no. / %			no	%
282/35	89/11	17-21	178	59	62	20	255	80	131	40	153	48	Adult	243	78
		22-25	43	14									Child	17	6
		26-29	22	7									Mental Health	29	9
		30-39	44	15									Learning Disability	21	7
		40+	15	5											

STUDENT SAMPLE n = 77

Female/Male		Age			Entry on UKCC DC Test		Entry on 5+ GCSEs		A-level(s), Degree (Additional qualifications)		Pre-vocational, vocational, other qualifications		Branch		
no	%		no	%	no	%	no	%	no.	%	no.	%		no	%
67/10	88/12	17-21	38	49	20	25	57	75	27	35	38	49	Adult	59	77
		22-25	8	11									Child	4	5
		26-29	5	6									Mental Health	7	9
		30-39	22	29									Learning Disability	7	9
		40+	4	5											

STUDENTS LEAVING THE SAMPLE n = 9

Female/Male		Age			Entry on UKCC DC Test		Entry on 5+ GCSEs		A-levels, Degree (Additional qualifications)		Pre-vocational, vocational (other qualifications)		Branch		
no	%		no	%	no	%	no	%	no	%	no	%		no	%
8/1	89/11	17-21	3	33	5	55	4	45	1	11	2	22	Adult	5	56
		22-25	0	0									Child	2	22
		26-29	1	11									Mental Health	0	0
		30-39	4	45									Learning Disability	2	22
		40+	1	11											

Appendix 4

SAMPLING THE PRACTICE-BASED STAFF

The difficult process of sample selection, given the vast number and variety of placement areas, is detailed below to clarify where the data were collected from. Essentially, the resultant sample comprised sisters/charge nurses and supervisors from each of the main hospital units taking the CFP Project 2000 students on allocation at that time in each of the six case-study Districts. In one District where practice staff did not assume an official 'supervisor' role until the first students entered their Branch programmes, the first-round interviewees were sisters/charge nurses and teacher-practitioners.

Particular wards/areas represented were selected at random from the lists of training areas senior nurse managers had provided. For community nursing settings, managers or team leaders of the main services (District Nursing, Health Visiting, Community Psychiatric and Community Learning Disabilities Nursing) were targeted. The total sample of 90 for the first round consisted of 29 sisters/charge nurses, four teacher practitioners, 35 student supervisors and 22 Community Nursing personnel. (The term supervisors was adopted by the researchers for staff designated to supervise and assess the students, variously titled mentors, practice supervisors, link nurses in the different schemes.)

For the second round of interviews in 1992, when the students were into their Branch programmes, every effort was made to see the same practice staff again. But a year is a long time in the Health Service and inevitably staff changes meant this was not always possible. (Senior nurses were not contacted on the second occasion, but in a number of places, their posts had ceased to exist by that time.) Where someone was working elsewhere within the same Unit, usually that person was interviewed again, provided he/she was still in a training area. In other cases, someone else from the original area selected was identified. Again, a total of 90 staff was interviewed, comprising 67 hospital-based and 23 community-based personnel. Twenty-four of the hospital-based staff and ten community staff were 'new' interviewees. The former included six practice supervisors in the scheme where that role had only been officially assumed for Branch students, as well as three teacher practitioners.

Promotions, either substantive or in an acting capacity, often accompanying staff movements, also meant that the division between 'ward managers' and 'supervisors' in the hospital-based sample had become increasingly blurred in places. Consequently, for purposes of reporting on this occasion, responses from the two sets of interviews were for the most part considered together, albeit identified as separate groups where appropriate.

Over half (13) of the 24 Community Nursing staff interviewed in 1992 were managers (mostly generic) of District Nursing, Health Visiting and other services such as School Nursing, several of them having a specific remit to liaise with colleges of nursing about student allocations. The remainder comprised four Community Psychiatric nurse (CPN) managers/team leaders (two responsible for community residential/day hospitals and other specialist services as well); three Community Learning Disabilities nurse (CMHN) managers, two ('G' grade) CMHNs, and two nurses supervising students in Learning Disabilities residential settings in the community. In one area, in addition to the interview with the district nursing manager, an informal discussion was conducted with a group of seven district nurses.

Where Project 2000 schemes involved more than one health authority, community personnel were selected to reflect experience in each District. The sample of practice areas was structured to represent the specialisms on offer to **the first group** of Project 2000 students, even though additional specialisms may have become available to subsequent intakes. Adult and Mental Health Branches were available to the first students in all six schemes; the Child and Learning Disability Branches in four and three schemes respectively.

LEAVERS FROM THE FIRST TWO INTAKES

FIRST INTAKE

	A	B	C	D	E	F	Total	% returning pro forma Total
Adult	I = 42 L = 10 F = 0	I = 73 L = 6 F = 4	I = 48 L = 13 F = 4	I = 92 L = 11 F = 4	I = 52* L = 14 F = 7	I = 46 L = 15 F = 5	353 69 26	37
Mental Health	I = 7 L = 3 F = 2	I = 15 L = 0 F = 4	I = 10 L = 2 F = 0	I = 13* L = 5 F = 2	—	I = 16 L = 12 F = 3	61 22 5	22
Learning Disability	I = 9 L = 1 F = 0	I = 12 L = 8 F = 2	—	—	—	—	21 8 2	25
Child	—	—	I = 9 L = 0 F = 0	—	I = 9* L = 0 F = 0	I = 10 L = 1 F = 0	28 2 0	0
Total	I = 58 L = 14 F = 2	I = 100 L = 13 F = 6	I = 67 L = 13 F = 4	I = 105* L = 16 F = 6	I = 61* L = 14 F = 7	I = 72 L = 28 F = 8	463 98 33	33

SECOND INTAKE

	A	B	C	D	E	F	Total	% returning pro forma Total
Adult	I = 33 L = 10 F = 2	I = 75 L = 8 F = 1	I = 48 L = 5 F = 1	I = 77 L = 6 F = 4	I = 47 L = 10 F = 7	I = 48 L = 9 F = 3	328 45 18	40
Mental Health	I = 4 L = 0 F = 0	I = 13 L = 1 F = 0	I = 12 L = 2 F = 0	—	—	I = 11 L = 2 F = 0	40 5 0	0
Learning Disability	—	—	I = 7 L = 0 F = 0	—	—	I = 7 L = 1 F = 0	14 1 0	0
Child	—	I = 12 L = 1 F = 0	I = 10 L = 1 F = 1	I = 8 L = 2 F = 0	I = 5 L = 0 F = 0	—	35 4 1	25
Total	I = 37 L = 10 F = 2	I = 100 L = 10 F = 1	I = 77 L = 8 F = 2	I = 85 L = 8 F = 4	I = 52 L = 10 F = 7	I = 66 L = 12 F = 3	417 58 19	32

I = Number in intake
L = Number of students leaving
F = Number returning proforma sent by research team

* These differ from the numbers in Interim Paper 2 because of 2 students who did not commence the course but were included on the original list given to the team.

* These recently provided figures differ from those provided to the team for Interim Paper 2.

150

Intake	Subgroup	A	B	C	D	E	F	Total
FIRST INTAKE	Adult	1 Pregnancy / 1 Dissatisfaction with the course	2 Failed assessment / 2 Personal	1 Failed assessment / 1 Pregnancy / 2 Dissatisfaction with the course	2 Dissatisfaction with the course / 2 Pregnancy	3 Dissatisfaction with the course / 2 Personal / 1 Illness / 1 Decided nursing was not for me	1 Thought would not pass assessments / 1 Decided nursing was not for me / 1 Personal	
	Mental Health	0	0	0			0	0
	Learning Disability	0	—	0	1 Failed assessment / 1 Dissatisfaction with course/decided nursing was not for me	—	—	—
	Child	—	2 Dissatisfaction with the course	—	—	—	1 Illness / 1 Other	
	Total	2	6	4	6	7	8	15 Dissastification with the course / 4 Pregnancy / 5 Personal / 5 Failed assessment / 2 Decided nursing was not for me / 1 Illness / 1 Other — **33**
SECOND INTAKE	Adult	1 Dissatisfaction with the course / 1 Pegnancy	1 Decided nursing was not to me	1 Failed assessment	1 Personal / 1 Failed assessment / 1 Decided nursing was not for me / 1 Reason not given	2 Illness / 4 Dissatisfaction with the course / 1 Pregnancy	2 Dissatisfaction with the course / 1 Personal	
	Mental Health	0	0	0		0	0	
	Learning Disability	—	—	0	—	—	0	
	Child	—	0	1 Pregnancy	0	0	—	1 Not given
	Total	2	1	2	4	7	3	7 Dissastisation with the course / 2 Personal / 2 Illness / 3 Pregnancy / 2 Personal / 2 Failed assessment / 1 Not given — **19**

FIRST INTAKE

S = number started course   C = number sucessfully completed course

	A	B	C	D	E	F	Total number	Total %
Adult	S = 42 C = 32	S = 73 C = 67*	S = 48 C = 35	S = 92 C = 81	S = 52 C = 38	S = 46 C = 31	S = 353 C = 284	80
Mental Health	S = 7 C = 4	S = 15 C = 15	S = 10* C = 10	S = 13 C = 8	—	S = 16 C = 4	S = 61 C = 41	67
Learning Disability	S = 9 C = 8	—	S = 9 C = 9	—	—	S = 10 C = 9	S = 28 C = 26	92
Child	—	S = 12 C = 5	—	—	S = 9 C = 9	—	S = 21 C = 14	66
Total number	S = 58 C = 44	S = 100 C = 87	S = 67 C = 54	S = 105 C = 89*	S = 61 C = 47	S = 72 C = 44	S = 463 C = 365	78
Total %	75	87	80	84	77	61	78	

* Includes one transferred from Adult to Child Branch

* Includes two transferred from Adult to Mental Health Branch

* In addition three joined a later set

152

S = number started course
C = number successfully completed course

	A	B	C	D	E	F	Total number	Total %
Adult	S = 33* C = 23	S = 75 C = 66	S = 48 C = 43	S = 77 C = 71	S = 47 C = 37	S = 48 C = 39	S = 328 C = 279	85
Mental Health	S = 4 C = 4	S = 13 C = 13	S = 12 C = 10	—	—	S = 11 C = 9	S = 40 C = 36	90
Learning Disability	—	—	S = 7 C = 7	—	—	S = 7 C = 6	S = 14 C = 13	92
Child	—	S = 12 C = 11	S = 10 C = 9	S = 8 C = 6	S = 5 C = 5	—	S = 35 C = 31	88
Total number	S = 37 C = 27	S = 100 C = 90	S = 77 C = 69	S = 85 C = 77*	S = 52 C = 42	S = 66 C = 54	S = 417 C = 359	86
Total %	72	90	89	90	80	81	86	

*Includes 2 who went back a set

*In addition 3 are awaiting a decision on whether they can make a third examination attempt